WHO'S WHO IN
AMERICAN FILM NOW

Also by James Monaco

The New Wave
How to Read a Film
Celebrity
Media Culture
Alain Resnais
American Film Now

WHO'S WHO
IN
AMERICAN FILM
NOW

James Monaco

Research and Editing: Sharon Boonshoft

Programming and Production: Robert Monaco

NEW YORK ZOETROPE

New York

1981

Copyright © 1981 by James Monaco

Reproduction by any means, electronic or otherwise, is
strictly forbidden under U.S. and international
copyright laws without the express written consent of
the publisher.

Library of Congress Catalogue card number: 81-47446.

ISBN: 0-918432-27-8 (paper)
       0-918432-34-0 (cloth)

New York Zoetrope
80 East 11th Street
New York 10003
Printed in the United States of America
First printing: March 1981
5 4 3 2 1

For Lucille
with affection

TABLE OF CONTENTS

Preface

Jean-Luc Godard wants to be a producer. François Truffaut says it's time to pay attention to all the other members of the crew. And after the artistic and financial disaster of *Heaven's Gate* those Hollywood studio executives still in office are clamping down hard on once powerful directors.

Whatever happened to the auteur theory—the idea that films were the sole artistic property of their directors? Godard and Truffaut both admit that the policy they set as critics in the 1950s now seems absurd to them as working professionals. In fact, the auteur *policy* was never more than just that — a strategy to arrogate more power to directors. And it certainly enjoyed enormous success throughout the 1960s in Europe and the 1970s in the U.S.

But as a way of looking at films, auteurism distorted our view of the art. Since the very beginning of movies this strange enterprise has been thoroughly communal in nature—moreso than any other art, even theater.

Who's Who in American Film Now is a reference guide to the American filmmaking community; it is also an attempt to give a true picture of how films are actually made in the real world: by scores of people working together to produce art objects that none of them as individuals could ever have conceived. This is not to suggest that each individual working on a particular film has the same value to the finished product as every one of his or her co-workers. Rather, that we as viewers never really know who was most responsible for the sum effect. The struggles between directors and actors, actors and cinematographers, editors and special effects people, et cetera, are the stuff of which all commercial and many independent productions are made.

Thirteen major crafts are listed in *Who's Who in American Film Now:* these are the people who *should* and usually do have significant input to a movie. Certainly there are great assistant directors, powerful continuity supervisors, and singularly talented casting experts at work in movies today, but for the most part such contributors work for the craftspeople we have included.

The order of the categories of filmmakers may at first seem arbitrary. It isn't. We've listed the crafts in the sequence usually followed in the process of film production. The script almost always comes first. The producer acquires it and begins the process of organizing the project. The director is usually first to be hired, and the major actors aren't far behind. With this "package" the producer can obtain financing from a studio or other source. Then, the rest of the crew comes on board. The editor is generally the last craftsperson on salary, often many months after the cast and crew have disbanded, and sometimes weeks or months after the producer and director have each gone on to other projects.

If you sense a subtle bias in favor of writers as the prime movers in movies—perhaps there is some truth in it. Remember, too, that editors by the nature of things are often the final authorities.

Because the film business is so thoroughly collaborative, certain organizational problems present themselves in a directory of this kind. In the first place, writers, producers, and all other craftspeople often share credit with one or more colleagues. In each such case that we've been able to identify, the appropriate title is accompanied by an asterisk (*) to indicate that at least one other person worked in a similar capacity on that particular film. (This procedure was not followed for actors and producers, for obvious reasons.)

Most of the categories (writers, directors, actors and actresses) are fairly well-defined. Some, however, are not.

The title of "producer" is the most problematical. Credits often list half a dozen people with various producer credits ("executive producer," "co-producer," "associate producer," "assistant producer," "production manager," and so forth). Moreover, unless you were intimately involved in the production of the film there is no way to tell who actually did what, if anything. Sometimes such a title is conferred as an honorarium.

We should expect "the producer" (no adjectives) to be the main force, but this is the case less often than you may think. Sometimes an assistant or associate — even a production manager — has the major authority in day-to-day production. Consequently, we've lumped these various titles together in a single category.

The same is true, although to a lesser extent, with various designers. Sound presents a slightly different problem. Recordists work both on and off the set as do mixers. Sound editing is a separate, identifiable task, but the film editor often has considerable control over this aspect of production. Anyone who works in sound has been included in this one category.

Any first edition of such a reference guide is always a "work in progress." Despite our best efforts, you are going to find errors in *Who's Who in American Film Now*. We would be very grateful if you would be kind enough to call them to our attention. (Please see the last page of the book for more information.)

Please note that no attempt has been made to be all-inclusive. With over four thousand filmmakers already listed, complete entries would have required a book several times the size of the present one. To include everyone who has ever worked in the American film industry during the last five years would require a multivolume encyclopedia. *Who's Who in American Film Now* is meant to be a manageable guide to *most* filmmakers, surveying *most* of their work. It is nevertheless true, however, that more than 90% of commercially-released American films made during the last three years have been included. For the years 1975 through 1977 the figure is approximately 70%; for the early 1970s, less. The total number of films cited is more than 2500.

Acknowledgements

Sharon Boonshoft helped to make sense of the massive amount of data from a confusing variety of sources. Robert Monaco designed the computer program to control the data base and oversaw production. I am extraordinarily grateful to both of them for their help.

The Type

Who's Who in American Film Now is set in a version of Garamond, a typeface with a long and honorable history. There are many contemporary versions of Garamond but all are based on the work of Claude Garamond (1480-1561). Garamond is characterized by a liveliness and authority that has made it a popular face throughout its 450 year history.

The book was set with photocomposition equipment by Alpha Publications, Center Square, Pennsylvania, under the supervision of Robert Monaco, and by Village Type and Graphics, New York. *Who's Who in American Film Now* was printed and bound by R. R. Donnelly & Sons Company, Harrisonburg, Virginia.

James Monaco
New York City
February 1981

Who Makes What in American Film Now?

Late in 1980, *Variety* announced that the average cost of an American feature film had risen to $10 million. In 1978 this figure was $6 million and in the early seventies $3 million. Inflation seems to have hit the film industry harder than most areas of the economy.

How does a film get to cost so much? For the answer to that question we have to take a quick look at the history of the American film industry. When film companies first established studios in Hollywood in the teens and twenties they operated on an industrial model. The studios were factories, employees were on annual salaries—even the stars—and clocked in every day. If a director finished his work on a particular film on a Thursday, he'd start a new one on Friday. In order to keep overhead under control each studio cranked out a specified number of features, "programmers," shorts, cartoons, newsreels, and two-reelers each year.

After the advent of television in the early fifties this system broke down rapidly. Today — *except* for series television, which does occupy a large number of workers in Hollywood—the American film industry has shifted to an "ad hoc" basis. Everyone, from stars to teamsters, operates on a freelance basis. Casts and crews are hired for individual films and when the particular project is finished, they are out of work once more. (The myth has it that they drive to the unemployment office in their Mercedeses.)

One economic result is that costs have risen rapidly. An average film can cost as much as $10 million not because "raw materials" have increased so dramatically in price but because star actors, directors, and even occasionally cinematographers can command high prices.

Take a basic old-fashioned $1 million movie, add a few stars at $2 or $3 million per, the extra expense involved in setting up an individual corporation for each separate project, and then figure the standard 35% studio overhead payment to the company that finances the film and — presto!— $1 million has been multiplied tenfold.

Are star actors being paid too much? Some analysts think so, yet a basic rule is operating. Steven Spielberg once put it this way: "Whatever they're paying you, it's not enough." If the producers of *Superman* pay Marlon Brando millions of dollars for a few days work it's because they expect to make even more than that as a direct result of his presence in the film. This has been true since the earliest days of the movie industry. In the teens Mary Pickford, Douglas Fairbanks, and Charles Chaplin (with D. W. Griffith) formed their own production company, United Artists, at least in part because their legitimate fees were so extraordinarily high that other production companies couldn't pay them. For thirty years, long-term contracts helped to keep star salaries under control, but now that actors are free agents once again and movies are making money once again, the stars ask—and get—large fees. The producers, however, make even more. In many cases it is still true that a star is the movie. People are paying to see Brando, not the movie he's in.

Crew members and technicians make what *appear* to be good salaries (see the figures below) but you must remember that free lance work is different in nature from full-time employment. A cinematographer on a feature film can easily expect to make $1000 or $2000 per week, but this doesn't mean he or she is making $50 to $100 thousand a year. The real annual income may be much less than half that, since the average shooting schedule for a film only lasts 12 weeks and even the successful freelancer may very well receive no more than two assignments a year.

Remember, too, that of the thousands of people that belong to any particular craft union, the majority are usually out of work. It's traditionally said that 85% of the Screen Actors Guild is unemployed at any one time.

With those provisos in mind, here are some of the basic pay rates for the various crafts and professions in the film industry.

Actors and Stars

The Screen Extras Guild represents people who appear in movies and television shows and don't talk. There are only three pay rates for extras and it's nearly impossible to make a career out of the job.

General extras are paid $73.50 per day (as of 1 February 1981). "Special ability" extras, who can, for example, ride a horse earn $83.50 per day. And "silent bits" — people who perform real actions in the film — get paid $133.50 per day. If somebody asks "Which way'd they go?" and you point, you're a silent bit and you get your $133.50. If you say "Thataway!" you're no longer an extra, you're an actor and your paycheck nearly doubles.

The Screen Actors Guild represents people who talk in movies. The basic day rate is $259 (plus a 9% payment for pension and welfare).

If an actor is hired for a full week's work that basic rate is $903. There is also a special 3-day minimum for television work only of $658.

Multiple picture players (actors hired for more than one appearance) work for a starting salary that depends on the type of show:

½-hour	$667/week
1-hour	$667
1½-hour	$786
2-hour	$926

"Term" players who get hired for the run of the production earn:

$774/week for a guaranteed 10 out of 13 weeks.

$644/week for a guaranteed 20 out of 26 weeks.

Of course these figures represent only the minimums allowed by contract. Many actors besides outright stars will be paid higher rates than these.

Salaries for stars are, fittingly, astronomical. During the mid-seventies Steve McQueen set a record by asking $3 million for any performance. He didn't work very often but when he did he got paid what he asked.

Many other star actors operate as co-producers and thus earn money as "bosses" as well as "workers." Any well-know actor will ask for and usually receive a percentage of the profits of the film. This is known in the trade as "points." Directors and even a few writers also commonly receive "points." Other craftspeople haven't reached that level yet.

Barbra Streisand, generally regarded as the highest priced female star received $3½ million (plus a hefty percentage of profits) for 10 weeks work on *All Night Long*. Burt Reynolds was rumored to have been paid $5 million for *Cannonball*.

Even second-rank stars can command million-dollar prices. Robert Duvall's current asking price is $2 million. James Caan demands the same.

Actors and others who receive a percentage of the profits, by the way, are always careful that the contract reads in terms of percentages of the gross income from a film. "Net points" — percentages of profits after the studio and producers have deducted their expenses — always have a way of evaporating, even on very successful films.

Actors are also interested in the expanding uses of film product. Since 1960 every Screen Actors Guild member has shared in the profits from television broadcast of films he has appeared in. "Residuals" can provide a small but steady income. The main point of the SAG strike of 1980 was to achieve a similar share of producers' profits from "supplementary markets" — videodiscs, videotape, pay television, cable, satellite, and so on. The actors won, and will be paid 3.6% of distributors' worldwide grosses on each film.

Directors

The Directors Guild of America negotiates for film and television directors. Their contracts with the members of the film industry provide for the following minimum rates of pay:

Feature Films

Budget under $500 thousand	$29,359 (as of 1 January 1981)
	($2669/week, 11 weeks guaranteed)
Budget $500 thousand-$1 million	$39,429
	($3033/week, 13 weeks)
Budget over $1.5 million	$55,185
	($4245/week, 13 weeks)

Directors also receive a percentage of television license money that amounts to less than 1%.

Of course most directors earn considerably more than the minimum. Straight $1 million salaries are not unheard of and points are common. Like actors, star directors earn money many different ways from the films in which they participate. Perhaps the record straight salary for a director is Francis Ford Coppola's reported $3 million for *Straight From the Heart,* but remember that points often mean more than salaries.

Television directors, like TV actors, are paid by the category of the show:

Primetime

½-hour	$6429 for minimum 7 days
1-hour	$10,918 for minimum 15 days
90-min	$18,226 for minimum 25 days
2-hour	$30,569 for minimum 42 days
4-hour	$61,138 for minimum 84 days

Television directors will not command star salaries like feature film directors, but twice the minimum payment is not uncommon—and then there are residuals.

Producers

It's a common misconception that all producers are bosses—or owners. Banks, investors, and studios own films. Very often producers are hired hands. As such, they are represented by the Producers Guild (which has contracts, at present, only with Paramount and Universal). The current contract calls for a guaranteed minimum of $450/week for associate producers and the following for full producers (a job description that includes "coproducers," "executive producers," and "staff producers," as well as plain producers):

Features budgeted at:

less than $1.5 million	$25,000
$1.5 to $2.5 million	$35,000
over $2.5 million	$50,000

Television: Non-episodic:

½-hour	$7,500
1-hour	$9,000

1½-hour	$12,500
2-hour	$15,000
2½-hour	$17,500
Television: Episodic:	
½-hour	$2,500
1-hour	$3,000
1½-hour	$4,250
2-hour	$5,500

Producers also commonly share in royalty payments each time a film is broadcast. This amounts to between $350 and $800 a show.

Writers

The Writers Guild of America sets standards and minimums for writers in film and television. Writers are the last in the chain to share directly in profits from a film (after producers, actors, and directors). Their fees are also often split. A writer who adapts a book or play to the screen will be paid less that the writer of an original screenplay. Writers, unlike directors, often work in teams and split fees. During the last year of a three-year contract which expired on 1 March 1981 the WGA fee structures looked like this:

	Budget under $1 million	over $1 million
Screenplay and treatment	$14,175	$26,326
Screenplay only	$8,861	$18,225
Story or treatment	$5,315	$8,100
Original treatment	$7,342	$12,151
Rewrite of screenplay	$5,315	$8,100
Polish of screenplay	$2,658	$4,050

You want to know what a "polish" is? So would a lot of practicing screenwriters.

Television

Experienced television writers received the following minimums under the WGA contract:

		Prime time bonus
½-hour	$4,718	$2,021
1-hour	$6,065	$3,369
1½-hour	$10,108	$3,369
2-hour	$12,128	$4,718

Writers on weekly salaries at studios earn at least $1000 per week, but there are few professionals in this category now.

For both features and television fees commonly exceed these bare minimums. $100,000 is not uncommon for screenwriters without a track record and experienced scenarists command three or four times that fee for feature films. Writers are less likely to get points than directors, producers or actors, but it does happen. Increasingly, writers are turning to producing in order to redress the balance between writer and director.

Agents

Producers, directors, actors, and writers form the top level of the motion picture industry. All of them are represented by agents who, during the past fifteen years, have emerged as the real power brokers in the business. After the studio factory system broke down it was clear that people with the knowledge of who was available to work on a particular film would hold the power. These people are agents.

Traditionally, the agent takes 10% of all fees, but this can mount up when it is the agent himself who is putting together the various elements of a film. The record seems to be ICM's performance with *Jaws* in 1975. The most powerful agency in the business represented so many cast and crew members on that film that they themselves were banking 10% of 53% of the profits. In other words, ICM had a direct 5.3% stake in that blockbuster.

Top agents like Sue Mengers (an employee of ICM) can earn $350,000 to $500,000 and up per year. At this level of course, the figures are relatively meaningless since real profit comes from stock option plans and the like.

Studio Executives

Increasingly, studio executives and agents are one and the same. The majority of studio executives started as agents. When they move to the other side of the desk they pay themselves quite well. A salary of less than $100,000 is now regarded as fit only for second- and third-level employees and the many vice-presidents at the studios earn much more than that. The average salary for the head of production at one of the major film companies in 1980 was $350,000. You can see why studios insist on a 35% cut as distribution fee: this sort of overhead mounts up.

Cinematographers

For several years now cinematographers—the people who actually photograph moving pictures—have been angling for admission to the charmed circles of producers, directors, writers, and actors. They haven't yet achieved this in terms of pay scales and percentages, but they are getting there in terms of publicity. Often the key bargaining points in a cinematographer's contract these days will have to do with getting their own mobile vans on location and guaranteed paid advertising rather than with salaries.

As of 1981 these were the base rates:

Director of Photography	$281.96/day
Camera operator	$162.12
Still photographer	$162.12
First assistant cameraman	$109.84

| Second assistant | $98.80 |
| Film loader | $80.44 |

Topflight cinematographers will be able to earn $6000-$8000 per week, a salary which is comparable with that of decently-paid writers. $10,000 per week with points is not unheard of.

Measured in terms of daily wages cinematographers who work on television commercials do as well as or better than nearly all feature film D.P.'s even if they aren't as well known. These rates go as high as $2500/day.

Mixers

Sound recordists and mixers don't have anywhere near the prestige of their visual opposite numbers. The basic salary for a mixer now averages $1000 per week although the better established mixers can command twice that amount and the best in the business can earn $60 or $70 thousand per year. A beginner starts at $537 per week.

Editors

Editors have as much to do with the ultimate effect of a film as cinematographers but they don't yet have the clout as a craft. This is reflected in lower pay scales. Film editors can earn a minimum of $981.74 per week (as of 31 July 1981). Assistants earn a minimum of $520.32. Sound effects and music editors earn at least $689.34. While it is possible for well-known editors to earn much more than this it is not common.

Composers and Musicians

Like cinematographers and editors, composers have been fighting for a larger share of the film pie in recent years. Like the Producers Guild, the Composers & Lyricists Guild is still fighting for recognition.

Top film composers like John Williams or Jerry Goldsmith will earn $35 to $50 thousand per feature film. Most composers earn half that and low-budget features will go for as little as $10 to $15 thousand. A lyricist can expect $5000 a song with leading lyricists like Alan and Marilyn Bergman getting much more.

For television, composers earn relatively more than you might expect, a reflection of the fact that so many television shows are produced with "wall-to-wall" music, unlike feature films where music is now usually intermittent. A half-hour sitcom will yield perhaps $2000, a movie-of-the-week, $6000 to $9000, a 4-hour miniseries $15,000.

Composers also share in performance royalties. That rate was recently raised to 4 cents per performance after many years at 2.75 cents. Composers only get half of this money (unlike their counterparts in the outside world): half goes to the producer.

Musicians are covered by an American Federation of Musicians contract that guarantees $115.51 for a minimum 3-hour call. A conductor will get double this amount. Add 15% for 1981.

Cartoonists

There are a dozen different job classifications for people who work in animated film: storywriting, storyboard, layout, design, animation, assistant animation, background painting for animation, animation checking, Xerox processing, cell service, cell painting, final checking, and so forth. A beginning painter will earn $300/week. A good layout person can earn perhaps $1000 per week.

Other Production Personnel

Sound recordist	$809.80/week
Head carpenter, props, or grip (electrician)	$677.75
Script supervisor	$659.72
Production coordinator	$413.40
Costumer	$668.75
Makeup or Hair stylist	$746.50
Teamster captain	$1048.63
Driver	$360.20
Art director	$1431.11
Costume designer	$871.12
Unit production manager	$1463 studio
	$1998 location

Behind the Scenes

People who work in the offices of film companies often earn less than people of comparable skills would earn in other businesses. The competition even for secretarial positions is intense since the job is regarded as prestigious and glamourous.

Traditionally, one of the best ways to break into the industry (besides entry-level secretarial positions) is the job of story analyst. All production companies have to deal with thousands of scripts and novels each year. It is the job of the story analyst to read, summarize, and evaluate these potential properties. Very few story analysts have staff positions. Most are freelance and the pay scale is minimal, ranging from $35 to $100 per script or book covered. Since the coverage involves reading the property and writing two to twenty pages of summary and evaluation, even efficient story analysts earn less than established secretaries — and there are no fringe benefits.

Publicity is another popular entree to the business side of film. The Screen Publicists Guild in New York has approximately 60 members. A senior publicist is guaranteed a minimum of $463.75 per week; a publicist earns at least $347.79; and the minimum for assistant publicist is $265.57.

Exhibition and Laboratories

Like an iceberg, most of the film business is not in production, but in distribution, exhibition, and ancillary services.

A head timer in a film processing laboratory, responsible for the color correction of the print, earns upwards of $12.30 per hour.

A projectionist at a neighborhood theatre in New York City will earn at least $14.67 per hour. If he is responsible for more than one screen, add 25% additional for each screen. If he can land a job at a first-run "Broadway Deluxe" house the minimum goes to $22.03.

Writers

AARON, SIDNEY: Altered States (80).

ABRAHAMS, JIM: Airplane (80).

ALDA, ALAN: The Seduction Of Joe Tynan (79).

ALLAN, TED: Falling In Love Again (80)*.

ALLEN, CHRIS: In God We Trust (80)*.

ALLEN, JANIS: Meatballs (79)*, Double Negative (80)*.

ALLEN, JAY PRESSON: The Prime of Miss Jean Brodie (69), Cabaret (72), Travels with My Aunt (72), Just Tell Me What You Want (79).

ALLEN, WOODY: What's New Pussycat? (65), What's Up Tiger Lily? (66)*, Take the Money and Run (69)*, Bananas (71)*, Everything You Always Wanted to Know About Sex (72), Play It Again, Sam (72), Sleeper (73)*, Love and Death (75), Annie Hall (77)*, Interiors (78), Manhattan (79), Stardust Memories (80).

ALLIN, MICHAEL: Flash Gordon (80)*.

ALTMAN, ROBERT: Bodyguard (48)*, The Delinquents (57), McCabe and Mrs. Miller (71)*, Images (72), Thieves Like Us (74)*, Buffalo Bill and the Indians (76)*, Three Women (77), A Wedding (78)*, A Perfect Couple (79)*, Health (80)*.

AMBROSE, DAVID: The Final Countdown (80)*.

AMIS, MARTIN: Saturn 3 (80).

ANDERSON, HESPER: Touched By Love (80).

ANHALT, EDWARD: A Girl Named Tamiko (63), Becket (64), Hour of the Gun (67), In Enemy Country (68), The Boston Strangler (68), The Madwoman of Chaillot (69), Jeremiah Johnson (72)*, Luther (73), Escape to Athena (79)*.

APPLEBAUM, HARVEY: The Little Dragons (80)*.

ATLEE, LOUIS G.: The Little Dragons (80)*.

AURTHUR, ROBERT ALAN: All That Jazz (79)*.

AUSTIN, RON: The Happening (67), Harry in Your Pocket (73).

AXELROD, GEORGE: The Seven Year Itch (55), Breakfast at Tiffany's

(61), The Manchurian Candidate (62), Goodbye Charlie (65), How to Murder Your Wife (65), Lord Love a Duck (66), The Secret Life of an American Wife (68), The Lady Vanishes (79).

AYKROYD, DAN: The Blues Brothers (80)*.

AYRES, GERALD: Foxes (80).

BAER, MAX, Jr.: Macon County Line (73).

BAIN, GARY L.: Ice Castles (78)*.

BAIRD, ROBERT: Seven (79)*.

BANCROFT, ANNE: Fatso (80).

BARHYDT, FRANK: Health (80)*.

BARRON, ARTHUR: Jeremy (73).

BARRON, FRED: Between the Lines (77), Something Short Of Paradise (79).

BARWOOD, HAL: The Sugarland Express (73)*, The Bingo Long Traveling All-Stars (76)*, McArthur (77)*, Corvette Summer (78)*.

BAUM, THOMAS: Carny (80).

BEATTS, ANNE: Gilda Live (80)*.

BEATTY, WARREN: Shampoo (75)*, Heaven Can Wait (78)*.

BELLWOOD, PETER: Phobia (80)*.

BELSON, JERRY: How Sweet It Is (68), The Grasshopper (69), Smile (75), Fun with Dick and Jane (77)*, The End (78), Smokey And The Bandit II (80)*.

BENCHLEY, PETER: The Island (80).

BENNER, RICHARD: Happy Birthday, Gemini (80).

BENSON, ROBBY: One on One (77), Die Laughing (80)*.

BENTON, ROBERT: Bonnie and Clyde (67), There Was a Crooked Man (70)*, Bad Company (72), What's Up, Doc? (72)*, The Late Show (77), Superman (78)*, Kramer vs. Kramer (79).

BERGMAN, ANDREW: Blazing Saddles (74)*, The In-Laws (79).

BERGREN, ERIC: The Elephant Man (80)*.

BERGSTEIN, ELEANOR: It's My Turn (80).

BERNSTEIN, WALTER: The Money Trap (66), The Molly Maguires (68), The Front (76), Semi-Tough (77), The Betsy (78)*, An Almost Perfect Affair (79)*, Yanks (79)*, Little Miss Marker (80).

BINDER, JOHN: Honeysuckle Rose (80)*.

BLATT, JERRY: Divine Madness (80)*.

BLATTY, WILLIAM PETER: Darling Lili (69), The Great Bank Robbery (69), The Exorcist (73), The Ninth Configuration (80).

BLEICH, BILL: The Hearse (80).

BLUM, LEN: Meatballs (79)*.

BOGDANOVICH, PETER: Targets (68), Directed by John Ford (71), The Last Picture Show (71)*, At Long Last Love (75), Nickelodeon (76), Saint Jack (79)*.

BOLOGNA, JOSEPH: Lovers and Other Strangers (69)*, Made for Each Other (71)*, Mixed Company (74)*, Woman of the Year (75)*.

BOORMAN, JOHN: Leo the Last (69), Zardoz (73).

BOOTH, JAMES: Sunburn (79)*.

BORCHERT, RUDOLPH: The Little Dragons (80)*.

BORETZ, ALVIN: Brass Target (78).

BRACKETT, LEIGH: El Dorado (67), Rio Lobo (70), The Long Goodbye (73), The Empire Strikes Back (80)*.

BRACKMAN, JACOB: The King of Marvin Gardens (72), Times Square (80).

BRALY, MALCOLM: On The Yard (79).

BRASCIA, JOHN F.: The Baltimore Bullet (80)*.

BREST, MARTIN: Going In Style (79).

BRICKMAN, MARSHALL: Sleeper (73), Annie Hall (77), Manhattan (79), Simon (80).

BRICKMAN, PAUL: Citizen's Band (Handle With Care) (77), The Bad News Bears in Breaking Training (77).

BRICUSSE, LESLIE: Sunday Lovers (80)*.

BRIDGES, JAMES: The Forbin Project (69), Limbo (72), The Baby Maker (73), The Paper Chase (73), September 30, 1955 (78), The China Syndrome (79)*, Urban Cowboy (80)*.

BRILEY, JOHN: Eagle's Wing (79).

BROOKS, ALBERT: Real Life (79).

BROOKS, JAMES L.: Starting Over (79).

BROOKS, JOSEPH: If Ever I See You Again (78).

BROOKS, MEL: The Twelve Chairs (70), Blazing Saddles (74), Young Frankenstein (74), Silent Movie (76).

BROOKS, RICHARD: Lord Jim (64), The Professionals (66), In Cold Blood (67), The Happy Ending (69), $ (71), Bite the Bullet (75).

BROWNING, ROD: Oh Heavenly Dog (80)*.

BRYANT, CHRIS: The Awakening (80)*.

BRYDEN, BILL: The Long Riders (80)*.

BUCHANAN, JAMES D.: The Happening (67), Midas Run (69), Harry in Your Pocket (73).

BUCHANAN, JOAN: H.O.T.S. (79)*.

BURNS, ALLAN: A Little Romance (79), Butch And Sundance (79).

BURNS, FRANCIS: Rough Cut (80).

BURNS, JACK: The Muppet Movie (79)*.

BYRUM, JOHN: Inserts (75), Mahogany (75), Harry and Walter Go to New York (76), Heart Beat (79).

CAFFARO, CHERI: H.O.T.S. (79)*.

CAMP, JOE: The Double Mcguffin (79), Oh Heavenly Dog (80)*.

CARLINO, LEWIS JOHN: The Brotherhood (68), Reflection of Fear (71), The Mechanic (72), Crazy Joe (74), The Sailor Who Fell from Grace with the Sea (76), I Never Promised You a Rose Garden (77), Resurrection (80), The Great Santini (80).

CAROTHERS, A. J.: Hero At Large (80).

CARPENTER, JOHN: Halloween (78), The Fog (80)*.

CARR, ALLAN: Can't Stop The Music (80)*.

CARROLL, J. LARRY: The Day Time Ended (80)*.

CARSON, L. M. KIT: The Last Word (79)*.

CASSAVETES, JOHN: Shadows (60), Too Late Blues (61)*, Faces (68), Husbands (70), Minnie and Moskowitz (71), A Woman Under the Influence (74), The Killing of a Chinese Bookie (76), Opening Night (77), Gloria (80).

CASTLE, NICK: Skatetown Usa (79).

CHAPMAN, GRAHAM: Life Of Brian (79)*.

CHAPMAN, JOHN: There Goes the Bride (80)*.

CHAPMAN, LEIGH: Boardwalk (79)*, Steel (80), The Octagon (80).

CHAYEFSKY, PADDY: Marty (55), The Americanization of Emily (64), Paint Your Wagon (69), The Hospital (71), Network (76), Altered States (80).

CHONG, THOMAS: Cheech And Chong's Next Movie (80)*.

CIMINO, MICHAEL: Silent Running (71), Thunderbolt and Lightfoot (74), Heaven's Gate (80).

CLEESE, JOHN: Life Of Brian (79)*.

CLEMENS, BRIAN: The Watcher In The Woods (80)*.

CLEMENT, DICK: The Prisoner Of Zenda (79)*.

CLOUSE, ROBERT: The Big Brawl (80).

COHEN, LARRY: The American Success Company (79)*.

COHEN, LAWRENCE D.: Carrie (76).

COHEN, LAWRENCE J.: Start the Revolution Without Me (69)*, SPYS (74)*, The Big Bus (76)*.

COLIN, SID: It's Not The Size That Counts (79).

COLLIER, JAMES F.: Joni (80).

CONSIDINE, JOHN: A Wedding (78)*.

CONWAY, TIM: The Prize Fighter (79)*, The Private Eyes (80)*.

COONEY, RAY: There Goes the Bride (80)*.

COPPOLA, FRANCIS: Come On Out (61), Tonight for Sure (61)*, Dementia 13 (63), Is Paris Burning? (66), This Property Is Condemned (66), You're a Big Boy Now (67), The Rain People (69), Patton (70), The Godfather (72)*, The Conversation (74), The Godfather, Part II (74)*, The Great Gatsby (74), Apocalypse Now (79)*.

COTLER, LANNY: The Earthling (80)

CRICHTON, MICHAEL: Westworld (73), Coma (78), The Great Train Robbery (79).

CRITTENDEN, JORDAN: Get to Know Your Rabbit (72).

CURTIN, VALERIE: ...And Justice For All (79)*.

DALY, JOHN: Sunburn (79)*.

DANA, BILL: The Nude Bomb (80)*.

DANUS, RICHARD CHRISTIAN: Xanadu (80)*.

DAVIES, JACK: ffolkes (80).
DAVIS, GERRY: The Final Countdown (80)*.
DAY, GERRY: The Black Hole (79)*.
DE PALMA, BRIAN: The Wedding Party (63)*, Greetings (68)*, Murder a la Mod (68), Hi, Mom! (70), Sisters (73)*, The Phantom of the Paradise (74), Dressed To Kill (80).
DEHN, PAUL: Goldfinger (64), The Spy Who Came in from The Cold (65), The Deadly Affair (66), Planet of the Apes (67), The Night of the Generals (67), Murder on the Orient Express (74).
DEMME, JONATHAN: Fighting Mad (76).
DENNIS, CHARLES: Double Negative (80)*.
DEVORE, CHRISTOPHER: The Elephant Man (80)*.
DIDION, JOAN: The Panic in Needle Park (71)*, Play It as It Lays (72)*, A Star is Born (76)*.
DILLON, ROBERT: Prime Cut (72), 99 44/100 Percent Dead (74), French Connection II (75).
DILORENZO, EDWARD: The Idolmaker (80).
DOCHTERMANN, RUDY: The Fiendish Plot Of Dr. Fu Manchu (80)*.
DOLINSKY, MEYER: The Fifth Floor (80).
DONNELLY, THOMAS MICHAEL: Defiance (80).
DONOVAN, MARTIN: Loving Couples (80).
DOOLEY, PAUL: Health (80)*.
DOWD, NANCY: Slapshot (77), Coming Home (78).
DRAGOTI, STAN: Dirty Little Billy (72)*.
DRAKE, T.Y.: Terror Train (80).
DRISKILL, WILLIAM: Seven (79)*.
DUNCAN, ELIZABETH: The War At Home (79).
DUNNE, JOHN GREGORY: The Panic in Needle Park (71)*, Play It as It Lays (72)*, A Star is Born (76)*.
EASTMAN, CAROL: see Joyce, Adrien.
EASTMAN, CHARLES: Little Fauss and Big Halsey (70), The All-American Boy (73), Second-Hand Hearts (80).
EASTMAN, SPENCER: Hide In Plain Sight (80).
EBERT, ROGER: Beyond the Valley of the Dolls (70).
EDWARDS, BLAKE: 10 (79).
EGLESON, JAN: Billy In The Lowlands (79).
ELIAS, MICHAEL: The Frisco Kid (79)*, The Jerk (79)*, Serial (80)*.
ELIASON, JOYCE: Tell Me a Riddle (80)*.
ESZTERHAS, JOE: F.I.S.T. (78)*.
EUSTIS, RICH: Serial (80)*.
EXTON, CLIVE: The Awakening (80)*.
FANAKA, JAMES: Penitentiary (79).
FARRIS, JOHN: The Fury (78).
FEIFFER, JULES: Carnal Knowledge (71), Little Murders (71), Popeye (80).

FEKE, STEVE: When A Stranger Calls (79)˙.

FELDMAN, MARTY: The Last Remake of Beau Geste (77)˙, In God We Trust (80)˙.

FENADY, ANDREW J.: The Man With Bogart's Face (80).

FERRIS, BETH: Heartland (80).

FISCHER, MAX: The Lucky Star (80)˙.

FISHBEIN, BARNET: Jesus (79).

FITZGERALD, BENEDICT: Wise Blood (79).

FLICKER, THEODORE: Up in the Cellar (70).

FLYNN, JOHN: The Outfit (73).

FONDA, PETER: Easy Rider (69).

FORBES, BRYAN: King Rat (65), The Raging Moon (70), The Slipper and the Rose (76), International Velvet (78), Hopscotch (80)˙.

FOREMAN, CARL: When Time Ran Out (80)˙.

FORMAN, MILOS: Taking Off (71).

FOSSE, BOB: All That Jazz (79)˙.

FOWLER, ROBERT: Below The Belt (80)˙.

FOX, FRED S.: Oh, God! Book II (80)˙.

FRANCOVICH, ALLAN: On Company Business (80).

FRANK, HARRIET, Jr.: Hud (63)˙, Hombre (67)˙, The Reivers (69)˙, The Cowboys (72)˙, Conrack (74)˙, The Spikes Gang (74)˙, Norma Rae (79)˙.

FRANK, MELVIN: A Funny Thing Happened on the Way to the Forum (66), Buona Sera Mrs. Campbell (68), A Touch of Class (73), The Duchess and the Dirtwater Fox (76)˙, Lost And Found (79)˙.

FREEDMAN, GERROLD: Borderline (80)˙.

FREEMAN, FRED: Start the Revolution Without Me (69)˙, SPYS (74)˙, The Big Bus (76)˙.

FREEMAN, LYN: Without Warning (80)˙.

FRIEDKIN, WILLIAM: Cruising (80).

FRIEDMAN, BRUCE JAY: Stir Crazy (80).

FRIEDMAN, STEPHEN: Lovin' Molly (73).

FULLER, SAMUEL: The Big Red One (80).

FURIE, SYDNEY J.: The Boys in Company C (78).

GAINES, CHARLES: Stay Hungry (76).

GALE, BOB: I Wanna Hold Your Hand (78), 1941 (79)˙, Used Cars (80)˙.

GALFAS, TIMOTHY: Sunnyside (79).

GARDNER, ROBERT: Clarence And Angel (80).

GARFIELD, BRIAN: Hopscotch (80)˙.

GARLAND, ROBERT: The Electric Horseman (79).

GELLER, STEPHEN: Slaughterhouse Five (72), The Valachi Papers (72).

GENT, PETER: North Dallas Forty (79)˙.

GETCHELL, ROBERT: Alice Doesn't Live Here Anymore (74), Bound for Glory (76).

GIDDING, NELSON: Beyond The Poseidon Adventure (79).

GILER, DAVID: The Parallax View (74), The Black Bird (75), Fun with Dick and Jane (77)*.

GILLIAM, TERRY: Life Of Brian (79)*.

GILROY, FRANK D.: The Subject Was Roses (68), The Only Game in Town (69), Desperate Characters (71), From Noon to Three (73), Once in Paris (78).

GLAZER, MITCHELL: Mr. Mikes Mondo Video (79)*.

GOLDBERG, DANNY: Meatballs (79)*.

GOLDMAN, BO: The Rose (79)*, Melvin and Howard (80).

GOLDMAN, HAL: Oh, God! Book II (80)*.

GOLDMAN, JAMES: A Lion in Winter (68), Nicholas and Alexandra (71), They Might Be Giants (71), Robin and Marian (76).

GOLDMAN, WILLIAM: Masquerade (65), Harper (66), Butch Cassidy and the Sundance Kid (69), The Hot Rock (72), The Stepford Wives (74), The Great Waldo Pepper (75), All the President's Men (76), Marathon Man (76), A Bridge Too Far (77), Magic (78).

GOLDRUP, RAY: Windwalker (80).

GOODHART, WILLIAM: Cloud Dancer (80).

GOODMAN, DAVID ZELAG: Lovers and Other Strangers (69), Monte Walsh (70), Straw Dogs (71), Man on a Swing (73), Farewell My Lovely (75), Logan's Run (76), Eyes of Laura Mars (78).

GORE, CHRISTOPHER: Fame (80).

GOTTLIEB, CARL: Jaws (75), Which Way is Up? (77), Jaws 2 (78), The Jerk (79)*.

GRAY, WILLIAM: Prom Night (80), The Changeling (80)*.

GREEN, WALON: Brinks (79).

GREENE, DAVID: Godspell (73).

GREENFELD, JOSH: Harry and Tonto (74), Oh, God! Book II (80)*.

GRIES, TOM: Will Penny (67), 100 Rifles (69).

GRODNIK, DANIEL: Without Warning (80)*.

GUARE, JOHN: Atlantic City U S A (80).

GUNN, BILL: Stop (70), The Angel Levine (70), Ganja and Hess (73).

HACKIN, DENNIS: Wanda Nevada (79), Bronco Billy (80).

HAILEY, OLIVER: Just You And Me, Kid (79)*.

HALES, JONATHAN: The Mirror Crack'd (80)*.

HALEY, JACK, Jr.: That's Entertainment (74).

HANSON, JOHN: Northern Lights (79).

HARPER, HENRY: Scavenger Hunt (79)*.

HARRIS, JAMES B.: Some Call It Loving (73).

HARRIS, TIMOTHY: Cheaper to Keep Her (80)*.

HARRISON, JOHN: Shock Waves (75)*.

HARVEY, RON: Fist of Fear Touch of Death (80).

HASS, CHARLIE: Over The Edge (79)*.

HEDLEY, THOMAS: Circle Of Two (80), Double Negative (80)*.

HEIMS, JO: Play Misty for Me (71), You'll Like My Mother (72), Breezy (73).

HENDERSHOT, ERIC: Take Down (79)*.

HENRY, BUCK: The Graduate (67), Candy (68), Catch-22 (70), The Owl and the Pussycat (70), What's Up, Doc? (72)*, The Day of the Dolphin (73), First Family (80).

HERNDON, VENABLE: Alice's Restaurant (69).

HESTON, FRASER CLARKE: The Mountain Men (80).

HIGGINS, COLIN: Harold and Maude (71), The Silver Streak (77), Foul Play (78), Nine To Five (80)*.

HILL, DEBRA: Halloween (78), The Fog (80)*.

HILL, WALTER: Hickey and Boggs (72), The Getaway (72), The Mackintosh Man (73), The Thief Who Came to Dinner (73), Hard Times (75), The Drowning Pool (75), The Driver (78), The Warriors (79)*.

HOPCRAFT, ARTHUR: Agatha (79)*.

HOPKINS, JOHN: Murder By Decree (79).

HOPPER, DENNIS: Easy Rider (69), The Last Movie (71).

HUNTER, EVAN: Walk Proud (79).

HUNTER, THOMAS: The Final Countdown (80)*.

HUNTER, TIM: Over The Edge (79)*.

HURWITZ, LEO: Dialogue With a Woman Departed (80).

HUSTON, JOHN: The Kremlin Letter (70).

HUYCK, WILLARD: American Graffiti (73)*, Lucky Lady (75)*, Havana (78)*, French Postcards (79)*, Radioland Murders (79)*.

HYAMS, PETER: Busting (74), Our Time (74), Telefon (77), Capricorn One (78), Hanover Street (79), The Hunter (80)*.

IDLE, ERIC: Life Of Brian (79)*.

ILLIDGE, PAUL: Head On (80)*.

IVORY, JAMES: The Guru (68).

JACKSON, LEWIS: You Better Watch Out (80).

JACOBS, JACK: In Search Of Historic Jesus (80)*.

JACOBS, SEAMAN: Oh, God! Book II (80)*.

JAGLOM, HENRY: Sitting Ducks (79).

JAMES, FREDERICK: Humanoids From The Deep (80).

JEWISON, NORMAN: Jesus Christ Superstar (73).

JHABVALA, RUTH PRAWER: Hullabaloo Over Georgie and Bonnie's Pictures (79), Jane Austen In Manhattan (80).

JOHNSON, DIANE: The Shining (80)*.

JOHNSON, MONICA: Americathon (79)*.

JONES, ROBERT C.: Coming Home (78).

JONES, TERRY: Life Of Brian (79)*.

JOUVENAT, GARY JULES: Out Of The Blue (80)*.

JOYCE, ADRIEN (CAROL EASTMAN): The Shooting (66), Five Easy Pieces (70), Puzzle of a Downfall Child (71), The Fortune (75).

Paul Schrader.   Robert Benton.

JUHL, JERRY: The Muppet Movie (79)*.
KANE, MICHAEL: Hot Stuff (79)*, Foolin' Around (80)*.
KANE, ROBERT G.: The Villain (79).
KANEW, JEFF: Natural Enemies (79).
KAPLAN, JONATHAN: White Line Fever (75).
KASDAN, LAWRENCE: The Empire Strikes Back (80)*.
KATZ, GLORIA: American Graffiti (73)*, Lucky Lady (75)*, Havana
    (78)*, French Postcards (79)*, Radioland Murders (79)*.
KAUFMAN, CHARLES: Mother's Day (80)*.
KAUFMAN, PHILIP: The Great Northfield Minnesota Raid (71), The
    Wanderers (79)*.
KAUFMAN, ROBERT: Getting Straight (70), I Love My Wife (70), Harry
    and Walter Go to New York (76), Love at First Bite (79), How To
    Beat The High Cost of Living (80), Nothing Personal (80).
KAUFMAN, ROSE: The Wanderers (79)*.
KAYE, JOHN: Rafferty and the Gold Dust Twins (75), American Hot
    Wax (78), Where The Buffalo Roam (80).
KAZIN, ELIA: America (63), The Arrangement (69), The Visitors (72).
KEACH, JAMES: The Long Riders (80)*.
KEACH, STACY: The Long Riders (80)*.
KELLOGG, MARJORIE: The Bell Jar (79).
KENNEDY, ADAM: Raise The Titanic (80).
KENNEDY, BURT: Young Billy Young (69), Hannie Caulder (71), The
    Train Robbers (73).
KERBY, BILL: The Rose (79)*.
KERN, RONNI: A Change of Seasons (80)*.
KING, JEFF: Sunnyside (79).
KINOY, ERNEST: Brother John (70), Buck and The Preacher (71),
    Leadbelly (75).

KLEINSCHMIDT, CARL: Middle Age Crazy (80).
KLINE, STEVE: Borderline (80)*.
KOENIG, LAIRD: Bloodline (79).
KOHN, JOHN: Goldengirl (79).
KORTCHMAR, MICHAEL: Love in a Taxi (80).
KORTY, JOHN: Oliver's Story (78)*.
KOSINSKI, JERZY: Being There (79).
KOTCHEFF, TED: North Dallas Forty (79)*.
KRANTZ, STEVE: Swap Meet (79).
KUBRICK, STANLEY: The Shining (80)*.
LA FRENAIS, IAN: The Prisoner Of Zenda (79)*.
LAGER, MARTIN: The Shape Of Things To Come (79).
LANCASTER, BILL: The Bad News Bears (76).
LANCASTER, BURT: The Midnight Man (74).
LANDIS, JOHN: The Blues Brothers (80)*.
LARDNER, RING, Jr.: The Cincinnati Kid (65), MASH (70), The Greatest
    (77).
LARNER, JEREMY: Drive, He Said (70)*, The Candidate (72).
LARSON, GLEN A.: Buck Rogers (79)*.
LATHAM, AARON: Urban Cowboy (80)*.
LAUGHLIN, TOM: Billy Jack (71), The Trial of Billy Jack (72).
LAURENTS, ARTHUR: The Way We Were (73), The Turning Point (77).
LEAR, NORMAN: Cold Turkey (70).
LEHMAN, ERNEST: Hello Dolly (69), Portnoy's Complaint (72), Family
    Plot (76), Black Sunday (77).
LEHMAN, LEW: Phobia (80)*.
LEIGHT, WARREN D.: Mother's Day (80)*.
LEIGHTON, TED: The Hunter (80)*.
LEVINSON, BARRY: ...And Justice For All (79)*.
LEWIS, ANDY and DAVE: Klute (71).
LIVINGSTON, HAROLD: Star Trek (79).
LOMMEL, ULLI: The Boogey Man (80).
LUCAS, GEORGE: THX 1138 (70)*, American Graffiti (73)*, Star Wars
    (77).
LURASCHI, TONY: The Outsider (79).
LYNCH, DAVID: The Elephant Man (80)*.
LYTLE, ALEV: Tell Me a Riddle (80)*.
MADDOX, DIANA: The Changeling (80)*.
MALICK, TERRENCE: Pocket Money (72), Badlands (73), The Gravy
    Train (74), Days of Heaven (78).
MANDEL, LORING: Promises In The Dark (79).
MANKIEWICZ, TOM: Live and Let Die (73), The Man with the Golden
    Gun (74), Mother, Jugs and Speed (76), The Cassandra Crossing
    (77), The Eagle Has Landed (77).
MANN, ABBY: A Child Is Waiting (62), The Detective (68), Report to

the Commissioner (74).

MANN, STANLEY: Circle Of Iron (79)*, Meteor (79)*.

MARCEL, TERENCE: Hawk the Slayer (80)*, There Goes the Bride (80)*.

MARCUS, LAWRENCE B.: Petulia (68), Justine (69), Alex and the Gypsy (76), The Stunt Man (80)*.

MARIN, ANDREW PETER: Hog Wild (80).

MARIN, CHEECH: Cheech And Chong's Next Movie (80)*.

MARTIN, MARDIK: Mean Streets (73)*, New York, New York (77)*, Valentino (77)*, Raging Bull (80)*.

MARTIN, STEVE: The Jerk (79)*.

MATHESON, RICHARD: Somewhere In Time (80).

MATHIS, STEVE: Without Warning (80)*.

MATHISON, MELISSA: The Black Stallion (79)*.

MAY, ELAINE: A New Leaf (71), Such Good Friends (71), Mikey and Nicky (76), Heaven Can Wait (78)*.

MAYES, WENDELL: Advise and Consent (62), In Harm's Way (65), Hotel (67), The Poseidon Adventure (72), The Revengers (72), Death Wish (74), The Bank Shot (74).

MAZURSKY, PAUL: I Love You, Alice B. Toklas (69)*, Alex in Wonderland (70)*, Blume in Love (73), Harry and Tonto (74)*, Next Stop, Greenwich Village (76), An Unmarried Woman (78), Willie & Phil (80).

McGUANE, THOMAS: Rancho De Luxe (74), 92 in the Shade (76), The Missouri Breaks (76), Tom Horn (80)*.

McINTYRE, TOM: Lady Grey (80), Living Legend (80).

McKAY, BRIAN: Brewster McCloud (70), McCabe and Mrs. Miller (71)*.

MEDLIN, BIG BOY: Roadie (80)*.

MERRILL, KEITH: Take Down (79)*.

MEYER, NICHOLAS: The Seven Percent Solution (76), Time After Time (79).

MEYERS, NANCY: Private Benjamin (80).

MICHAELS, LORNE: Gilda Live (80)*.

MIDLER, BETTE: Divine Madness (80)*.

MILIUS, JOHN: Evel Knivel (71), Jeremiah Johnson (72), The Life and Times of Judge Roy Bean (72), Dillinger (73), Magnum Force (73), The Wind and the Lion (75), Big Wednesday (78), Apocalypse Now (79)*.

MILLER, HARVEY: Private Benjamin (80).

MILLER, MELISSA: Oh, God! Book II (80)*.

MILLER, VICTOR: Friday the 13th (80).

MISLOVE, MICHAEL: Americathon (79)*.

MOLONEY, JIM: The Fiendish Plot Of Dr. Fu Manchu (80)*.

MONASH, PAUL: The Friends of Eddie Coyle (73).

MORTIMER, JOHN: John and Mary (69).

MURPHY, RICHARD: The Kidnapping Of The President (80).

MUTRUX, FLOYD: The Christian Licorice Store (70), Freebie and The Bean (74), Aloha Bobby and Rose (75), American Me (79), Happy Hour (79), The Hollywood Knights (80).

MYHERS, JOHN: The Prize Fighter (79)*, The Private Eyes (80)*.

NAKANO, DESMOND: Boulevard Nights (79).

NANKIN, MICHAEL: Midnight Madness (80)*.

NATKIN, RICK: Night Of The Juggler (80)*.

NELSON, DUSTY: Effects (79).

NELSON, RALPH: Flight of the Doves (71).

NETT, BEN: Without Warning (80)*.

NEWMAN, DAVID: Bonnie and Clyde (67), There Was a Crooked Man (70)*, Bad Company (72), What's Up, Doc? (72)*, The Crazy American Girl (75), Superman (78)*, Superman II (80)*.

NEWMAN, LESLIE: Superman (78)*, Superman II (80)*.

NEWMAN, WALTER: Cat Ballou (67)*, Bloodbrothers (78).

NICHOLLS, ALLAN: A Perfect Couple (79)*.

NICHOLSON, JACK: Drive, He Said (70)*.

NILSSON, ROB: Northern Lights (79).

NORTH, EDMUND H.: Meteor (79)*.

NORTON, B.W.L.: More American Graffiti (79).

NORTON, BILL, Sr.: Night Of The Juggler (80)*.

NOVELLO, DON: Gilda Live (80)*.

NUNEZ, VICTOR: Gal Young Un (79).

O DONOGHUE, MICHAEL: Mr. Mikes Mondo Video (79)*.

O'BANNON, DAN: Alien (79).

O'NEILL, ROBERT VINCENT: The Baltimore Bullet (80)*.

OLIANSKY, JOEL: The Competition (80).

OLIVER, STEPHEN: Sunburn (79)*.

ORMSBY, ALAN: My Bodyguard (80), The Little Dragons (80)*.

PALIN, MICHAEL: Life Of Brian (79)*.

PARENT, GAIL: The Main Event (79)*.

PARKER, SCOTT: Die Laughing (80)*, He Knows You're Alone (80).

PATCHETT, TOM: Up The Academy (80)*.

PAUL, STEVEN: Falling In Love Again (80)*.

PAULSEN, DAVID: Schizoid (80).

PECK, KIMI: Little Darlings (80)*.

PECKINPAH, SAM: The Wild Bunch (69)*, Straw Dogs (71)*.

PENN, ARTHUR: Alice's Restaurant (69).

PERKINS, TONY: The Last of Sheila (73)*.

PERRY, ELEANOR: David and Lisa (62), The Swimmer (68), Last Summer (69), The Lady in the Car With Glasses... (69), Diary of a Mad Housewife (70), The Man Who Loved Cat Dancing (73).

PIERSON, FRANK: Cat Ballou (67)*, Cool Hand Luke (67), The

Happening (67), The Looking Glass War (69), The Anderson Tapes (71), Dog Day Afternoon (75), King of the Gypsies (78).

PLATT, POLLY: Pretty Baby (78).

POLONSKY, ABRAHAM: Avalanche Express (79).

PONICSAN, DARRYL: Cinderella Liberty (74).

POWELL, PETER: The Final Countdown (80)*.

PRAGER, EMILY: Mr. Mikes Mondo Video (79)*.

PUZO, MARIO: Superman (78)*, Superman II (80)*.

RAFELSON, BOB: Head (68), Stay Hungry (76).

RAMIS, HAROLD: Meatballs (79)*.

RAUCH, EARL MAC: New York, New York (77).

RAUCHER, HERMAN: Sweet November (68), Watermelon Man (69), Summer of '42 (71), Class of '44 (73), Ode to Billie Joe (76), The Other Side of Midnight (77)*, There Should Have Been Castles (79).

RAVETCH, IRVING: Hud (63)*, Hombre (67)*, The Reivers (69)*, The Cowboys (72)*, Conrack (74)*, The Spikes Gang (74)*, Norma Rae (79)*.

RAYFIEL, DAVID: Castle Keep (68), Valdez is Coming (70), Three Days of the Condor (75)*, Lipstick (76).

REICHERT, MARK: Union City (80).

REINER, CARL: The Comic (69).

RESNICK, PATRICIA: Nine To Five (80)*.

RICHERT, WILLIAM: The American Success Company (79)*, Winter Kills (79).

RICHLER, MORDECAI: Life at the Top (65), The Apprenticeship of Duddy Kravitz (74), Fun with Dick and Jane (77)*.

RICHTER, W.D.: Slither (72), Peeper (75), Nickelodeon (76), Invasion of The Bodysnatchers (78), Dracula (79), Brubaker (80).

RICKMAN, TOM: Coal Miner's Daughter (80).

ROBBINS, MATTHEW: The Sugarland Express (73)*, The Bingo Long Traveling All-Stars (76)*, McArthur (77)*, Corvette Summer (78)*.

ROBERTS, MARGUERITE: Norwood (69), True Grit (69).

ROBERTS, WILLIAM: The Magnificent Seven (68), The Last American Hero (73).

ROBERTSON, HARRY: Hawk the Slayer (80)*.

ROEMER, MICHAEL: Pilgrim, Farewell (80).

ROMERO, GEORGE: Martin (78).

ROSE, JACK: Lost And Found (79)*.

ROSE, REGINALD: The Sea Wolves (80).

ROSE, WILLIAM: It's a Mad, Mad, Mad, Mad World (63), The Russians Are Coming, The Russians Are Coming (66), Guess Who's Coming to Dinner? (67), The Flim Flam Man (67), The Secret of Santa Vittoria (69).

ROSEBROOK, JEB: The Black Hole (79)*.

ROSEN, MARC: Final Assignment (80).

ROSENBERG, JEANNE: The Black Stallion (79)*.
ROSENTHAL, JACK: The Lucky Star (80)*.
ROSS, JUDITH: Rich Kids (79).
ROTH, ERIC: The Concorde-Airport '79 (79).
RUBEL, MARC REID: Xanadu (80)*.
RUBIN, MANN: First Deadly Sin (80).
RUDOLPH, ALAN: Buffalo Bill and the Indians (76)*, Welcome to L.A. (77), Remember My Name (78).
RUSH, RICHARD: The Stunt Man (80)*.
SACHS, WILLIAM: Galaxina (80).
SACKS, EZRA: A Small Circle Of Friends (80).
SALMINI, AMBROSE: American Odyssey (80).
SALT, WALDO: Midnight Cowboy (69), The Gang That Couldn't Shoot Straight (71), Serpico (73), The Day of the Locust (75), Coming Home (78).
SANDERSON, JAMES: Head On (80)*.
SANDLER, BARRY: Gable and Lombard (76), The Duchess and the Dirtwater Fox (76)*, The Mirror Crack'd (80)*.
SANGSTER, JAMES: The Legacy (79)*, Phobia (80)*.
SARGENT, ALVIN: The Stalking Moon (68), The Sterile Cuckoo (69), I Walk the Line (70), Love, Pain and the Whole Damn Thing (72), The Effect of Gamma Rays (72), Paper Moon (73), Bobby Deerfield (77), Julia (77), Ordinary People (80).
SARNE, MIKE: Myra Breckinridge (70).
SAYLES, JOHN: Alligator (80), Battle Beyond The Stars (80), Return Of The Secaucus Seven (80).
SCHELL, MAXIMILIAN: End of the Game (76).
SCHMIDT, WAYNE: The Day Time Ended (80)*.
SCHMOELLER, DAVID: The Day Time Ended (80)*.
SCHNEIDER, BARRY: Roller Boogie (79).
SCHRADER, LEONARD: The Yakuza (75), Blue Collar (78)*, Old Boyfriends (79)*.
SCHRADER, PAUL: The Yakuza (75), Obsession (76), Taxi Driver (76), Rolling Thunder (77), Blue Collar (78)*, Hardcore (79), Old Boyfriends (79)*, American Gigolo (80), Raging Bull (80)*.
SCHULMAN, ARNOLD: Players (79).
SCHUMACHER, JOEL: Carwash (76), The Wiz (78).
SCORSESE, MARTIN: What's a Nice Girl Like You... (63), It's Not Just You, Murray (64)*, The Big Shave (67), Who's That Knocking at My Door (69), Mean Streets (73)*.
SCOTT, ALLAN: The Awakening (80)*.
SEATON, GEORGE: What's So Bad About Feeling Good (68), Airport (69).
SEGAL, ERICH: Yellow Submarine (68), Love Story (70), R.P.M. (70), Oliver's Story (78)*, Oliver's Story (78), A Change of Seasons (80)*.

SEGAL, FRED: A Change of Seasons (80)*.

SEGAL, JERRY: Die Laughing (80)*.

SELTZER, DAVID: King, Queen, Knave (72), One Is a Lonely Number (72), The Other Side of the Mountain (75), The Omen (76), Damien-Omen II (78), Prophecy (79).

SEMPLE, LORENZO, Jr.: Daddy's Gone A-Hunting (69), Pretty Poison (69), The Marriage of a Young Stockbroker (71), Papillon (73), The Parallax View (74), The Super Cops (74), The Drowning Pool (75)*, Three Days of the Condor (75)*, King Kong (76), Dick Tracy (79), Hurricane (79), Flash Gordon (80)*.

SHABER, DAVID: The Warriors (79)*, Those Lips Those Eyes (80).

SHAGAN, STEVE: Save the Tiger (72), Hustle (75), Nightwing (78), Nightwing (79)*, The Formula (80).

SHANER, JOHN HERMAN: The Last Married Couple In America (80).

SHARP, ALAN: The Hired Hand (71), The Last Run (71), Ulzana's Raid (72), Night Moves (75).

SHAVELSON, MELVILLE: The War Between Men and Women (72), Mixed Company (74).

SHAW, FRANK: The Frisco Kid (79)*.

SHERMAN, GARY: Phobia (80)*.

SHERMAN, STANFORD: Any Which Way You Can (80).

SHRAKE, BUD: Kid Blue (73), Nightwing (79)*, Tom Horn (80)*.

SHUSETT, RONALD: Phobia (80)*.

SHUSTER, ROSIE: Gilda Live (80)*.

SHYER, CHARLES: Private Benjamin (80).

SIEGEL, BARRY: Windows (80).

SILLIPHANT, STIRLING: In the Heat of the Night (67), Charly (68), A Walk in the Spring Rain (69), Marlowe (69), The Liberation of L.B. Jones (70), Murphy's War (71), The New Centurions (72), The Poseidon Adventure (72), Shaft in Africa (73), The Towering Inferno (74), The Killer Elite (75), The Enforcer (76), Telefon (77), The Swarm (78), Circle Of Iron (79)*, When Time Ran Out (80)*.

SILVER, JOAN MICKLIN: Hester Street (74), Head Over Heels (79).

SIMON, MAYO: Marooned (69), Futureworld (76).

SIMON, NEIL: After the Fox (66), Barefoot in the Park (67), Sweet Charity (68), The Odd Couple (68), The Out of Towners (70), Plaza Suite (71), The Star Spangled Girl (71), The Heartbreak Kid (72), The Last of the Red Hot Lovers (72), The Prisoner of Second Avenue (75), The Sunshine Boys (75), Murder by Death (76), California Suite (78), The Cheap Detective (78), The Goodbye Girl (78), Chapter Two (79), Seems Like Old Times (80).

SIMON, PAUL: One Trick Pony (80).

SISSON, ROSEMARY ANNE: The Watcher In The Woods (80)*.

SLADE, BERNARD: Tribute (80).

SMITH, ANDREW: The Main Event (79)*.

SMITH, GREG: The Last Word (79)*.
SMITH, MARTIN CRUZ: Nightwing (79)*.
SMITH, STEVEN PHILLIP: The Long Riders (80)*.
SOBIESKI, CAROL: Honeysuckle Rose (80)*.
SONDHEIM, STEPHEN: The Last of Sheila (73)*.
SONNETT, SHERRY: Below The Belt (80)*.
SOUTHERN, TERRY: The Cincinnati Kid (65), The Loved One (65),
    Easy Rider (69), The Magic Christian (70).
SPALDING, HARRY: The Watcher In The Woods (80)*.
SPIELBERG, STEVEN: Close Encounters of the Third Kind (77).
STALLONE, SYLVESTER: Rocky (76), F.I.S.T. (78), Paradise Alley (78),
    Rocky II (79).
STARKES, JAISON: The Fish That Saved Pittsburgh (79)*.
STERN, LEONARD: Just You And Me, Kid (79)*, Two of a Kind (79),
    The Nude Bomb (80)*.
STERN, SANDOR: The Amityville Horror (79).
STERN, STEVEN: Running (79).
STEVENS, EDMOND: The Fish That Saved Pittsburgh (79)*.
STEVENS, LESLIE: Buck Rogers (79)*.
STEWART, DOUGLAS DAY: Blue Lagoon (80).
STONE, OLIVER: Midnight Express (78), Born on the Fourth of July
    (79), The Platoon (79).
STONE, PETER: Charade (63), Father Goose (64), Mirage (65), The
    Secret War of Harry Frigg (67), Sweet Charity (68), The Skin Game
    (71), 1776 (72), The Taking of Pelham 1-2-3 (74), Silver Bears (77),
    Who Is Killing the Great Chef's of Europe (78), Why Would I Lie?
    (80).
STOPPARD, TOM: The Human Factor (79).
SULTAN, ARNE: The Nude Bomb (80)*.
SWIFT, DAVID: Foolin' Around (80)*.
TAIT, DON: Herbie Goes Bananas (80).
TARADASH, DANIEL: Hawaii (66), Castle Keep (68), The Other Side of
    Midnight (77)*.
TARSES, JAY: Up The Academy (80)*.
TAYLOR, RENEE: Lovers and Other Strangers (69)*, Made for Each
    Other (71)*, Mixed Company (74)*, Woman of the Year (75)*.
TESICH, STEVE: Breaking Away (79).
TEWKESBURY, JOAN: Thieves Like Us (74)*, Nashville (75).
THEROUX, PAUL: Saint Jack (79).
THOM, ROBERT: Bloody Mama (70), Crazy Mama (75).
THOMAS, GUY: Wholly Moses! (80).
THOMPSON, ROB: Hearts of the West (75).
THORNLEY, STEVEN: Hangar 18 (80).
TIDYMAN, ERNEST: Shaft (71), The French Connection (71), High
    Plains Drifter (72), Shaft's Big Score (72), Report to the

Commissioner (74), Street People (79).

TILLEY, PATRIC: The Legacy (79)*.

TOBACK, JAMES: The Gambler (75), Fingers (78).

TOWNE, ROBERT: Villa Rides (68), The Last Detail (73), Chinatown (74), Shampoo (75), The Yakuza (75), Greystoke (79).

TRUMBO, DALTON: Exodus (60), Spartacus (60), Hawaii (66), The Fixer (68), The Horsemen (70), Johnny Got His Gun (71), Executive Action (73), Papillon (73).

TUGGLE, RICHARD: Escape From Alcatraz (79).

TYNAN, KATHLEEN: Agatha (79)*.

UDOFF, YALE: Bad Timing (80).

USTINOV, PETER: Lady L (65).

VAIL, STEVEN A.: Scavenger Hunt (79)*.

VARHOL, MICHAEL: The Last Word (79)*.

VEBER, FRANCIS: Sunday Lovers (80)*.

VENTURA, MICHAEL: Roadie (80)*.

VERONA, STEPHEN: Pipe Dreams (76), Boardwalk (79)*.

VILANCH, BRUCE: Divine Madness (80)*.

VINT, JESSE: Hometown USA (79).

WAGNER, JANE: Moment By Moment (78).

WAITE, RALPH: On The Nickel (80).

WALD, MARVIN: In Search Of Historic Jesus (80)*.

WALSH, JOSEPH: California Split (74).

WALTON, FRED: When A Stranger Calls (79)*.

WAMBAUGH, JOSEPH: The Black Marble (80).

WARD, DAVID S.: Steelyard Blues (72), The Sting (73).

WASHBURN, DERIC: The Deer Hunter (78).

WECHTER, DAVID: Midnight Madness (80)*.

WEIDERHORN, KEN: Shock Waves (75)*.

WEINGROD, HERSCHEL: Cheaper to Keep Her (80)*.

WEISER, STANLEY: Coast To Coast (80).

WELLAND, COLIN: Yanks (79)*.

WELLER, MICHAEL: Hair (79).

WESLEY, RICHARD: Uptown Saturday Night (74), Let's Do It Again (75).

WESTLAKE, DONALD: Cops and Robbers (73), Hot Stuff (79)*.

WEXLER, HASKELL: Medium Cool (69).

WEXLER, NORMAN: Joe (70), Serpico (73), Mandingo (75), Saturday Night Fever (77).

WHEAT, JIM: Silent Scream (80)*.

WHEAT, KEN: Silent Scream (80)*.

WHEELER, HUGH: Nijinsky (80).

WHEELER, PAUL: The Legacy (79)*.

WILDER, BILLY: The Private Life of Sherlock Holmes (70), The Front Page (74).

WILDER, GENE: Young Frankenstein (74), The Adventure of Sherlock Holmes (75), Sunday Lovers (80)*.

WILLIAMSON, TONY: Breakthrough (79).

WILLINGHAM, CALDER: The Graduate (67), Little Big Man (70), Thieves Like Us (74)*.

WINNER, MICHAEL: The Big Sleep (78).

WITTENBORN, DIRK: Mr. Mikes Mondo Video (79)*.

WITTLIFF, WILLIAM D.: The Black Stallion (79)*, Honeysuckle Rose (80)*.

WOHL, IRA: Best Boy (79).

WOOD, CHARLES: Cuba (79).

WOOD, CHRISTOPHER: Moonraker (79).

WOODARD, BRONTE: Can't Stop The Music (80)*.

WRYE, DONALD: Ice Castles (78)*.

WURLITZER, RUDOLPH: Two-Lane Blacktop (71), Pat Garrett and Billy The Kid (73).

WYNN, TRACY KEENAN: The Autobiography of Ms. Jane Pitman (73), The Longest Yard (74), The Drowning Pool (75)*, The Deep (77).

YABLANS, FRANK: North Dallas Forty (79)*.

YAKIR, LEONARD: Out Of The Blue (80)*.

YATES, BROCK: Smokey And The Bandit II (80)*.

YATES, PETER: Robbery (67).

YORK, SUSANNAH: Falling In Love Again (80)*.

YOUNG, BURT: Uncle Joe Shannon (78).

YOUNG, DALENE: Little Darlings (80)*.

YOUNG, TERENCE: The Christmas Tree (69).

ZACHARIAS, ALFREDO: The Bees (78).

ZEMECKIS, ROBERT: I Wanna Hold Your Hand (78), 1941 (79), Used Cars (80)*.

ZUCKER, DAVID: Airplane (80).

ZUCKER, JERRY: Airplane (80).

Producers
of all sorts

ABRAHAMS, JIM: Airplane (80).

ABRAMSON, RICHARD C.: The Last Word (79).

ADAMS, BERLE: Brass Target (78).

ADAMS, TONY: 10 (79).

ADELSON, MERV: The Big Red One (80).

ADLER, GIL: Home Movies (79).

AFFRIME, MINDY: Tell Me a Riddle (80).

ALDRICH, ROBERT: The Killing of Sister George (68), Too Late the Hero (69), The Grissom Gang (71), Ulzana's Raid (72), Hustle (75).

ALLEN, IRWIN: The Big Circus (59), Voyage to the Bottom of the Sea (61), The Wrecking Crew (68), The Poseidon Adventure (72), The Swarm (78), Beyond The Poseidon Adventure (79), When Time Ran Out (80).

ALLEN, JAY PRESSON: It's My Turn (80), Just Tell Me What You Want (80).

ALTMAN, ROBERT: The Late Show (77), Welcome to L.A. (77), Remember My Name (78), A Perfect Couple (79), Rich Kids (79), Health (80).

ARBEID, BEN: Eagle's Wing (79).

ARKIN, ALAN: The In-Laws (79).

ARKOFF, SAMUEL Z.: The Amityville Horror (79), Dressed To Kill (80), How To Beat The High Cost of Living (80).

ASSEYEV, TAMARA: Norma Rae (79).

ASTAIRE, JARVIS: Agatha (79).

AURTHUR, ROBERT ALAN: All That Jazz (79).

AVEDIS, HOWARD: The Fifth Floor (80).

AVILDSEN, JOHN: Slow Dancing in the Big City (78).

AVNET, JON: Coast To Coast (80).

AXELROD, GEORGE: How to Murder Your Wife (65), Lord Love a Duck (66), The Secret Life of an American Wife (68).

AYDELOTT, WILLIAM: Return Of The Secaucus Seven (80).

AYRES, GERALD: Foxes (80).

AZOFF, IRVING: Urban Cowboy (80).

BACH, STEVEN: Butch And Sundance (79).

BAER, MAX, Jr.: Macon County Line (73), The McCulloughs (75), Ode to Billie Joe (76).

BALLARD, THOMAS E.: Windwalker (80).

BAND, CHARLES: The Day Time Ended (80).

BART, PETER: Fun with Dick and Jane (77)*, Islands in the Stream (77)*.

BBS: Head (68), Easy Rider (69), Drive, He Said (70), Five Easy Pieces (70), A Safe Place (71), The Last Picture Show (71), The King of Marvin Gardens (72), Hearts and Minds (74), Stay Hungry (76).

BEATTY, WARREN: Bonnie and Clyde (67), Shampoo (75), Heaven Can Wait (78).

BEAUDINE, WILLIAM, Jr.: The Magic Of Lassie (78).

BECKERMAN, SIDNEY: Bloodline (79), Serial (80).

BEFFA, SUZANNE: American Odyssey (80).

BEGELMAN, DAVID: Wholly Moses! (80).

BELIN, GRAHAM: Union City (80).

BELKIN, ALAN: The Octagon (80).

BELLAFONTE, HARRY: The Angel Levine (70), Buck and The Preacher (71).

BELOLO, HENRI: Can't Stop The Music (80).

BELSON, JERRY: How Sweet It Is (68), The Grasshopper (69).

BENESON, BILL: Boulevard Nights (79).

BENSON, ROBBY: Die Laughing (80).

BERMAN, LESTER: Something Short Of Paradise (79).

BERNSTEIN, JACK B.: North Dallas Forty (79).

BERNSTEIN, JAY: Sunburn (79), Nothing Personal (80).

BERNSTEIN, WALTER: The Molly Maguires (68).

BERUH, JOSEPH: He Knows You're Alone (80).

BICK, JERRY: The Long Goodbye (73), Thieves Like Us (74), Russian Roulette (75).

BILL, TONY: Deadhead Miles (70), Steelyard Blues (72), The Sting (73), Hearts of the West (75), Harry and Walter Go to New York (76), Boulevard Nights (79), Going In Style (79), The Little Dragons (80).

BLATT, DANIEL H.: The American Success Company (79).

BLATTY, WILLIAM PETER: The Ninth Configuration (80).

BLOCH, CHARLES B.: The Fog (80).

BOGDANOVICH, PETER: What's Up, Doc? (72), Paper Moon (73), Daisy Miller (74), At Long Last Love (75), Nickelodeon (76).

BOORMAN, JOHN: Deliverance (72), Zardoz (73).

BOX, BETTY E.: It's Not The Size That Counts (79).

BRABOURNE, JOHN: The Mirror Crack'd (80).

BRACKMAN, JACOB: Times Square (80).

BRANDT, JERROLD, Jr.: The Bell Jar (79).

BRASCIA, JOHN F.: The Baltimore Bullet (80).

BRAUN, ZEV: The Fiendish Plot Of Dr. Fu Manchu (80).

BRAUNSBERG, ANDREW: Being There (79).

BRAUNSTEIN, GEORGE: Fade to Black (80).

BREGMAN, MARTIN: Serpico (73), Dog Day Afternoon (75), The Next Man (76), The Seduction Of Joe Tynan (79), Simon (80).

BREMSON, ROBERT: Alligator (80), The Little Dragons (80).

BRIGHT, RICHARD S.: Tribute (80).

BRILLSTEIN, BERNIE: The Blues Brothers (80), Up The Academy (80).

BROCCOLI, ALBERT R.: Moonraker (79).

BRODSKY, JACK: Little Murders (71), Everything You Always Wanted to Know About Sex (72), Summer Wishes, Winter Dreams (73).

BROOKS, JAMES L.: Starting Over (79).

BROOKS, JOSEPH: If Ever I See You Again (78).

BROOKS, MEL: The Elephant Man (80).

BROOKS, RICHARD: In Cold Blood (67), The Happy Ending (69).

BROWN, BARRY: The War At Home (79), Cloud Dancer (80).

BROWN, DAVID: The Sting (73), The Sugarland Express (73), The Black Windmill (74), Jaws (75), MacArthur (77), Jaws 2 (78), The Island (80).

BROWN, HOWARD: Cheech And Chong's Next Movie (80).

BROWN, WILLIAM F.: Joni (80).

BRUCKHEIMER, JERRY: American Gigolo (80), Defiance (80).

BUBA, PASQUALE: Effects (79).

CAFFEY, RICHARD: Buck Rogers (79).

CAINE, MICHAEL: Pulp (72).

CAMP, JOE: The Double Mcguffin (79), Oh Heavenly Dog (80).

CAMRAS, ROGER: Hometown USA (79).

CANTON, MARK: Die Laughing (80).

CAPRA, FRANK, Jr.: The Black Marble (80).

CARD, LAMAR: Terror Train (80).

CARDONA, RENE, Jr.: Guyana:Cult Of The Damned (80).

CARELLI, JOANN: Heaven's Gate (80).

CARLIN, ED: Battle Beyond The Stars (80).

CARLINO, LEWIS JOHN: The Mechanic (72).

CARR, ALLAN: Can't Stop The Music (80).

CARR, TERRY: Coast To Coast (80).

CARRERAS, MICHAEL: The Lady Vanishes (79).

CARROLL, GORDON: Alien (79).

CARUSO, FRED: Winter Kills (79).

CATES, GILBERT: I Never Sang for My Father (69), Oh, God! Book II (80), The Last Married Couple In America (80).

CATES, JOSEPH: The Last Married Couple In America (80).

CHAPIN, DOUG: When A Stranger Calls (79).

CHARTOFF, ROBERT: The Split (68), Leo the Last (69), They Shoot Horses, Don't They? (69), The Strawberry Statement (70), The Gang That Couldn't Shoot Straight (71), The Mechanic (72), The New Centurions (72), Up the Sandbox (72), SPYS (74), Peeper (75), The Gambler (75), Nickelodeon (76), Rocky (76), New York, New York (77), Comes a Horseman (78), Sons (78), Uncle Joe Shannon (78), Rocky II (79), Raging Bull (80).

CHASE, BRANDON: Alligator (80).

CHRISAFIS, CHRIS: The Sea Wolves (80).

CHRISTIANSEN, ROBERT: Hide In Plain Sight (80).

CIMINO, MICHAEL: The Deerhunter (78).

CLARK, BOB: Murder By Decree (79).

CLARK, GREYDON: Without Warning (80).

COBLENZ, WALTER: All the President's Men (76), The Onion Field (79).

COHEN, MARTIN B.: Humanoids From The Deep (80).

COHEN, RONALD: Running (79), Middle Age Crazy (80).

CONCORAN, KEVIN: Herbie Goes Bananas (80).

CONWAY, JAMES L.: In Search Of Historic Jesus (80).

COONEY, RAY: There Goes the Bride (80).

COOPER, ROBERT: Running (79), Middle Age Crazy (80).

COPPOLA, FRANCIS: THX 1138 (70), American Graffiti (73), The Conversation (74), The Godfather, Part II (74), Apocalypse Now (79), The Black Stallion (79).

CORMAN, GENE: The Big Red One (80).

CORMAN, ROGER: Bloody Mama (70), Gas-s-s (70), Von Richtofen and Brown (71), Boxcar Bertha (72), I Escaped from Devil's Island (73), Cockfighter (74), Death Race 2000 (75), Fighting Mad (76), Moving Violation (76), Thunder and Lightning (76), Piranha (78), Saint Jack (79), Battle Beyond The Stars (80), Humanoids From The Deep (80).

CORNFELD, STUART: Fatso (80), The Elephant Man (80).

CRAWFORD, ROBERT L.: A Little Romance (79).

CROSFIELD, PAUL: The Human Factor (79).

CUNNINGHAM, SEAN S.: Friday the 13th (80).

CURTIS, BRUCE COHN: Roller Boogie (79).

D'ANTONI, PHILIP: Bullitt (68), The French Connection (71), The Seven Ups (73).

DALEY, ROBERT: Play Misty for Me (71), High Plains Drifter (72), Breezy (73), Magnum Force (73), Thunderbolt and Lightfoot (74), The Enforcer (76), The Outlaw Josey Wales (76), Every Which Way But Loose (78), Escape From Alcatraz (79), Any Which Way You Can (80), Bronco Billy (80).

DALY, JOHN: Sunburn (79).

DASHEY, DAVID: The Fish That Saved Pittsburgh (79).

DAVID, PIERRE: Hog Wild (80).

DAVIDSON, WILLIAM: The Shape Of Things To Come (79).

DAVIS, PETER S.: Steel (80).

DAVIS, W. TERRY: H.O.T.S. (79).

DAVISON, JON: Piranha (78), Airplane (80).

DE LAURENTIIS, DINO: Barbarella (68), Waterloo (70), The Valachi Papers (72), Serpico (73), The Stone Killer (73), Death Wish (74), Mandingo (75), Three Days of the Condor (75), King Kong (76), Lipstick (76), The Shootist (76), The Serpent's Egg (77), King of the Gypsies (78), Brinks (79), The Great Train Robbery (79), Flash Gordon (80).

DE PALMA, BRIAN: Home Movies (79).

DE SILVA, DAVID: Fame (80).

DELL, WANDA: The Prize Fighter (79), The Private Eyes (80).

DEUTSCH, STEPHEN: Somewhere In Time (80).

DEVLIN, DON: My Bodyguard (80).

DIMILLA, ROBERT: He Knows You're Alone (80).

DIRECTORS COMPANY: Paper Moon (73), Daisy Miller (74), The Conversation (74).

DOBROFSKY, NEAL: Wanda Nevada (79), Bronco Billy (80).

DONEN, STANLEY: Charade (63), Arabesque (66), Two for the Road (67), Bedazzled (68), Staircase (69), The Little Prince (74), Lucky Lady (75), Movie Movie Baxter's Beauties (78), Movie Movie Dynamite Hands (78), Saturn 3 (80).

DOR, MEIRA ATTIA: Sitting Ducks (79).

DOUGLAS, KIRK: The Light at the End of the World (71), Posse (75).

DOUGLAS, MICHAEL: One Flew Over the Cuckoo's Nest (75), The China Syndrome (79), Running (79).

DOUGLAS, PETER VINCENT: The Final Countdown (80).

DRABINSKY, GARTH B.: The Changeling (80), Tribute (80).

DREYFUSS, LORIN: Skatetown Usa (79).

DREYFUSS, RICHARD: The Big Fix (78).

DUBS, ARTHUR R.: Windwalker (80).

DUNCAN, ELIZABETH: The War At Home (79).

DUNNE, GRIFFIN: Head Over Heels (79).

DUPONT, RENE: Murder By Decree (79).

DURAND, RUDY: Tilt (79).

ECKERT, JOHN: Middle Age Crazy (80).

EDWARDS, BLAKE: 10 (79).

EGLESON, NICK: Billy In The Lowlands (79).

ELFAND, MARTIN: Serpico (73), Dog Day Afternoon (75), The Next Man (76), It's My Turn (80).

ELLIOTT, LANG: The Prize Fighter (79), The Private Eyes (80).

ENGELBERG, MORT: Hot Stuff (79), The Villain (79), Smokey And The Bandit II (80), The Hunter (80).

ERICKSON, C.O.: Popeye (80), Urban Cowboy (80).

EVANS, ROBERT: Chinatown (74), The Great Gatsby (74), Marathon Man (76), Black Sunday (77), Players (79), Popeye (80), Urban Cowboy (80).

FANAKA, JAMES: Penitentiary (79).

FEIN, IRVING: Just You And Me, Kid (79).

FEITSHANS, BUZZ: 1941 (79), Hardcore (79).

FEKE, STEVE: When A Stranger Calls (79).

FELDMAN, EDWARD S.: The Other Side of the Mountain (75), The Last Married Couple In America (80).

FENADY, ANDREW J.: The Man With Bogart's Face (80).

FIELD, CONNIE: The Life and Times of Rosie the Riveter (80).

FIELDS, FREDDIE: Lipstick (76), Citizen's Band (Handle With Care) (77), Looking for Mr. Goodbar (77), American Gigolo (80), Wholly Moses! (80).

FIRST ARTISTS: A Warm December (72), Pocket Money (72), The Getaway (72), Up the Sandbox (72), Uptown Saturday Night (74), Let's Do It Again (75), A Star is Born (76), An Enemy of the People (76), The Gumball Rally (76), Straight Time (78).

FITZGERALD, KATHY: Wise Blood (79).

FITZGERALD, MICHAEL: Wise Blood (79).

FLEURY, ANDRE: The Lucky Star (80).

FONDA, PETER: Easy Rider (69), The Hired Hand (71).

FOREMAN, JOHN: W.U.S.A (70), They Might Be Giants (71), The Effect of Gamma Rays (72), The Life and Times of Judge Roy Bean (72), The Man Who Would Be King (75).

FOSTER, DAVID: The Legacy (79), Tribute (80).

FOWLER, ROBERT: Below The Belt (80).

FRANK, MELVIN: A Funny Thing Happened on the Way... (66), Buona Sera Mrs. Campbell (68), A Touch of Class (73), The Prisoner of Second Avenue (75), The Duchess and the Dirtwater (76), Lost And Found (79).

FRANKEL, JERRY: Cheaper to Keep Her (80).

FRANKENHEIMER, JOHN: I Walk the Line (70), The Horsemen (70).

FRANKOVICH, MIKE: Bob & Carol & Ted & Alice (69), Cactus Flower (69), Marooned (69), Doctors' Wives (70), $ (71), Butterflies Are Free (72), Forty Carats (73), Report to the Commissioner (74), The Shootist (76).

FREDERICKSON, GARY: Apocalypse Now (79).

FREEMAN, JOEL: The Octagon (80).

FRENCH, ROBIN: Blue Collar (78).

FRIEDMAN, STEPHEN: Lovin' Molly (73), Hero At Large (80), Little Darlings (80).

FRYE, WILLIAM: Raise The Titanic (80).

FUCHS, LEO: Sunday Lovers (80).

FURIE, SYDNEY J.: Little Fauss and Big Halsey (70), Lady Sings the Blues (72).

GAINES, LEONARD: Going In Style (79).

GALE, BOB: Used Cars (80).

GALLO, FRED T.: Going In Style (79).

GEISINGER, ELLIOT: The Amityville Horror (79).

GEORGE, GEORGE W.: Rich Kids (79).

GILBERT, BRUCE: Nine To Five (80).

GILER, DAVID: Alien (79).

GILMORE, WILLIAM S., Jr.: Defiance (80).

GLOBUS, YORAM: Schizoid (80).

GOLAN, MENAHEM: Schizoid (80).

GOLDBERG, DANNY: Meatballs (79), No Nukes (80).

GOLDBERG, LEONARD J.: Winter Kills (79).

GOLDSTONE, JOHN: Life Of Brian (79).

GOODWIN, RICHARD: The Mirror Crack'd (80).

GORDON, LAWRENCE: Hard Times (75), Rolling Thunder (77), Hooper (78), The Driver (78), The End (78), It's Not The Size That Counts (79), The Warriors (79), Xanadu (80).

GORDY, BERRY: Mahogany (75), The Bingo Long Traveling All-Stars (76).

GOTTFRIED, HOWARD: The Hospital (71), Network (76), Altered States (80).

GOTTLIEB, MORTON: Sleuth (72), Same Time Next Year (78).

GRADE, LORD LEW: Saturn 3 (80).

GRANT, MICHAEL: Head On (80).

GRANVILLE WRATHER, BONITA: The Magic Of Lassie (78).

GREEN, GERALD: Sunburn (79).

GREENBERG, HAROLD: Terror Train (80).

GREENHUT, ROBERT: Stardust Memories (80).

GREISMAN, ALAN: Heart Beat (79).

GROSBARD, ULU: Who Is Harry Kellerman .... (71).

GRUSKOFF, MICHAEL: Silent Running (71), Young Frankenstein (74), Lucky Lady (75), Rafferty and the Gold Dust Twins (75).

GUCCIONE, BOB: Caligula (79).

GUERCIO, JAMES WILLIAM: Second-Hand Hearts (80).

GUTMAN, JAMES C.: Something Short Of Paradise (79).

HACKIN, DENNIS: Wanda Nevada (79), Bronco Billy (80).

HACOBSON, FRANK R.: Joni (80).

HALEY, JACK, Jr.: That's Entertainment (74).

HAMADY, RON: Fade to Black (80).

HAMEL, ALAN: Nothing Personal (80).

HAMILTON, GUY: Force 10 from Navarone (78).

HANSON, CURTIS: The Little Dragons (80).
HANSON, JOHN: Northern Lights (79).
HARLAN, JAN: The Shining (80).
HARRIS, BURT: Just Tell Me What You Want (80).
HARRIS, DENNY: Silent Scream (80).
HARRIS, JAMES B.: The Killing (56), Paths of Glory (57), Lolita (62), Some Call It Loving (73), Telefon (77).
HARRIS, JOAN: Silent Scream (80).
HARRISON, GEORGE: Life Of Brian (79).
HARRISON, JOHN: Effects (79).
HARTWIG, WOLF C.: Breakthrough (79).
HAUSMAN, MICHAEL: Rich Kids (79), One Trick Pony (80).
HAWN, GOLDIE: Private Benjamin (80).
HAYWARD, WILLIAM: Wanda Nevada (79).
HEFNER, HUGH M.: The Fiendish Plot Of Dr. Fu Manchu (80).
HELLER, ROSILYN: Ice Castles (78).
HELLMAN, JEROME: The World of Henry Orient (64), A Fine Madness (66), Midnight Cowboy (69), The Day of the Locust (75), Coming Home (78), Promises In The Dark (79).
HELLMAN, MONTE: The Shooting (66).
HELPERN, DAVID, Jr.: Something Short Of Paradise (79).
HEMPSTEAD, HANNAH: The Little Dragons (80).
HENSON, JIM: The Muppet Movie (79).
HERBERMAN, LEN: Murder By Decree (79).
HERMAN, NORMAN T.: In God We Trust (80).
HEROUX, CLAUDE: Hog Wild (80).
HERROD, GERRY: Boardwalk (79).
HERTZBERG, MICHAEL: The Twelve Chairs (69), Blazing Saddles (74), Silent Movie (76).
HERTZOG, LAWRENCE: Final Assignment (80).
HEYMAN, JOHN: Jesus (79).
HILL, DEBRA: Halloween (78), The Fog (80).
HILL, WALTER: Alien (79).
HILLER, ARTHUR: The In-Laws (79).
HIRSCHFIELD, NORMAN: Nothing Personal (80).
HITZIG, RUPERT: Happy Birthday, Gemini (80).
HODGES, MIKE: Pulp (72), The Terminal Man (74).
HOWARD, SANDY: Circle Of Iron (79), Meteor (79), Terror Train (80).
HUNTER, ROSS: Thoroughly Modern Millie (67), Airport (69), Lost Horizon (73).
HUSTON, JOHN: The Mackintosh Man (73).
IRVINE, RICH: Why Would I Lie? (80).
ISENBERG, LENNY: Cheaper to Keep Her (80).
JACOBS, NEWTON P.: The Hearse (80).

JAFFE, HERB: Time After Time (79), Motel Hell (80), Those Lips Those Eyes (80).

JAFFE, HOWARD B.: Reflection of Fear (71), Man on a Swing (73).

JAFFE, ROBERT: Motel Hell (80).

JAFFE, STANLEY: Goodbye Columbus (69), A New Leaf (71), Bad Company (72), Man on a Swing (73), The Bad News Bears (76), Kramer vs. Kramer (79).

JAFFE, STEVEN CHARLES: Motel Hell (80), Those Lips Those Eyes (80).

JANNI, JOSEPH: Yanks (79).

JEFFREY, HOWARD: Divine Madness (80).

JEKEL, WILLIAM D.: The Baltimore Bullet (80).

JEWISON, NORMAN: The Russians Are Coming.... (66), In the Heat of the Night (67), The Thomas Crown Affair (68), Gaily, Gaily (69), Fiddler on the Roof (71), Jesus Christ Superstar (73), Rollerball (75), F.I.S.T. (78), ...And Justice For All (79).

JOFFE, CHARLES: Take the Money and Run (69), Bananas (71), Everything You Always Wanted to Know About Sex (72), Sleeper (73), Love and Death (75), The Front (76), Annie Hall (77), Stardust Memories (80).

JONES, L. Q.: The Brotherhood of Satan (70).

KAMERON, PETE: You Better Watch Out (80).

KASSAR, MARIO: The Changeling (80).

KASTNER, ELLIOT: The Night of the Following Day (68), The Walking Stick (69), Where Eagles Dare (69), A Severed Head (70), The Night Comers (71), Villain (71), When Eight Bells Toll (71), Fear is the Key (72), Zee and Co. (72), Cops and Robbers (73), The Long Goodbye (73), 11 Harrowhouse (74), Rancho De Luxe (74), Breakheart Pass (75), Farewell My Lovely (75), Love and Death (75), Russian Roulette (75), 92 in the Shade (76), Swashbuckler (76), The Big Sleep (78), Goldengirl (79), ffolkes (80), First Deadly Sin (80), Saturn 3 (80).

KATZ, GLORIA: French Postcards (79).

KATZKA, GABRIEL: Soldier Blue (70), The Taking of Pelham 1-2-3 (74), Butch And Sundance (79), Meteor (79).

KAUFMAN, CHARLES: Mother's Day (80).

KAUFMAN, ROBERT: I Love My Wife (70), Love at First Bite (79), How To Beat The High Cost of Living (80).

KAY, NORA: Nijinsky (80).

KAZANJIAN, HOWARD: More American Graffiti (79).

KAZIN, ELIA: America (63), The Arrangement (69).

KEACH, JAMES: The Long Riders (80).

KEACH, STACY: The Long Riders (80).

KELLEY, PATRICK: A Little Romance (79).

KEMENY, JOHN: Ice Castles (78).

KING, ALAN: Happy Birthday, Gemini (80).

Robert Evans.   Amy Robinson.

KING, ZALMAN: Roadie (80).
KINGHAM, BERNARD J.: Hawk the Slayer (80).
KIRKWOOD, GENE: The Idolmaker (80).
KLEINER, BURT: You Better Watch Out (80).
KLEISER, RANDAL: Blue Lagoon (80).
KOCH, HOWARD W., Jr.: Plaza Suite (71), Badge 373 (73), Once is Not
    Enough (75), The Other Side of Midnight (77), Heaven Can Wait
    (78), Greystoke (79), The Frisco Kid (79), The Idolmaker (80).
KOHNER, PANCHO: Why Would I Lie? (80).
KOPELSON, ARNOLD: Lost And Found (79), The Legacy (79), Final
    Assignment (80), Foolin' Around (80), Night Of The Juggler (80).
KRAMER, LEE: Xanadu (80).
KRAMER, STANLEY: Judgment at Nuremberg (62), It's a Mad, Mad, Mad,
    Mad World (64), Ship of Fools (65), Guess Who's Coming to Dinner?
    (67), The Secret of Santa Vittoria (69), R.P.M. (70), Bless the Beasts
    and Children (71), Oklahoma Crude (73), The Domino Principle
    (77), The Runner Stumbles (79).
KRANTZ, STEVE: Swap Meet (79).
KRAVITZ, MICHAEL: Mother's Day (80).
KROFFT, MARTY: Middle Age Crazy (80).
KROFFT, SID: Middle Age Crazy (80).
KROST, BARRY: When A Stranger Calls (79).
KUBRICK, STANLEY: The Shining (80).
KURTZ, GARY: American Graffiti (73), Star Wars (77), The Empire
    Strikes Back (80).
LADD, ALAN, Jr.: The Night Comers (71), Fear is the Key (72).
LANCASTER, BURT: The Midnight Man (74).
LANDAU, EDIE: Hopscotch (80).

LANDAU, ELY: Hopscotch (80).

LANDERS, HAL: The Gypsy Moths (69), Monte Walsh (70), The Hot Rock (72), Death Wish (74), Joyride (77).

LANG, JENNINGS: The Concorde-Airport '79 (79), Little Miss Marker (80), The Nude Bomb (80).

LANGER, CAROLE: Joe Albany ... a Jazz Life (80).

LANSBURY, EDGAR: He Knows You're Alone (80).

LARSEN, RIKK: Billy In The Lowlands (79).

LARSON, BOB: Coal Miner's Daughter (80).

LARSON, GLEN A.: Buck Rogers (79).

LAUGHLIN, TOM: Born Losers (67), Billy Jack (71), The Trial of Billy Jack (72).

LAZARUS, PAUL N.: Hanover Street (79).

LAZER, DAVID: The Muppet Movie (79).

LEAR, NORMAN: Divorce American Style (67), The Night They Raided Minsky's (68), Start the Revolution Without Me (69), Cold Turkey (70), The Thief Who Came to Dinner (73).

LEDERER, RICHARD: The Hollywood Knights (80).

LEGER, CLAUDE: The Lucky Star (80).

LEHMAN, ERNEST: Hello Dolly (69), Portnoy's Complaint (72).

LEONE, MICHAEL: The Octagon (80).

LEVENE, TERRY: Fist of Fear Touch of Death (80).

LEVEY, WILLIAM A.: Skatetown Usa (79).

LEVINE, JOSEPH E.: The Graduate (67), The Producers (67), The Lion in Winter (68), Soldier Blue (70), Sunflower (70), Carnal Knowledge (71), Day of the Dolphin (73), A Bridge Too Far (77).

LEWIS, ARTHUR: Brass Target (78).

LEWIS, PAUL: Out Of The Blue (80).

LINSON, ART: Rafferty and the Gold Dust Twins (75), Carwash (76), American Hot Wax (78), Melvin and Howard (80), Where The Buffalo Roam (80).

LITTO, GEORGE: Over The Edge (79), Dressed To Kill (80).

LLOYD, EUAN: The Sea Wolves (80).

LOBELL, MICHAEL: Windows (80).

LOMMEL, ULLI: The Boogey Man (80).

LOSEY, GAVRIK: Agatha (79).

LOVELL, DYSON: The Champ (79).

LOWRY, HUNT: Humanoids From The Deep (80).

LUCAS, GEORGE: More American Graffiti (79), The Empire Strikes Back (80).

LUMET, SIDNEY: The Deadly Affair (67), Bye Bye Braverman (68), Just Tell Me What You Want (80).

LYON, RACHEL: Tell Me a Riddle (80).

MacLAINE, SHIRLEY: The Other Half of the Sky.... (75).

MALICK, TERRENCE: Badlands (73).

MANASSE, GEORGE: He Knows You're Alone (80).
MANES, FRITZ: Any Which Way You Can (80).
MANKIEWICZ, JOSEPH L.: There Was a Crooked Man (70).
MANN, TED: Brubaker (80).
MARSHALL, ALAN: Fame (80).
MARSHALL, BILL: Circle Of Two (80).
MARSHALL, FRANK: The Warriors (79).
MASLANSKY, PAUL: Circle Of Iron (79), Hot Stuff (79), Scavenger Hunt (79), The Villain (79).
MATHER, GEORGE E.: Galaxina (80).
MATTHAU, WALTER: Little Miss Marker (80).
MAYES, WENDELL: Hotel (67).
MAZURSKY, PAUL: Willie & Phil (80).
McCORMICK, KEVIN: Times Square (80).
McEUEN, WILLIAM E.: The Jerk (79).
McQUEEN, STEVE: An Enemy of the People (76), Tom Horn (80).
MELNICK, DANIEL: All That Jazz (79), Altered States (80), First Family (80).
MENDELUK, GEORGE: The Kidnapping Of The President (80).
MERCHANT, ISMAIL: Hullabaloo Over Georgie and Bonnie's Pictures (79), Jane Austen In Manhattan (80).
MERRICK, DAVID: Child's Play (72), The Great Gatsby (74), Semi-Tough (77), Rough Cut (80).
MERRILL, KEITH: Take Down (79).
METCALF, MARK: Head Over Heels (79).
MEYERS, NANCY: Private Benjamin (80).
MICHAELS, JOEL B.: The Changeling (80), Tribute (80).
MICHAELS, LORNE: Mr. Mikes Mondo Video (79), Gilda Live (80).
MILIUS, JOHN: 1941 (79), Hardcore (79), Used Cars (80).
MILLER, DANIEL: Today Is For The Championship (80).
MILLER, HARVEY: Private Benjamin (80).
MILLER, JOSEPH: Below The Belt (80).
MILLER, RON: The Black Hole (79), Herbie Goes Bananas (80), Midnight Madness (80), The Watcher In The Woods (80).
MILLER, STEPHEN: Hog Wild (80).
MIRISCH, MARVIN E.: Dracula (79).
MIRISCH, WALTER: In the Heat of the Night (67), The Thomas Crown Affair (68), The Hawaiians (70), The Landlord (70), The Organization (70), The Private Life of Sherlock Holmes (70), They Call Me Mister Tibbs (70), Scorpio (72), Mr. Majestyk (74), The Spikes Gang (74), Midway (76), Same Time Next Year (78), Dracula (79), The Prisoner Of Zenda (79).
MISSEL, RENEE: The Main Event (79), Resurrection (80).
MONASH, PAUL: Butch Cassidy and the Sundance Kid (69), Slaughterhouse Five (72), The Friends of Eddie Coyle (73), The

Front Page (74), Carrie (76).

MOONJEAN, HANK: Smokey And The Bandit II (80).

MORALI, JACQUES: Can't Stop The Music (80).

MULLIGAN, ROBERT: Inside Daisy Clover (66), Up the Down Staircase (67), Same Time Next Year (78).

MUTRUX, FLOYD: Freebie and The Bean (74).

NEILL, STEVE: The Day Time Ended (80).

NELSON, JAMES: Borderline (80).

NELSON, JEFFREY: Return Of The Secaucus Seven (80).

NELSON, RALPH: Flight of the Doves (71).

NEUFELD, MACE: The Frisco Kid (79).

NEWMAN, PAUL: Rachel, Rachel (68), W.U.S.A. (70), Sometimes a Great Notion (71), They Might Be Giants (71), The Effect of Gamma Rays (72), The Mackintosh Man (73).

NICOLELLA, JOHN: Times Square (80).

NILSSON, ROB: Northern Lights (79).

NIVEN, DAVID, Jr.: Escape To Athena (79).

NOLAN, LELAND: The Fiendish Plot Of Dr. Fu Manchu (80).

NUNEZ, VICTOR: Gal Young Un (79).

O'BRIEN, DENIS: Life Of Brian (79).

O'CONNELL, SUSAN: Tell Me a Riddle (80).

O'DELL, DENIS: Cuba (79).

O'DONOGHUE, MICHAEL: Mr. Mikes Mondo Video (79).

O'DONOVAN, DANNY: Goldengirl (79).

O'TOOLE, STANLEY: Nijinsky (80).

ORENTREICH, CATHERINE: The Wizard Of Waukesha (80).

ORGOLINI, ARNOLD: Meteor (79).

OWENSBY, EARL: Lady Grey (80), Living Legend (80).

PAKULA, ALAN J.: Fear Strikes Out (57), Love with the Proper Stranger (63), To Kill a Mockingbird (63), Baby the Rain Must Fall (65), Inside Daisy Clover (66), Up the Down Staircase (67), The Stalking Moon (68), The Sterile Cuckoo (69), Klute (71), Love, Pain and the Whole Damn Thing (72), Pain and the Whole Damn Thing (72), The Parallax View (74), Starting Over (79).

PALEVSKY, MAX: Fun with Dick and Jane (77)*, Islands in the Stream (77)*.

PALMER, PATRICK: ...And Justice For All (79).

PANZER, WILLIAM N.: Steel (80).

PAPPAS, GEORGE: First Deadly Sin (80).

PARVIN, THEODORE: Meteor (79).

PAUL, HANK: Falling In Love Again (80).

PAUL, STEVEN: Falling In Love Again (80).

PAUL, WILLIAM: The Ninth Configuration (80).

PEARLMAN, NAN: He Knows You're Alone (80).

PEERCE, LARRY: The Other Side of the Mountain (75).

PERLMUTTER, DAVID: Double Negative (80), Nothing Personal (80).

PERRY, ELEANOR: The Man Who Loved Cat Dancing (73).

PERRY, FRANK: Ladybug (63), Diary of a Mad Housewife (70), Doc (71).

PERSKY, LESTER: The Last Detail (73), For Pete's Sake (74), Bite the Bullet (75), Shampoo (75), The Killer Elite (75), The Man Who Would Be King (75), Bound for Glory (76), Taxi Driver (76), The Front (76), The Missouri Breaks (76), Equus (77), Hair (79), Yanks (79).

PETERS, JON: A Star is Born (76), Eyes of Laura Mars (78), The Main Event (79), Die Laughing (80).

PFEIFFER, CAROLYN: Roadie (80).

PHILLIPS, DON: Melvin and Howard (80).

PHILLIPS, JULIA and MICHAEL: Steelyard Blues (72), The Sting (73), Taxi Driver (76), Close Encounters of the Third Kind (77).

PICKER, DAVID V.: Juggernaut (74), Lenny (74), Royal Flash (75), Smile (75), Oliver's Story (78), The One and Only (78), Bloodline (79), The Jerk (79).

PINE, HOWARD: The Competition (80).

PLASCHKES, OTTO: Hopscotch (80).

PLATT, POLLY: Pretty Baby (78).

PLOTNICK, STANLEY: Pilgrim, Farewell (80).

POLLACK, SYDNEY: Honeysuckle Rose (80).

PRATT, CHARLES A.: The Great Santini (80).

PREMINGER, OTTO: The Human Factor (79).

PRESSMAN, EDWARD R.: The Revolutionary (70), Dealing (72), Badlands (73), Sisters (73), Phantom of The Paradise (74), Nunzio (78), Paradise Alley (78), Heart Beat (79), Old Boyfriends (79), The Secret Life of Plants (79), You Better Watch Out (80).

PRESSMAN, MICHAEL: Those Lips Those Eyes (80).

PUTTNAM, DAVID: Foxes (80).

QUESTED, JOHN: Sunburn (79).

RADNITZ, ROBERT B.: And Now Miguel (65), My Side of the Mountain (68), The Little Ark (71), Sounder (72).

RAFELSON, BOB: Stay Hungry (76).

RANSOHOFF, MARTIN: The Cincinnati Kid (65), The Sandpiper (65), Castle Keep (68), Ice Station Zebra (68), Catch-22 (70), The Moonshine War (70), Save the Tiger (72), The White Dawn (73), The Other Side of Midnight (77), The Silver Streak (77), Nightwing (78), The Invasion of the Body Snatchers (78), The Wanderers (79), A Change of Seasons (80), The Mountain Men (80).

RAPPAPORT, MICHELE: Old Boyfriends (79).

RAVETCH, IRVING: Hud (63), Hombre (67), The Reivers (69), Conrack (74).

RAY, TONY: The Rose (79), Willie & Phil (80).

REDFORD, ROBERT: Downhill Racer (69), The Candidate (72), All the President's Men (76).

REITMAN, IVAN: National Lampoon's Animal House (78), Meatballs (79).

REYNOLDS, BURT: Hooper (78), The End (78).

RICH, LEE: The Big Red One (80).

RICHMOND, TED: Breakthrough (79).

RISSNER, DANTON: Up The Academy (80).

RITCHIE, MICHAEL: Divine Madness (80).

RITT, MARTIN: Hombre (67), The Molly Maguires (68)*.

ROBERTS, BOBBY: The Gypsy Moths (69), Monte Walsh (70), The Hot Rock (72), Death Wish (74), Joyride (77).

ROBERTS, WILLIAM: The Last American Hero (73).

ROBERTSON, CLIFF: Charly (68), The Great Northfield Minnesota Raid (71), J.W. Coop (72).

ROBERTSON, ROBBIE: The Last Waltz (78), Carny (80).

ROBINSON, AMY: Head Over Heels (79).

ROBSON, MARK: Avalanche Express (79).

RODDENBERRY, GENE: Star Trek (79).

ROLLINS, JACK: Take the Money and Run (69), Bananas (71), Everything You Always Wanted to Know About Sex (72), Sleeper (73), Love and Death (75), The Front (76), Annie Hall (77), Stardust Memories (80).

ROOS, FRED: Apocalypse Now (79), The Black Stallion (79).

ROSE, ALEX: Norma Rae (79).

ROSEN, EDWARD: Americathon (79).

ROSEN, ROBERT L.: Prophecy (79).

ROSENBERG, MICHAEL: Tell Me a Riddle (80).

ROSENBERG, RICK: Hide In Plain Sight (80).

ROSENBERG, STUART: The Laughing Policeman (73).

ROSENMAN, HOWARD: The Main Event (79), Resurrection (80).

ROSS, HERBERT: The Last of Sheila (73).

ROSSELLINI, FRANCO: Caligula (79).

ROTH, JOE: Americathon (79).

ROTHMAN, MOSES: ffolkes (80).

ROTHSTEIN, ROGER M.: Chapter Two (79), Seems Like Old Times (80).

ROUSSET-ROUARD, YVES: A Little Romance (79).

RUBAN, AL: Opening Night (77).

RUDDY, ALBERT S.: Little Fauss and Big Halsey (70), The Godfather (72), The Longest Yard (74), Coonskin (75), Matilda (78).

RUDMAN, NORMAN G.: The Baltimore Bullet (80).

RUSH, RICHARD: Getting Straight (70), Freebie and The Bean (74), The Stunt Man (80).

RUSSELL, CHARLES: The Hearse (80).

Clint Eastwood and friend.

Julia Phillips.

RUSSO, AARON: The Rose (79).

RYAN, JOHN: The Kidnapping Of The President (80).

RYDELL, MARK: The Cowboys (72), Cinderella Liberty (74).

SACHS, TOM: The Lady Vanishes (79).

SACKHEIM, WILLIAM: The In-Laws (79).

SALAND, RONALD: The Amityville Horror (79).

SALKIND, ILYA and ALEXANDER: The Light at the End of the World
(71), The Three Musketeers (73), The Four Musketeers (74),
Superman (78), Superman II (78).

SALTZMAN, HARRY: Nijinsky (80).

SANGER, JONATHAN: The Elephant Man (80).

SAVAGE, PETER: Raging Bull (80).

SCHAEFER, GEORGE: An Enemy Of The People (76).

SCHAFFEL, ROBERT L.: Sunnyside (79).

SCHAIN, DON: H.O.T.S. (79).

SCHATZBERG, JERRY: Sweet Revenge (77).

SCHECHTMAN, JEFF: Piranha (78).

SCHEINMAN, ANDREW: The Awakening (80), The Mountain Men (80).

SCHELL, MAXIMILIAN: End of the Game (76).

SCHERICK, EDGAR J.: For Love of Ivy (68), Jenny (70), Sleuth (72),
The Heartbreak Kid (72), Gordon's War (73), The Stepford Wives
(74), The Taking of Pelham 1-2-3 (74), I Never Promised You a Rose
Garden (77), The American Success Company (79).

SCHICK, ELLIOT: The Earthling (80).

SCHLOSSBERG, JULIAN: No Nukes (80).

SCHMIDT, MARLENE: The Fifth Floor (80).

SCHMIDT, WAYNE: The Day Time Ended (80).

SCHMIDT, WOLF: The Boogey Man (80).

SCHNEIDER, BERT: Hearts and Minds (75), Days of Heaven (78).

SCHNEIDER, HAROLD: Goin' South (78).
SCHNEIDER, STANLEY: Three Days of the Condor (75).
SCHRADER, PAUL: Old Boyfriends (79).
SCHRAGER, SHELDON: Promises In The Dark (79).
SCHULMAN, ARNOLD: Players (79).
SCHUTE, MARTIN: There Goes the Bride (80).
SCHWARTZ, BERNARD: Coal Miner's Daughter (80).
SCHWARTZMAN, JACK: Being There (79).
SCHWARY, RONALD L.: Ordinary People (80).
SEATON, GEORGE: What's So Bad About Feeling Good (68), Showdown (72).
SEFEL, JOSEPH: The Kidnapping Of The President (80).
SELLERS, ARLENE: Cuba (79), The Lady Vanishes (79).
SELLIER, CHARLES E., Jr.: Hangar 18 (80), In Search Of Historic Jesus (80).
SELLUS, ACHIM: Breakthrough (79).
SEMPLE, LORENZO, Jr.: Hurricane (79).
SERPE, RALPH: Brinks (79).
SHAFER, MARTIN: The Awakening (80), The Mountain Men (80).
SHAGAN, STEVE: Save the Tiger (72), The Formula (80).
SHAMBERG, MICHAEL: Heart Beat (79).
SHANER, JOHN HERMAN: The Last Married Couple In America (80).
SHANKER, MARK: First Deadly Sin (80).
SHAPIRO, GEORGE: In God We Trust (80).
SHARMAT, STEPHEN: The Earthling (80).
SHAVELSON, MELVILLE: Mixed Company (74).
SHAVICK, JAMES: Final Assignment (80).
SHAW, PETER: Eagle's Wing (79).
SHAW, SAM: A Woman Under the Influence (74), Opening Night (77), Gloria (80).
SHERMAN, ROBERT: Scarecrow (73), Night Moves (75), The Missouri Breaks (76).
SHUSETT, RONALD: Alien (79).
SHYER, CHARLES: Private Benjamin (80).
SICKINGER, ROBERT: Love in a Taxi (80).
SIDARIS, ANDY: Seven (79).
SIEGEL, DONALD: Escape From Alcatraz (79).
SILBER, GLENN: The War At Home (79).
SILVER, JOAN MICKLIN: On The Yard (79).
SILVER, RAPHAEL D.: Hester Street (74), Bernice Bobs Her Hair (76), Between the Lines (77).
SILVERMAN, RON: Brubaker (80).
SILVERSTEIN, ELLIOT: The Car (77).
SIMMONDS, ALAN: Head On (80).
SIMON, JEROME: Double Negative (80).

SIMON, MELVIN: Love At First Bite (79), Scavenger Hunt (79), Seven (79), The Runner Stumbles (79), When A Stranger Calls (79), Cloud Dancer (80), My Bodyguard (80), The Man With Bogart's Face (80), The Stunt Man (80).

SIMPSON, PETER: Prom Night (80).

SINATRA, FRANK: First Deadly Sin (80).

SINDELL, GERALD: H.O.T.S. (79).

SOLNICKI, VICTOR: Hog Wild (80).

SOLO, ROBERT: Invasion Of The Bodysnatchers (78), The Awakening (80).

SPEIGEL, SAM: Bridge over the River Kwai (57), Lawrence of Arabia (62), The Swimmer (68), Nicholas and Alexandra (71), The Last Tycoon (76).

SPENGLER, PIERRE: Superman (78), Superman II (80).

SPIELBERG, STEVEN: I Want to Hold Your Hand (77), Used Cars (80).

ST. JACQUES, RAYMOND: The Book of Numbers (73).

ST. JOHNS, RICHARD: Circle Of Iron (79), Nightwing (79), The Wanderers (79), A Change of Seasons (80), The Final Countdown (80), The Mountain Men (80).

STALLONE, SYLVESTER: Rocky II (79).

STARGER, MARTIN: Movie Movie Baxter's Beauties (78), Movie Movie Dynamite Hands (78), The Muppet Movie (79), Borderline (80), Raise The Titanic (80), Saturn 3 (80).

STARK, RAY: Reflections in a Golden Eye (67), The Owl and the Pussycat (70), Fat City (72), The Way We Were (73), Funny Lady (75), The Sunshine Boys (75), Murder by Death (76), Smokey and the Bandit (77), California Suite (78), The Cheap Detective (78), The Goodbye Girl (78), Chapter Two (79), The Electric Horseman (79), The Hunter (79), Seems Like Old Times (80).

STERLING, ROBERT: Winter Kills (79).

STERNBERG, TOM: The Black Stallion (79).

STEWART, JAMES L.: Why Would I Lie? (80).

STIGWOOD, ROBERT: Jesus Christ Superstar (73), Tommy (75), Bugsy Malone (76), Survive (76), Saturday Night Fever (77), Grease (78), Moment By Moment (78), Sergeant Pepper's Lonely Hearts Club Band (78), Times Square (80).

STRAUSS, PETER E.: Skatetown Usa (79), Touched By Love (80).

STROLLER, LOUIS A.: The Seduction Of Joe Tynan (79), Simon (80).

STROMBERG, GARY: The Fish That Saved Pittsburgh (79).

SUSSKIND, DAVID: A Raisin in the Sun (61), Lovers and Other Strangers (69), Alice Doesn't Live Here Anymore (74), All Creatures Great and Small (74), Buffalo Bill and the Indians (76), Loving Couples (80).

TABET, SYLVIO: Fade to Black (80).

TAFT, GENE: Honeysuckle Rose (80).

TAIT, DON: Herbie Goes Bananas (80).

TANNEN, MICHAEL: One Trick Pony (80).
TAPLIN, JONATHAN: Carny (80).
TEMCHIN, JACK: Home Movies (79).
TENNANT, WILLIAM: The Hollywood Knights (80).
TENSER, MARILYN J.: Galaxina (80).
TENSER, MARK: The Hearse (80).
TEPPER, WILLIAM: Heart Beat (79).
THOMAS, JEREMY: Bad Timing (80).
THOMPSON, TOMMY: A Perfect Couple (79).
THOMSON, GAIL: Final Assignment (80).
TISCH, STEVE: Coast To Coast (80).
TODD, MICHAEL, Jr.: The Bell Jar (79).
TOWERS, HARRY ALAN: The Shape Of Things To Come (79).
TRANE, REUBEN: Shock Waves (75).
TRUMBULL, DOUGLAS: Silent Running (71).
TUCKER, LARRY: Bob & Carol & Ted & Alice (69).
TUCKER, MELVILLE: Stir Crazy (80).
TURMAN, LAWRENCE: The Flim Flam Man (67), The Graduate (67),
    Pretty Poison (69), The Great White Hope (70), The Marriage of a
    Young Stockbroker (71), The Drowning Pool (75), First Love (77),
    Heroes (77), Walk Proud (79), Tribute (80).
VAIL, STEVEN A.: Scavenger Hunt (79).
VAINA, ANDREW: The Changeling (80).
VALENTE, RENEE: Loving Couples (80).
VAN DER KOLK, HENK: Circle Of Two (80).
VARHOL, MICHAEL: The Last Word (79).
VERONA, STEPHEN: Pipe Dreams (76).
VINER, MICHAEL: Touched By Love (80).
VINT, JESSE: Hometown USA (79).
WAITE, RALPH: On The Nickel (80).
WALSH, JOSEPH: California Split (74).
WAYNE, MICHAEL: McLintock (63), The Green Berets (68), Chisum
    (70), Big Jake (71), Cahill (73), The Train Robbers (73).
WEILL, CLAUDIA: Girl Friends (78).
WEINSTEIN, HANNAH: Claudine (74), Greased Lightning (77), Stir
    Crazy (80).
WEINTRAUB, FRED: The Big Brawl (80), Tom Horn (80).
WEINTRAUB, JERRY: Cruising (80).
WEISBURD, DAN: Today Is For The Championship (80).
WEISS, ROBERT K.: The Blues Brothers (80).
WEST, HOWARD: In God We Trust (80).
WESTON, JAY: Night Of The Juggler (80).
WILDER, BILLY: The Private Life of Sherlock Holmes (70).
WILLIAMS, BERNARD: Flash Gordon (80).
WILLOUGHBY, GEORGE: Boardwalk (79).

WILSON, MICHAEL G.: Moonraker (79).

WINITSKY, ALEX: Breakthrough (79), Cuba (79), The Lady Vanishes (79).

WINKLER, IRWIN: The Split (68), Leo the Last (69), They Shoot Horses, Don't They? (69), The Strawberry Statement (70), The Gang That Couldn't Shoot Straight (71), The Mechanic (72), The New Centurions (72), Up the Sandbox (72), SPYS (74), Peeper (75), The Gambler (75), Nickelodeon (76), Rocky (76), New York, New York (77), Comes a Horseman (78), Sons (78), Uncle Joe Shannon (78), Rocky II (79), Raging Bull (80).

WINNER, MICHAEL: Lawman (70), The Stone Killer (73), Death Wish (74)*, Won Ton Ton, The Dog Who Saved Hollywood (76), The Big Sleep (78).

WISEMAN, FREDERICK: Manoeuvre (79).

WIZAN, JOE: Jeremiah Johnson (72), Junior Bonner (72), Prime Cut (72), The Last American Hero (73), 99 44/100 Percent Dead (74), Audrey Rose (77), ...And Justice For All (79), Voices (79).

WOHL, IRA: Best Boy (79).

WORTH, MARVIN: The Rose (79), Up The Academy (80).

WUNSCH, ROBERT J.: Defiance (80).

YABLANS, FRANK: The Other Side of Midnight (77), The Silver Streak (77), The Fury (78), North Dallas Forty (79).

YABLANS, IRWIN: Halloween (78), Roller Boogie (79), Fade to Black (80).

YATES, PETER: Murphy's War (71), Breaking Away (79).

YORKIN, BUD: The Thief Who Came to Dinner (73).

ZACHARIAS, ALFREDO: The Bees (78).

ZANUCK, RICHARD D.: The Sting (73), The Sugarland Express (73), The Black Windmill (74), Jaws (75), MacArthur (77), Jaws 2 (78), The Island (80).

ZEITMAN, JEROME M.: Just You And Me, Kid (79), How To Beat The High Cost of Living (80).

ZIEFF, HOWARD: Hearts of the West (75).

ZINNEMANN, TIM: A Small Circle Of Friends (80), The Long Riders (80).

ZUCKER, DAVID: Airplane (80).

ZUCKER, JERRY: Airplane (80).

Directors

ABRAHAMS, JIM: Airplane (80).

ALDRICH, ROBERT: The Dirty Dozen (67), The Killing of Sister George (68), The Legend of Lylah Clare (68), Too Late the Hero (69), The Grissom Gang (71), Ulzana's Raid (72), The Emperor of the North Pole (73), The Longest Yard (74), Hustle (75), The Twilight's Last Gleaming (77), The Choirboys (78), The Frisco Kid (79).

ALLEN, IRWIN: Voyage to the Bottom of the Sea (61), The Swarm (78), Beyond The Poseidon Adventure (79).

ALLEN, WOODY: What's Up Tiger Lily? (66), Take the Money and Run (69), Bananas (71), Everything You Always Wanted to Know About Sex (72), Sleeper (73), Love and Death (75), Annie Hall (77), Interiors (78), Manhattan (79), Stardust Memories (80).

ALMOND, PAUL: Final Assignment (80).

ALTMAN, ROBERT: The Delinquents (57), The James Dean Story (57)*, Countdown (68), Nightmare in Chicago (69), That Cold Day in the Park (69), Brewster McCloud (70), MASH (70), McCabe and Mrs. Miller (71), Images (72), The Long Goodbye (73), California Split (74), Thieves Like Us (74), Nashville (75), Buffalo Bill and the Indians (76), Three Women (77), A Wedding (78), Quintet (78), A Perfect Couple (79), Health (80), Popeye (80).

ANNAKIN, KEN: Cheaper to Keep Her (80).

APTED, MICHAEL: Agatha (79), Coal Miner's Daughter (80).

ARKIN, ALAN: Little Murders (71).

ASHBY, HAL: The Landlord (70), Harold and Maude (71), The Last Detail (73), Shampoo (75), Bound for Glory (76), Coming Home (78), Being There (79), Second-Hand Hearts (80).

ATTENBOROUGH, RICHARD: Magic (78).

AVAKIAN, ARAM: The End of the Road (71), Cops and Robbers (73), 11 Harrowhouse (74).

AVEDIS, HOWARD: The Fifth Floor (80).

AVILDSEN, JOHN: Turn On to Love (67), OK Bill (68), Guess What We Learned at School (69), Joe (70), Cry Uncle (71), Roger the Stoolie (72), Save the Tiger (72), W.W. And the Dixie Dancekings (75), Rocky (76), Slow Dancing in the Big City (78), The Formula (80).

AXELROD, GEORGE: Lord Love a Duck (66).

BADHAM, JOHN: The Bingo Long Traveling All-Stars (76), Saturday Night Fever (77), Dracula (79).

BAER, MAX, Jr.: The McCulloughs (75), Ode to Billie Joe (76), Hometown USA (79).

BAKSHI, RALPH: Fritz the Cat (72), Heavy Traffic (73), Coonskin (75), Wizards (77), Lord of the Rings (78).

BALLARD, CARROLL: The Black Stallion (79).

BANCROFT, ANNE: Fatso (80).

BARRON, ARTHUR: Jeremy (73), Brothers (77).

BARTEL, PAUL: Private Parts (72), Death Race 2000 (75), Cannonball (76).

BEAN, ROBERT B.: Made for Each Other (71), "2" (73).

BEATTY, WARREN: Heaven Can Wait (78)*.

BECKER, HAROLD: The Onion Field (79), The Black Marble (80).

BENNER, RICHARD: Happy Birthday, Gemini (80).

BENTON, ROBERT: Bad Company (72), The Late Show (77), Kramer vs. Kramer (79).

BERNSTEIN, WALTER: Little Miss Marker (80).

BERRY, JOHN: Maya (66), Claudine (74), Thieves (77).

BERTOLUCCI, BERNARDO: Luna (79).

BILL, TONY: My Bodyguard (80).

BILSON, BRUCE: The North Avenue Irregulars (79).

BIRD, STEWART: The Wobblies (79)*.

BLACK, NOEL: Pretty Poison (69), Skater Dater (73), I'm a Fool (76), A Man, A Woman, and a Bank (79), Two Minks in a Cage (79).

BLATTY, WILLIAM PETER: The Ninth Configuration (80).

BLOOMFIELD, GEORGE: Double Negative (80), Nothing Personal (80).

BOGART, PAUL: Halls of Anger (68), Marlowe (69), Cancel My Reservation (71), The Skin Game (71), Class of '44 (73), Mr. Ricco (75).

BOGDANOVICH, PETER: Targets (68), The Last Picture Show (71), What's Up, Doc? (72), Paper Moon (73), Daisy Miller (74), At Long Last Love (75), Nickelodeon (76), Saint Jack (79).

BOORMAN, JOHN: Catch Us if You Can (65), Point Blank (67), Hell in the Pacific (68), Leo the Last (69), Deliverance (72), Zardoz (73), Exorcist II-The Heretic (77).

BOULTING, ROY: The Last Word (79).

BOWERS, GEORGE: The Hearse (80).

BOX, EVEL: Benji (74).

BRASS, GIOVANNI TINTO: Caligula (79).

BREST, MARTIN: Going In Style (79).

BRICKMAN, MARSHALL: Simon (80).

BRIDGES, JAMES: The Baby Maker (73), The Paper Chase (73), September 30, 1955 (78), The China Syndrome (79), Urban Cowboy (80).

BROCKMAN, SUSAN: The Wizard Of Waukesha (80)*.

BROOKS, ALBERT: Real Life (79).

BROOKS, JOSEPH: You Light Up My Life (77), If Ever I See You Again (78).

BROOKS, MEL: The Producers (67), The Twelve Chairs (70), Blazing Saddles (74), Young Frankenstein (74), Silent Movie (76), High Anxiety (77).

BROOKS, RICHARD: Elmer Gantry (60), Sweet Bird of Youth (62), Lord Jim (64), The Professionals (66), In Cold Blood (67), The Happy Ending (69), $ (71), Bite the Bullet (75), Looking for Mr. Goodbar (77).

BROWN, BARRY: The War At Home (79)*, Cloud Dancer (80).

BUTLER, ROBERT: Night Of The Juggler (80).

BYRUM, JOHN: Inserts (75), Heart Beat (79).

CAAN, JAMES: Hide In Plain Sight (80).

CAMP, JOE: The Double Mcguffin (79), Oh Heavenly Dog (80).

CAMPUS, MICHAEL: The Education of Sonny Carson (74).

CARDONA, RENE, Jr.: Guyana:Cult Of The Damned (80).

CARDOS, JOHN: The Day Time Ended (80).

CARLINO, LEWIS JOHN: The Sailor Who Fell from Grace.... (76), The Great Santini (80).

CARPENTER, JOHN: Halloween (78), The Fog (80).

CARRADINE, DAVID: You And Me (73).

CARVER, STEVEN: Steel (80).

CASSAVETES, JOHN: Shadows (60), Too Late Blues (61), A Child is Waiting (62), Faces (68), Husbands (70), Minnie and Moskowitz (71), A Woman Under the Influence (74), The Killing of a Chinese Bookie (76), Opening Night (77), Gloria (80).

CATES, GILBERT: I Never Sang for My Father (69), Summer Wishes, Winter Dreams (73), The Promise (79), Oh, God! Book II (80), The Last Married Couple In America (80).

CHAFFEY, DON: The Magic Of Lassie (78).

CHONG, THOMAS: Cheech And Chong's Next Movie (80).

CIMINO, MICHAEL: Thunderbolt and Lightfoot (74), The Deerhunter (78), Heaven's Gate (80).

CLARK, BOB: Murder By Decree (79), Tribute (80).

CLARK, GREYDON: Without Warning (80).

CLAYTON, JACK: Room at the Top (58), The Innocents (61), The Pumpkin Eater (64), Our Mother's House (67), The Great Gatsby (74).

Hal Ashby.

CLOUSE, ROBERT: The Big Brawl (80).

COE, FRED: Me, Natalie (68).

COE, GEORGE: De Duve (68).

COHEN, ROB: A Small Circle Of Friends (80).

COLLIER, JAMES F.: Joni (80).

COLLINS, ROBERT: Walk Proud (79).

COLLINSON, PETER: The Earthling (80).

CONNOR, KEVIN: Motel Hell (80).

CONWAY, JAMES L.: Hangar 18 (80).

COOLIDGE, MARTHA: An Old Fashioned Woman (74), Not a Pretty Picture (76).

COPPOLA, FRANCIS: Come On Out (61), Tonight for Sure (61), Battle Beyond the Sun (63), Dementia 13 (63), You're a Big Boy Now (67), Finian's Rainbow (68), The Rain People (69), The Godfather (72), The Conversation (74), The Godfather, Part II (74), Apocalypse Now (79).

CORMAN, ROGER: The St. Valentine's Day Massacre (67), Bloody Mama (70), Gas-s-s (70), Von Richtofen and Brown (71).

COSMATOS, GEORGE P.: Escape To Athena (79).

COX, NELL: Liza's Pioneer Diary (76).

CRICHTON, MICHAEL: Westworld (73), Coma (78), The Great Train Robbery (79).

CUKOR, GEORGE: The Chapman Report (62), My Fair Lady (64), Justine (69), Travels with My Aunt (72), Love Among the Ruins (75), The Blue Bird (76).

CULP, ROBERT: Hickey and Boggs (72).

CUNNINGHAM, SEAN S.: Friday the 13th (80).

D'ANTONI, PHILIP: The Seven Ups (73).

DANTE, JOE: Hollywood Boulevard (76), Piranha (78).

DARLING, JOAN: First Love (77).

DASSIN, JULES: Never on Sunday (60), Topkapi (64), Survival (68), Uptight (68), Promise at Dawn (70), A Dream of Passion (78), Circle Of Two (80).

DAVIDSON, MARTIN: The Lords of Flatbush (73), Almost Summer (78), Hero At Large (80).

DAVIS, OSSIE: Cotton Comes to Harlem (70), Kongi's Harvest (70), Black Girl (72), Gordon's War (73), Countdown at Kusini (74).

DAVIS, PETER: Hearts and Minds (74).

DAY, ROBERT: The Man With Bogart's Face (80).

DE LUISE, DOM: Hot Stuff (79).

DE PALMA, BRIAN: The Wedding Party (63)*, Greetings (68), Murder a la Mod (68), Dionysus in 69 (70)*, Hi, Mom! (70), Get to Know Your Rabbit (72), Sisters (73), The Phantom of the Paradise (74), Carrie (76), Obsession (76), The Fury (78), Home Movies (79), Dressed To Kill (80).

DEMME, JONATHAN: Caged Heat (74), Crazy Mama (75), Fighting Mad (76), Citizen's Band (Handle With Care) (77), Last Embrace (79), Melvin and Howard (80).

DONEN, STANLEY: Charade (63), Arabesque (66), Two for the Road (67), Bedazzled (68), Staircase (69), The Little Prince (74), Lucky Lady (75), Movie Movie Baxter's Beauties (78), Movie Movie Dynamite Hands (78), Saturn 3 (80).

DONNER, CLIVE: The Nude Bomb (80).

DONNER, RICHARD: Salt and Pepper (68), Twinky (69), The Omen (76), Superman (78).

DOUGLAS, KIRK: Posse (75).

DOWNEY, ROBERT: Greaser's Palace (72), Up The Academy (80).

DRAGOTI, STAN: Dirty Little Billy (72), Love at First Bite (79).

DUKE, DARRYL: Payday (72).

DURAND, RUDY: Tilt (79).

DYLAN, BOB: Ranaldo and Clara (78).

EASTMAN, CHARLES: The All-American Boy (73).

EASTWOOD, CLINT: Play Misty for Me (71), High Plains Drifter (72), Breezy (73), The Eiger Sanction (75), The Outlaw Josey Wales (76), The Gauntlet (77), Bronco Billy (80).

EDWARDS, BLAKE: 10 (79).

EGLESON, JAN: Billy In The Lowlands (79).

ELLIOTT, LANG: The Private Eyes (80).

FANAKA, JAMES: Penitentiary (79).

FARGO, JAMES: Caravans (78), Every Which Way But Loose (78).

FELDMAN, MARTY: The Last Remake of Beau Geste (77), In God We Trust (80).

FIELD, CONNIE: The Life and Times of Rosie the Riveter (80).

George Roy Hill.   Albert Brooks.

FISCHER, MAX: The Lucky Star (80).

FLEISCHER, RICHARD: Fantastic Voyage (66), The Boston Strangler (68), Che! (69), Tora! Tora! Tora! (70), 10 Rillington Place (71), See No Evil (71), The Last Run (71), Soylent Green (72), The New Centurions (72), The Don is Dead (73), Mr. Majestyk (74), The Spikes Gang (74), Mandingo (75), The Incredible Sarah (76), The Prince and the Pauper (77), Ashanti (79).

FLICKER, THEODORE: The Troublemaker (64), The President's Analyst (67), Up in the Cellar (70).

FLYNN, JOHN: The Sergeant (68), The Jerusalem File (71), The Outfit (73), Rolling Thunder (77), Defiance (80).

FONDA, PETER: The Hired Hand (71), Wanda Nevada (79).

FORBES, BRYAN: King Rat (65), The Madwoman of Chaillot (69), The Raging Moon (70), The Stepford Wives (74), The Slipper and the Rose (76), International Velvet (78), Sunday Lovers (80)*.

FORMAN, MILOS: The Firemen's Ball (67), Taking Off (71), The Decathlon (73), One Flew Over the Cuckoo's Nest (75), Hair (79).

FOSSE, BOB: Sweet Charity (69), Cabaret (72), Lenny (74), All That Jazz (79).

FOWLER, ROBERT: Below The Belt (80).

FRAKER, WILLIAM A.: Monte Walsh (70), Reflection of Fear (71).

FRANCOVICH, ALLAN: On Company Business (80).

FRANK, MELVIN: Buona Sera Mrs. Campbell (68), A Touch of Class (73), The Prisoner of Second Avenue (75), The Duchess and the Dirtwater Fox (76), Lost And Found (79).

FRANKENHEIMER, JOHN: The Fixer (68), The Extraordinary Seaman (69), The Gypsy Moths (69), I Walk the Line (70), The Horsemen (70), Impossible Object (73), The Iceman Cometh (73), 99 44/100

Percent Dead (74), French Connection II (75), Black Sunday (77), Prophecy (79).

FRAWLEY, JAMES: The Christian Licorice Store (70), Kid Blue (73), The Big Bus (76), The Muppet Movie (79).

FREEDMAN, GERROLD: Kansas City Bomber (72), Borderline (80).

FREEMAN, AL, Jr.: A Fable (71).

FRIEDKIN, WILLIAM: Good Times (67), The Night They Raided Minsky's (68), The Boys in the Band (70), The French Connection (71), The Exorcist (73), Sorcerer (77), Brinks (79), Cruising (80).

FULLER, SAMUEL: The Big Red One (80).

FURIE, SYDNEY J.: The Leather Boys (63), The Ipcress File (65), The Appaloosa (66), The Naked Runner (67), The Lawyer (69), Little Fauss and Big Halsey (70), Lady Sings the Blues (72), Sheila Levine Is Dead and Living in New York (75), Gable and Lombard (76), The Boys in Company C (78).

GALFAS, TIMOTHY: Sunnyside (79).

GARDNER, ROBERT: Clarence And Angel (80).

GILBERT, LEWIS: Moonraker (79).

GILER, DAVID: The Black Bird (75).

GILROY, FRANK D.: Desperate Characters (71), From Noon to Three (73), Once in Paris (78).

GODMILOW, JILL: Antonia (74), Louise Nevelson in Process (77).

GOLAN, MENAHEM: What's Good for the Goose (69), Lepke (74).

GOLDBERG, DANNY: No Nukes (80)*.

GOLDSTONE, JAMES: A Man Called Gannon (69), Winning (69), Brother John (70), Red Sky at Morning (70), The Gang That Couldn't Shoot Straight (72), They Only Kill Their Masters (72), Swashbuckler (76), Rollercoaster (77), When Time Ran Out (80).

GORDY, BERRY: Mahogany (75).

GRANT, LEE: Tell Me a Riddle (80).

GRANT, MICHAEL: Head On (80).

GREENE, DAVID: Sebastian (68), The People Next Door (70), Godspell (73).

GREENWALD, ROBERT: Xanadu (80).

GRIES, TOM: Will Penny (67), 100 Rifles (69), The Hawaiians (70), Lady Ice (73), Breakheart Pass (75), The Greatest (77).

GROSBARD, ULU: The Subject Was Roses (68), Who Is Harry Kellerman .... (71), Straight Time (78).

GUILLERMIN, JOHN: The Blue Max (66), House of Cards (68), P.J. (68), The Bridge at Remegen (69), El Condor (70), Skyjacked (72), Shaft in Africa (73), The Towering Inferno (74), King Kong (76), Death on the Nile (78).

GUNN, BILL: Stop (70), Ganja and Hess (73).

HACKFORD, TAYLOR: The Idolmaker (80).

HAGGARD, PIERS: The Fiendish Plot Of Dr. Fu Manchu (80).

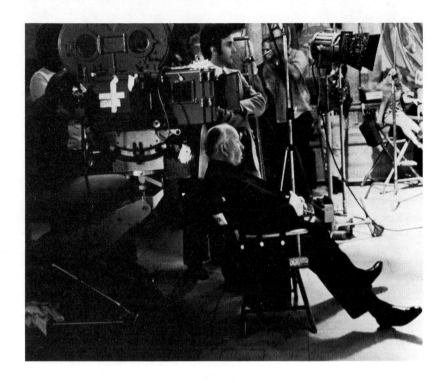

HAGMANN, STUART: The Strawberry Statement (70), Believe in Me (71).

HALEY, JACK, Jr.: Norwood (69), The Love Machine (71), That's Entertainment (74).

HALLER, DANIEL: Buck Rogers (79).

HAMILTON, GUY: Force 10 from Navarone (78), The Mirror Crack'd (80).

HANCOCK, JOHN: Let's Scare Jessica to Death (71), Bang the Drum Slowly (73), Baby Blue Marine (76), California Dreaming (78).

HANSON, CURTIS: The Little Dragons (80).

HANSON, JOHN: Northern Lights (79)*.

HARRIS, DENNY: Silent Scream (80).

HARRIS, JAMES B.: Some Call It Loving (73).

HARVEY, ANTHONY: Eagle's Wing (79), Players (79).

HEFFRON, RICHARD T.: Newman's Law (74), Futureworld (76), Trackdown (76), Outlaw Blues (77), Foolin' Around (80).

HELLMAN, JEROME: Promises In The Dark (79).

HELLMAN, MONTE: The Beast from Haunted Cave (59), Back Door to Hell (65), Flight to Fury (65), Ride the Whirlwind (66), The Shooting (66), Two-Lane Blacktop (71), Cockfighter (74), Shatter (74).

HELPERN, DAVID, Jr.: Something Short Of Paradise (79).

HENRY, BUCK: Heaven Can Wait (78)*, First Family (80).

HIGGINS, COLIN: Foul Play (78), Nine To Five (80).

HILL, GEORGE ROY: Period of Adjustment (62), Toys in the Attic (63), The World of Henry Orient (64), Hawaii (66), Thoroughly Modern Millie (67), Butch Cassidy and the Sundance Kid (69), Slaughterhouse Five (72), The Sting (73), The Great Waldo Pepper (75), Slapshot (77), A Little Romance (79).

HILL, WALTER: Hard Times (75), The Driver (78), The Warriors (79), The Long Riders (80).

HILLER, ARTHUR: Popi (69), Love Story (70), The Out of Towners (70), Plaza Suite (71), The Hospital (71), Man of La Mancha (73), The Crazy World of Julius Vrooder (74), The Man in the Glass Booth (75), The Silver Streak (77), Nightwing (78), The In-Laws (79).

HITCHCOCK, ALFRED: Torn Curtain (66), Topaz (69), Frenzy (72), Family Plot (76).

HODGES, MIKE: Get Carter (71), Pulp (72), The Terminal Man (74), Flash Gordon (80).

HOPPER, DENNIS: Easy Rider (69), The Last Movie (71), Kid Blue (73), Out Of The Blue (80).

HOUGH, JOHN: Dirty Mary, Crazy Larry (74), Brass Target (78), The Watcher In The Woods (80).

HOWARD, CY: Lovers and Other Strangers (69).

HOWARD, RON: Grand Theft Auto (77).

HURWITZ, HARRY: The Projectionist (71).

HURWITZ, LEO: Dialogue With a Woman Departed (80).

HUSTON, JOHN: The List of Adrian Messenger (63), The Night of the Iguana (64), Reflections in a Golden Eye (67), A Walk with Love and Death (69), Sinful Davey (69), The Kremlin Letter (70), Fat City (72), The Life and Times of Judge Roy Bean (72), The Mackintosh Man (73), The Man Who Would Be King (75), Wise Blood (79), Phobia (80).

HUTTON, BRIAN: Fargo (65), The Pad (66), Sol Madrid (67), Where Eagles Dare (68), Kelly's Heroes (70), Zee and Co. (71), Night Watch (73), First Deadly Sin (80).

HUYCK, WILLARD: The Devil's Eight (75), The Second Coming (77), French Postcards (79).

HYAMS, PETER: Busting (74), Our Time (74), Peeper (75), Capricorn One (78), Hanover Street (79).

ISRAEL, NEIL: Americathon (79).

IVORY, JAMES: The Householder (63), Shakespeare Wallah (64), The Guru (68), Bombay Talkie (70), Adventures of a Brown Man.... (72), Savages (72), The Wild Party (74), Autobiography of a Princess (75), Roseland (77), Hullabaloo Over Georgie and Bonnie's Pictures (79), Jane Austen In Manhattan (80).

JACKSON, LEWIS: You Better Watch Out (80).

JAGLOM, HENRY: A Safe Place (71), Tracks (77), Other People (79), Sitting Ducks (79).

JAMES, J. FRANK: The Sweet Creek County War (79).

JAMESON, JERRY: Raise The Titanic (80).

JARROT, CHARLES: Anne of the Thousand Days (70), Mary, Queen of Scots (71), Lost Horizon (72), The Dove (74), The Littlest Horse Thieves (77), The Other Side of Midnight (77).

JEWISON, NORMAN: Forty Pounds of Trouble (62), The Thrill of It All (63), Send Me No Flowers (64), The Art of Love (65), The Cincinnati Kid (65), The Russians Are Coming, The Russians Are Coming (66), In the Heat of the Night (67), The Thomas Crown Affair (68), Gaily, Gaily (69), Fiddler on the Roof (71), Jesus Christ Superstar (73), Rollerball (75), F.I.S.T. (78), ...And Justice For All (79).

JOHNSON, LAMONT: Covenant with Death (67), A Gunfight (70), The Mackenzie Break (70), The Groundstar Conspiracy (72), You'll Like My Mother (72), The Last American Hero (73), Visit to a Chief's Son (74), Lipstick (76), One on One (77), Somebody Killed Her Husband (78).

JONES, TERRY: Life Of Brian (79).

KADAR, JAN: A Shop on Main Street (64), The Angel Levine (70), Adrift (71), Lies My Father Told Me (75).

KAGAN, JEREMY PAUL: The What-Did-You-Think-of-the-Movie Movie (72), The Love Song of Charles Faber (74), Katherine (75), Scott Joplin (76), Heroes (77), The Big Fix (78).

KANEW, JEFF: Natural Enemies (79).

KAPLAN, JONATHAN: White Line Fever (75), Mr. Billion (77), Over The Edge (79).

KARLSON, PHIL: The Silencers (66), A Time for Killing (67), The Wrecking Crew (68), Hornet's Nest (69), Ben (72), Walking Tall (73), Framed (75).

KARSON, ERIC: The Octagon (80).

KATSELAS, MILTON: Butterflies Are Free (72), Forty Carats (73), Report to the Commissioner (74).

KATZ, GLORIA: French Postcards (79).

KATZIN, LEE J.: Heaven with a Gun (69), Whatever Happened to Aunt Alice (69), The Phynx (70), Le Mans (71), The Salzburg Connection (72).

KAUFMAN, CHARLES: Mother's Day (80).

KAUFMAN, PHILIP: The Great Northfield Minnesota Raid (71), The White Dawn (74), Invasion of the Bodysnatchers (78), The Wanderers (79).

KAYLOR, ROBERT: Carny (80).

KAZIN, ELIA: America (63), The Arrangement (69), The Visitors (72),

Stanley Kubrick.

The Last Tycoon (76).

KEETER, WORTH: Lady Grey (80), Living Legend (80).

KENNEDY, BURT: The Money Trap (66), The Return of the Seven (66), Welcome to Hard Times (67), Support Your Local Sheriff (68), The Good Guys and the Bad Guys (69), Young Billy Young (69), Dirty Dingus Magee (70), The Dubious Patriots (70), Hannie Caulder (71), Support Your Local Gunfighter (71), The Deserter (71), The Train Robbers (73).

KERSHNER, IRVIN: The Hoodlum Priest (61), A Face in the Rain (63), The Luck of Ginger Coffey (64), A Fine Madness (66), The Flim Flam Man (67), Loving (70), Up the Sandbox (72), SPYS (74), Return of a Man Called Horse (76), Eyes of Laura Mars (78), The Empire Strikes Back (80).

KING, WOODIE, Jr.: The Long Night (75).

KIRSH, JOHN: Jesus (79)*.

KLANE, ROBERT: Thank God It's Friday (78).

KLEIN, WILLIAM: Far from Vietnam (66), Qui Etes-Vous Polly Magoo (67), Mr. Freedom (68).

KLEISER, RANDAL: All Together Now (76), Grease (78), Blue Lagoon (80).

KOCH, HOWARD W., Jr.: Badge 373 (73).

KOPPLE, BARBARA: Harlan County, U.S.A (76).

KORTY, JOHN: The Language of Faces (61), The Crazy Quilt (65), Funnyman (67), Riverrun (68), The Autobiography of Ms. Jane

Pitman (73), Silence (74), The Electric Flag (74), Alex and the Gypsy (76), Oliver's Story (78).

KOTCHEFF, TED: Tiara Tahiti (62), Life at the Top (65), Two Gentlemen Sharing (70), Billy Two Hats (73), The Apprenticeship of Duddy Kravitz (74), Fun with Dick and Jane (77), Who Is Killing the Great Chef's of Europe (78), North Dallas Forty (79).

KRAMER, STANLEY: Judgment at Nuremberg (62), It's a Mad, Mad, Mad, Mad World (64), Ship of Fools (65), Guess Who's Coming to Dinner? (67), The Secret of Santa Vittoria (69), R.P.M. (70), Bless the Beasts and Children (71), Oklahoma Crude (73), The Domino Principle (77), The Runner Stumbles (79).

KUBRICK, STANLEY: Fear and Desire (53), Killer's Kiss (55), The Killing (56), Paths of Glory (57), Spartacus (60), Lolita (62), Dr. Strangelove (63), 2001: A Space Odyssey (68), A Clockwork Orange (71), Barry Lyndon (75), The Shining (79).

KULIK, BUZZ: The Hunter (80).

LANCASTER, BURT: The Midnight Man (74).

LANDAU, SAUL: Report on Torture in Brazil (71)*.

LANDIS, JOHN: Schlock (76), Kentucky Fried Movie (77), National Lampoon's Animal House (78), A Connecticut Yankee (79), The Blues Brothers (80).

LANG, RICHARD: A Change of Seasons (80), The Mountain Men (80).

LAUGHLIN, TOM: The Young Sinner (65), Born Losers (67), Billy Jack (71), The Trial of Billy Jack (72).

LEAF, PAUL: Bach to Bach (73), I Never Promised You a Long Run (73).

LEAR, NORMAN: Cold Turkey (70).

LEE-THOMPSON, J.: MacKenna's Gold (69), The Chairman (69), St. Ives (73), Huckleberry Finn (74), The Reincarnation of Peter Proud (74), The Greek Tycoon (78).

LEHMAN, ERNEST: Portnoy's Complaint (72).

LEMMON, JACK: Kotch (71).

LESTER, MARK L.: Roller Boogie (79).

LESTER, RICHARD: The Running, Jumping, Standing Still Film (59), It's Trad, Dad (62), The Mouse on the Moon (63), A Hard Day's Night (64), Help (65), The Knack (65), A Funny Thing Happened on the Way... (66), How I Won the War (67), Petulia (68), The Bed-Sitting Room (69), The Three Musketeers (73), Juggernaut (74), The Four Musketeers (74), Royal Flash (75), Robin and Marian (76), The Ritz (76), Butch And Sundance (79), Cuba (79), Superman II (80).

LEVEY, WILLIAM A.: Skatetown Usa (79).

LINSON, ART: Where The Buffalo Roam (80).

LODEN, BARBARA: Wanda (70).

LOMMEL, ULLI: The Boogey Man (80).

LOSEY, JOSEPH: Boom (68), Secret Ceremony (68), Figures in a Landscape (70), The Go-Between (71), The Assassination of Trotsky

Terrence Malick.

(72), A Doll's House (73), Galileo (74), The Romantic
Englishwoman (75), Mr. Klein (76), Don Giovanni (79).
LOVER, ANTHONY: Distance (76).
LUCAS, GEORGE: THX 1138 (70), American Graffiti (73), Star Wars
(77).
LUMET, SIDNEY: The Group (66), The Deadly Affair (67), Bye Bye
Braverman (68), The Appointment (68), The Seagull (68), Blood Kin
(69), The Anderson Tapes (71), Child's Play (72), The Offence (72),
Lovin' Molly (73), Serpico (73), Murder on the Orient Express (74),
Dog Day Afternoon (75), Network (76), Equus (77), The Wiz (78),
Just Tell Me What You Want (80).
LURASCHI, TONY: The Outsider (79).
LYNCH, DAVID: The Elephant Man (80).
LYNCH, PAUL: Prom Night (80).
LYNE, ADRIAN: Foxes (80).
MACK, BRICE: Swap Meet (79).
MALICK, TERRENCE: Badlands (73), Days of Heaven (78).
MALLE, LOUIS: Atlantic City U S A (80).
MALLINSON, MATTHEW: Fist of Fear Touch of Death (80).
MANKIEWICZ, JOSEPH L.: Cleopatra (63), There Was a Crooked Man
(70), Sleuth (72).
MARCEL, TERENCE: Hawk the Slayer (80), There Goes the Bride (80).
MARQUAND, RICHARD: The Legacy (79).
MASTROIANNI, ARMAND: He Knows You're Alone (80).

MAXWELL, RONALD F.: Little Darlings (80).

MAY, ELAINE: A New Leaf (71), The Heartbreak Kid (72), Mikey and Nicky (76).

MAYSLES, ALBERT and DAVID: The Youth of Poland (57), Kenya (61), Safari Ya Gari (61), Showman (63), What's Happening (64), Meet Marlon Brando (65), Truman Capote (66), Salesman (69), Gimme Shelter (71), Grey Gardens (75), Running Fence (77).

MAZURSKY, PAUL: Bob & Carol & Ted & Alice (69), Alex in Wonderland (70), Blume in Love (73), Harry and Tonto (74), Next Stop, Greenwich Village (76), An Unmarried Woman (78), Willie & Phil (80).

McBRIDE, JIM: My Girlfriend's Wedding (74).

McCARTY, ROBERT: I Could Never Have Sex With Any Man (73).

McCOWAN, GEORGE: The Shape Of Things To Come (79).

McEVEETY, VINCENT: Herbie Goes Bananas (80).

McGUANE, THOMAS: 92 in the Shade (76).

McLAGLEN, ANDREW V.: Bandolero (68), The Ballad of Josie (68), The Devil's Brigade (68), Hellfighters (69), The Undefeated (69), Chisum (70), Fool's Parade (71), One More Train to Rob (71), Something Big (71), The Last Hard Men (76), Breakthrough (79), ffolkes (80), The Sea Wolves (80).

MEDAK, PETER: The Changeling (80).

MEDFORD, DON: The Hunting Party (71), The Organization (71).

MENDELUK, GEORGE: The Kidnapping Of The President (80).

MERRILL, KEITH: Take Down (79), Windwalker (80).

MEYER, NICHOLAS: Time After Time (79).

MEYER, RUSS: Finders Keepers Lovers Weepers (68), Vixen (68), Cherry (69), Harry and Raquel (69), Beyond the Valley of the Dolls (70), The Seven Minutes (71), Black Snake (73), The Supervixens (73), Up (76).

MILIUS, JOHN: Dillinger (73), The Wind and the Lion (75), Big Wednesday (78).

MILLER, ROBERT ELLIS: Any Wednesday (66), Sweet November (68), The Heart is a Lonely Hunter (68), The Buttercup Chain (70), The Baltimore Bullet (80).

MINNELLI, VINCENTE: The Sandpiper (65), On a Clear Day You Can See Forever (70), A Matter of Time (76).

MOLINARO, EDOUARD: Sunday Lovers (80)*.

MOORE, RICHARD: Circle Of Iron (79).

MOORE, ROBERT: Murder by Death (76), The Cheap Detective (78), Chapter Two (79).

MORRISEY, PAUL: Flesh (68), Trash (70), Heat (72), Women in Revolt (72).

MOSES, GILBERT: The Fish That Saved Pittsburgh (79).

MOYLE, ALAN: Times Square (80).

Michael Ritchie.

MULLIGAN, ROBERT: Inside Daisy Clover (66), Up the Down Staircase
(67), The Stalking Moon (68), The Piano Sport (69), Bad Times,
Good Times (70), The Pursuit of Happiness (70), Summer of '42
(71), The Other (72), The Nickel Ride (74), Bloodbrothers (78),
Same Time Next Year (78).

MURAKAMI, JIMMY T.: Battle Beyond The Stars (80).

MUTRUX, FLOYD: Dusty and Sweets McGee (71), Aloha Bobby and
Rose (75), American Hot Wax (78), American Me (79), Dick Tracy
(79), Happy Hour (79), The Hollywood Knights (80).

NANKIN, MICHAEL: Midnight Madness (80)*.

NEAME, RONALD: The Prime of Miss Jean Brodie (69), Scrooge (70),
The Poseidon Adventure (72), The Odessa File (74), Meteor (79),
Hopscotch (80).

NEEDHAM, HAL: Smokey and the Bandit (77), Hooper (78), The Villain
(79), Smokey And The Bandit II (80).

NELSON, DUSTY: Effects (79).

NELSON, GARY: The Black Hole (79).

NELSON, RALPH: Counterpoint (67), Charly (68), Tick, Tick, Tick...
Soldier Blue (70), Flight of the Doves (71), The Wrath of God (72),
Wilby Conspiracy (75), Embryo (76).

NEWELL, MIKE: The Awakening (80).

NEWMAN, DAVID: The Crazy American Girl (75).

NEWMAN, PAUL: Rachel, Rachel (68), Sometimes a Great Notion (71),
The Effect of Gamma Rays (72).

The one you don't recognize is director Alan Pakula.

NICHOLS, MIKE: Who's Afraid of Virginia Woolf (66), The Graduate (67), Catch-22 (70), Carnal Knowledge (71), The Day of the Dolphin (73), The Fortune (75), Gilda Live (80).

NICHOLSON, JACK: Drive, He Said (70), Goin' South (78).

NILSSON, ROB: Northern Lights (79)*.

NORTON, B.W.L.: More American Graffiti (79).

NOSSECK, NOEL: Dreamer (79).

NUNEZ, VICTOR: Gal Young Un (79).

O'DONOGHUE, MICHAEL: Mr. Mikes Mondo Video (79).

OLIANSKY, JOEL: The Competition (80).

ORENTREICH, CATHERINE: The Wizard Of Waukesha (80)*.

PAGE, ANTHONY: The Lady Vanishes (79).

PAKULA, ALAN J.: The Sterile Cuckoo (69), Klute (71), Love, Pain the Whole Damn Thing (72), The Parallax View (74), All the President's Men (76), Comes a Horseman (78), Starting Over (79).

PARIS, JERRY: Don't Raise the Bridge, Lower the River (67), Never a Dull Moment (67), How Sweet It Is (68), The Grasshopper (69), Viva Max (69), The Star Spangled Girl (71).

PARKER, ALAN: Midnight Express (78), Fame (80).

PARKS, GORDON, Jr.: Superfly (72).

PARKS, GORDON, Sr.: The Learning Tree (69), Shaft (71), Flavio (72), Shaft's Big Score (72), The Super Cops (74), Leadbelly (75).

PASSER, IVAN: A Boring Afternoon (64), Intimate Lighting (66), The Legend of Beautiful Julia (68), Born to Win (71), Law and Disorder

(74), Silver Bears (78).

PAUL, STEVEN: Falling In Love Again (80).

PAULSEN, DAVID: Schizoid (80).

PEARCE, RICHARD: Heartland (80).

PECKINPAH, SAM: The Wild Bunch (69), The Ballad of Cable Hogue (70), Straw Dogs (71), Junior Bonner (72), The Getaway (72), Pat Garrett and Billy The Kid (73), Bring Me the Head of Alfredo Garcia (74), The Killer Elite (75), Cross of Iron (77), Convoy (78).

PEERCE, LARRY: One Potato, Two Potato (66), Goodbye Columbus (69), A Separate Peace (73), Ash Wednesday (73), The Other Side of the Mountain (75), Two-Minute Warning (76), The Bell Jar (78), Why Would I Lie? (80).

PEETERS, BARBARA: Humanoids From The Deep (80).

PENN, ARTHUR: The Left Handed Gun (58), The Miracle Worker (62), Mickey One (65), The Chase (65), Bonnie and Clyde (67), Alice's Restaurant (69), The Highest (73), Night Moves (75), The Missouri Breaks (76), Altered States (80).

PERRY, FRANK: David and Lisa (62), Ladybug (63), The Swimmer (68), Trilogy (68), Last Summer (69), Diary of a Mad Housewife (70), Doc (71), Play It as It Lays (72), Man on a Swing (73), Rancho De Luxe (74).

PERSKY, BILL: Serial (80).

PETRIE, DANIEL: A Raisin in the Sun (61), The Spy with the Cold Nose (67), The Neptune Factor (72), Buster and Billie (74), Lifeguard (76), The Betsy (77), Resurrection (80).

PIERSON, FRANK: The Looking Glass War (69).

POITIER, SIDNEY: Buck and The Preacher (71), A Warm December (72), Uptown Saturday Night (74), Let's Do It Again (75), Stir Crazy (80).

POLLACK, SYDNEY: The Electric Horseman (79).

POTENZA, ANTHONY: No Nukes (80)*.

PREECE, MICHAEL: The Prize Fighter (79).

PREMINGER, OTTO: The Human Factor (79).

PRESSMAN, MICHAEL: Boulevard Nights (79), Those Lips Those Eyes (80).

QUINE, RICHARD: The Prisoner Of Zenda (79).

RAFELSON, BOB: Stay Hungry (76).

RAINER, YVONNE: Journeys From Berlin 1971 (80).

REDFORD, ROBERT: Ordinary People (80).

REICHERT, MARK: Union City (80).

REINER, CARL: The Comic (69), The Jerk (79).

REITMAN, IVAN: Meatballs (79).

REYNOLDS, BURT: The End (78).

RICH, DAVID LOWELL: The Concorde-Airport '79 (79).

RICHARDS, DICK: The Culpepper Cattle Company (72), Rafferty and the Gold Dust Twins (74), Farewell My Lovely (75), March or Die (77), Double Exposure (78), No Knife (79).

RICHERT, WILLIAM: The American Success Company (79), Winter Kills (79).

RISI, DINO: Sunday Lovers (80)*.

RITCHIE, MICHAEL: Downhill Racer (69), Prime Cut (72), The Candidate (72), Smile (75), The Bad News Bears (76), Semi-Tough (77), An Almost Perfect Affair (79), Divine Madness (80), The Island (80).

RITT, MARTIN: The Spy Who Came in from the Cold (65), Hombre (67), The Brotherhood (68), The Molly Maguires (68), The Great White Hope (70), Pete 'n Tillie (72), Sounder (72), Conrack (74), The Front (76), Casey's Shadow (77).

ROBERTSON, CLIFF: J.W. Coop (72).

ROBSON, MARK: Avalanche Express (79).

ROEG, NICOLAS: Bad Timing (80).

ROEMER, MICHAEL: Pilgrim, Farewell (80).

ROMERO, GEORGE: The Night of the Living Dead (68), Hungry Wives (73), The Crazies (73), Martin (78).

ROOKS, CONRAD: Chappaqua (66), Siddhartha (72).

ROSE, LES: Hog Wild (80).

ROSENBERG, STUART: Cool Hand Luke (67), The April Fools (69), Move (70), W.U.S.A (70), Pocket Money (72), The Laughing Policeman (73), The Drowning Pool (75), Voyage of the Damned (76), The Amityville Horror (79), Brubaker (80).

ROSS, HERBERT: Goodbye Mr. Chips (69), The Owl and the Pussycat (70), T.R. Baskin (71), Play It Again, Sam (72), The Last of Sheila (73), Funny Lady (75), The Sunshine Boys (75), The Seven Percent Solution (76), The Turning Point (77), California Suite (78), The Goodbye Girl (78), Nijinsky (80).

RUDOLPH, ALAN: Welcome to L.A. (77), Remember My Name (78), Roadie (80).

RUSH, RICHARD: Hell's Angels on Wheels (69), Getting Straight (70), Freebie and The Bean (74), The Stunt Man (80).

RUSSELL, KEN: Altered States (80).

RYDELL, MARK: The Fox (68), The Reivers (69), The Cowboys (72), Cinderella Liberty (74), Harry and Walter Go to New York (76), The Rose (78).

SACHS, WILLIAM: Galaxina (80).

SAGAL, BORIS: The Thousand Plane Raid (69), Mosquito Squadron (70), The Omega Man (71).

SAKS, GENE: Barefoot in the Park (67), The Odd Couple (68), Cactus Flower (69), The Last of the Red Hot Lovers (72), Mame (74).

SALMINI, AMBROSE: American Odyssey (80).

SANDRICH, JAY: Seems Like Old Times (80).

Peters Benchley and Yates.

Frederick Wiseman.

SARAFIAN, RICHARD: Run Free, Run Wild (69), Fragment of Fear (70), Ashanti (71), Man in the Wilderness (71), The Next Man (71), Vanishing Point (71), Lolly Madonna XXX (73), The Man Who Loved Cat Dancing (73), Sunburn (79).

SARGENT, JOSEPH: The Hell with Heroes (68), The Forbin Project (69), White Lightning (73), The Taking of Pelham 1-2-3 (74), MacArthur (77), Goldengirl (79), Coast To Coast (80).

SARNE, MIKE: Myra Breckinridge (70).

SAYLES, JOHN: Return Of The Secaucus Seven (80).

SCHAEFER, GEORGE: An Enemy Of The People (76).

SCHAFFNER, FRANKLIN: The Stripper (63), The Best Man (64), The War Lord (65), Planet of the Apes (68), The Double Man (68), Patton (69), Nicholas and Alexandra (71), Papillon (73), Islands in the Stream (77), The Boys from Brazil (78).

SCHATZBERG, JERRY: Puzzle of a Downfall Child (70), The Panic in Needle Park (71), Scarecrow (73), Dandy the All American Girl (76), Sweet Revenge (77), The Seduction Of Joe Tynan (79), Honeysuckle Rose (80).

SCHEERER, ROBERT: How To Beat The High Cost of Living (80).

SCHELL, MAXIMILIAN: End of the Game (76), The Pedestrian (78).

SCHELLERUP, HENNING: In Search Of Historic Jesus (80).

SCHLESINGER, JOHN: A Kind of Loving (62), Billy Liar (63), Darling (65), Far From the Madding Crowd (67), Midnight Cowboy (69), Sunday, Bloody Sunday (71), The Longest (73), The Day of the Locust (75), Marathon Man (76), Yanks (79).

SCHLOSSBERG, JULIAN: No Nukes (80)*.

SCHRADER, PAUL: Blue Collar (78), Hardcore (79), American Gigolo (80).

SCHULTZ, MICHAEL: Cooley High (75), Carwash (76), Greased Lightning (77), Which Way Is Up? (77), Sergeant Pepper's Lonely Hearts Club Band (78), Scavenger Hunt (79).

SCORSESE, MARTIN: What's a Nice Girl Like You... (63), It's Not Just You, Murray (64), The Big Shave (67), Who's That Knocking at My Door (69), Boxcar Bertha (72), Mean Streets (73), Alice Doesn't Live Here Anymore (74), Italian American (74), Taxi Driver (76), New York, New York (77), American Boy: A Profile (78), The Last Waltz (78), Raging Bull (80).

SCOTT, GEORGE C.: Rage (72), The Savage Is Loose (74).

SCOTT, RIDLEY: The Duellists (77), Alien (79).

SEATON, GEORGE: What's So Bad About Feeling Good (68), Airport (69), Showdown (72).

SHAFFER, DEBORAH: The Wobblies (79)*.

SHAVELSON, MELVILLE: Yours, Mine and Ours (68), The War Between Men and Women (72), Mixed Company (74).

SHEAR, BARRY: Wild in the Streets (68), The Todd Killings (70), Across 110th Street (72), The Deadly Trackers (73).

SHERIN, EDWIN: Valdez is Coming (70), Glory Boy (71).

SICKINGER, ROBERT: Love in a Taxi (80).

SIDARIS, ANDY: Seven (79).

SIEGEL, DONALD: Coogan's Bluff (68), Madigan (68), Death of a Gunfighter (69), Two Mules for Sister Sara (69), Dirty Harry (71), The Beguiled (71), Charley Varrick (72), The Black Windmill (74), The Shootist (76), Telefon (77), Escape From Alcatraz (79), Rough Cut (80).

SILBER, GLENN: The War At Home (79)*.

SILVER, JOAN MICKLIN: Hester Street (74), Bernice Bobs Her Hair (76), Between the Lines (77), Head Over Heels (79).

SILVER, RAPHAEL D.: On the Yard (79).

SILVERSTEIN, ELLIOT: Cat Ballou (65), The Happening (67), A Man Called Horse (70), The Car (77).

SINDELL, GERALD: H.O.T.S. (79).

SMIGHT, JACK: Harper (66), The Secret War of Harry Frigg (67), No Way to Treat a Lady (68), The Illustrated Man (69), The Traveling Executioner (69), Rabbit Run (70), Airport 75 (75), Midway (76), Damnation Alley (77), Fast Break (79), Loving Couples (80).

SONTAG, SUSAN: Duet for Cannibals (69), Promised Lands (73).

SPIELBERG, STEVEN: Duel (71), Sugarland Express (73), Jaws (75), Close Encounters of the Third Kind (77), 1941 (79).

SPOTTISWOODE, ROGER: Terror Train (80).

ST. JACQUES, RAYMOND: The Book of Numbers (73).

Howard Zieff.

Jerry Schatzberg.

STALLONE, SYLVESTER: Paradise Alley (78), Rocky II (79).

STERN, LEONARD: Just You And Me, Kid (79), Two of a Kind (79).

STERN, STEVEN: Running (79).

STRICK, JOSEPH: The Savage Eye (59), The Balcony (64), Ulysses (67), Tropic of Cancer (69), Janice (73), A Portrait of the Artist.... (77).

STUART, MEL: If It's Tuesday This Must Be Belgium (69), I Love My Wife (70), Willy Wonka and the Chocolate.... (71), One Is a Lonely Number (72).

STURGES, JOHN: The Magnificent Seven (60), The Great Escape (63), The Hour of the Gun (67), Ice Station Zebra (68), Marooned (69), Joe Kidd (72), McQ (74), The Eagle Has Landed (77).

SYKES, PETER: Jesus (79)*.

SYLBERT, PAUL: The Steagle (71).

SZWARC, JEANNOT: The Extreme Closeup (73), Bug (75), Jaws 2 (78), Somewhere In Time (80).

TAYLOR, DON: The Final Countdown (80).

TEAGUE, LEWIS: Alligator (80).

TEWKESBURY, JOAN: Old Boyfriends (79).

THOMAS, RALPH: It's Not The Size That Counts (79).

TILL, ERIC: Hot Millions (68), The Walking Stick (70), A Fan's Notes (72), It Shouldn't Happen to a Vet (76).

TOBACK, JAMES: Fingers (78).

TRENT, JOHN: Middle Age Crazy (80).

TRIKONIS, GUS: Touched By Love (80).

TROELL, JAN: The Emigrants (72), The New Land (73), Zandy's Bride (74), Hurricane (79).

TRUMBO, DALTON: Johnny Got His Gun (71).

TRUMBULL, DOUGLAS: Silent Running (71), Brainstorm (78).

Claudia Weill.   Paul Mazursky.

TURMAN, LAWRENCE: The Marriage of a Young Stockbroker (71).
USTINOV, PETER: Lady L (65), Hammersmith Is Out (72).
VAN HORN, BUDDY: Any Which Way You Can (80).
VAN PEEBLES, MELVIN: The Story of a Three Day Pass (67),
    Watermelon Man (69), Sweet Sweetback's Baadasssss Song (71).
VERONA, STEPHEN: Pipe Dreams (76), Boardwalk (79).
WADLEIGH, MICHAEL: Woodstock (79).
WAGNER, JANE: Moment By Moment (78).
WAITE, RALPH: On The Nickel (80).
WALKER, NANCY: Can't Stop The Music (80).
WALTON, FRED: When A Stranger Calls (79).
WARHOL, ANDY: The Chelsea Girls (66), My Hustler (67), Women in
    Revolt (72), Bad (76).
WAYNE, JOHN: The Green Berets (68).
WECHTER, DAVID: Midnight Madness (80)*.
WEILL, CLAUDIA: Joyce at 34 (72), The Other Half of the Sky.... (75),
    Girl Friends (78), It's My Turn (80).
WEIS, GARY: Wholly Moses! (80).
WEISBURD, DAN: Today Is For The Championship (80).
WENDKOS, PAUL: Angel Baby (60), Guns of the Magnificent Seven
    (69), Cannon for Cordoba (70), The Mephisto Waltz (71), Special
    Delivery (76).
WERNER, JEFF: Die Laughing (80).
WEXLER, HASKELL: The Bus (64), Medium Cool (69), Interview with
    President Allende (71)*, Report on Torture in Brazil (71)*,
    Introduction to the Enemy (74).
WIARD, WILLIAM: Tom Horn (80).
WIEDERHORN, KEN: Shock Waves (75).

WILDER, BILLY: The Private Life of Sherlock Holmes (70), Avanti (72), The Front Page (74), The Fortune Cookie (76), Fedora (78).

WILDER, GENE: The Adventure of Sherlock Holmes (75), Sunday Lovers (80)*.

WILLIAMS, OSCAR: Five on the Black Hand Side (73).

WILLIAMS, PAUL: Out of It (69), The Revolutionary (70), Dealing (72), Nunzio (78).

WILLIS, GORDON: Windows (80).

WINNER, MICHAEL: The Jokers (67), Hannibal Brooks (68), The Games (69), Lawman (70), Chato's Land (71), The Nightcomers (71), Scorpio (72), The Mechanic (72), The Stone Killer (73), Death Wish (74), Won Ton Ton, The Dog Who Saved Hollywood (76), The Sentinel (77), The Big Sleep (78), Firepower (79).

WISE, ROBERT: West Side Story (60), The Sound of Music (65), The Andromeda Strain (70), Two People (73), The Hindenburg (75), Audrey Rose (77), Star Trek (79).

WISEMAN, FREDERICK: Titicut Follies (67), High School (68), Law and Order (69), Hospital (70), Basic Training (71), Essene (72), Juvenile Court (73), Primate (74), Welfare (75), Meat (76), Canal Zone (77), Sinai Field Mission (78), Manoeuvre (79).

WOHL, IRA: Best Boy (79).

WRYE, DONALD: Ice Castles (78).

WYLER, WILLIAM: How to Steal a Million (66), Funny Girl (68), The Liberation of L.B. Jones (70).

YATES, PETER: Summer Holiday (62), One Way Pendulum (64), Robbery (67), Bullitt (68), John and Mary (69), Murphy's War (71), The Hot Rock (72), The Friends of Eddie Coyle (73), For Pete's Sake (74), Mother, Jugs and Speed (76), The Deep (77), Breaking Away (79).

YORKIN, BUD: Come Blow Your Horn (63), Divorce American Style (67), Inspector Clouseau (68), Start the Revolution Without Me (69), The Thief Who Came to Dinner (73).

YOUNG, ROBERT M.: Short Eyes (77), Alambrista (78), Rich Kids (79), One Trick Pony (80).

YOUNG, TERENCE: Dr. No (62), From Russia with Love (63), Thunderball (65), The Poppy Is Also a Flower (66), Wait Until Dark (67), You Only Live Twice (67), Mayerling (68), The Christmas Tree (69), Cold Sweat (70), Grand Slam (70), Red Sun (71), The Valachi Papers (72), War Goddess (73), The Klansman (74), Bloodline (79).

ZACHARIAS, ALFREDO: The Bees (78).

ZAPPA, FRANK: 200 Motels (71).

ZEFFIRELLI, FRANCO: The Champ (79).

ZEMECKIS, ROBERT: I Wanna Hold Your Hand (78), Used Cars (80).

ZIEFF, HOWARD: Slither (72), Hearts of the West (75), House Calls (78), The Main Event (79), Private Benjamin (80).

ZINNEMANN, FRED: Behold a Pale Horse (64), A Man For All Seasons (66), The Day of the Jackal (73).

ZUCKER, DAVID: Airplane (80).

ZUCKER, JERRY: Airplane (80).

Actors and Actresses

ABBOTT, DIAHNNE: Taxi Driver (76), New York, New York (77), Welcome to L.A. (77).

ABDUL-JABBAR, KAREEM: Airplane (80).

ACKLAND, JOSS: Rough Cut (80).

ACKROYD, DAVID: The Mountain Men (80).

ADAMES, JOHN: Gloria (80).

ADAMS, BROOKE: Shock Waves (75), Days of Heaven (78), Invasion Of The Bodysnatchers (78), A Man, A Woman, and a Bank (79), Cuba (79), Tell Me a Riddle (80).

ADAMS, CATLIN: The Jerk (79).

ADAMS, DON: The Nude Bomb (80).

ADAMS, JULIE: The Fifth Floor (80).

ADAMS, MAUDE: The Man with the Golden Gun (74), Rollerball (75).

AGUTTER, JENNY: Logan's Run (76), The Eagle Has Landed (77).

AIELLO, DANNY: Defiance (80), Hide In Plain Sight (80).

ALBERT, EDDIE: The Concorde-Airport '79 (79), Foolin' Around (80), How To Beat The High Cost of Living (80).

ALBERT, EDWARD: Butterflies Are Free (72), Forty Carats (73), Midway (76), The Domino Principle (77), The Greek Tycoon (78), When Time Ran Out (80).

ALDA, ALAN: Paper Lion (68), The Extraordinary Seaman (69), Jennie (70), The Moonshine War (70), The Mephisto Waltz (71), To Kill a Clown (71), California Suite (78), Same Time Next Year (79), The Seduction Of Joe Tynan (79).

ALDEN, GINGER: Lady Grey (80), Living Legend (80).

ALDEN, NORMAN: Cloud Dancer (80).

ALEXANDER, JANE: A Gunfight (70), The Great White Hope (70), The New Centurions (72), All the President's Men (76), Eleanor and Franklin (76), The Betsy (77), Kramer vs. Kramer (79), Brubaker (80).

ALLEN, KAREN: The Wanderers (79), A Small Circle Of Friends (80), Cruising (80).

ALLEN, NANCY: 1941 (79), Home Movies (79), Dressed To Kill (80).

ALLEN, PENELOPE: On The Nickel (80), Resurrection (80).

ALLEN, PHILLIP R.: The Onion Field (79).

ALLEN, SHEILA: When Time Ran Out (80).

ALLEN, WOODY: What's New Pussycat? (65), Casino Royale (67), Take the Money and Run (69), Everything You Always Wanted to Know About Sex (72), Play It Again, Sam (72), Sleeper (73), Love and Death (75), The Front (76), Annie Hall (77), Manhattan (79), Stardust Memories (80).

ALTMAN, RICHARD: The Main Event (79).

ALVARADO, TRINI: Rich Kids (79), Times Square (80).

ALVARENGA, TONY: Walk Proud (79).

AMBRIZ, DOMINGO: Walk Proud (79).

AMOS, JOHN: Touched By Love (80).

AMSLER, JOE: The Main Event (79).

ANDERSON, JEAN: The Lady Vanishes (79).

ANDERSON, JOHN: In Search Of Historic Jesus (80).

ANDERSON, MELODY: Flash Gordon (80).

ANDERSSON, BIBI: Duel At Diablo (66), The Kremlin Letter (70), The Touch (71), An Enemy of the People (76), I Never Promised You a Rose Garden (77), Quintet (79), The Concorde-Airport '79 (79).

ANDREWS, BRIAN: The Great Santini (80).

ANDREWS, HARRY: Superman (78), Hawk the Slayer (80).

ANDREWS, JULIE: 10 (79), Little Miss Marker (80).

ANN-MARGRET: Mr. Kinky (68), C.C. and Company (70), R.P.M. (70), Carnal Knowledge (71), The Outside Man (73), The Train Robbers (73), Tommy (75), The Last Remake of Beau Geste (77), Joseph Andrews (78), Magic (78), The Cheap Detective (78), The Villain (79), Middle Age Crazy (80).

ANSPACH, SUSAN: Five Easy Pieces (70), The Landlord (70), Play It Again, Sam (72), Blume in Love (73), Nashville (75), The Big Fix (78), Running (79).

ANTON, SUSAN: Goldengirl (79).

ARBUS, ALLAN: The Electric Horseman (79), The Last Married Couple In America (80).

ARCHER, ANNE: Cancel My Reservation, Good Guys Wear Black, Lifeguard, The All-American Boy, The Honkers, Trackdown, Paradise Alley (78), Hero At Large (80), Raise The Titanic (80).

ARKIN, ALAN: The Russians Are Coming, The Russians Are Coming (66), Wait Until Dark (67), Woman Times Seven (67), Inspector Clouseau (68), The Heart is a Lonely Hunter (68), Popi (69), The Monitors (69), Catch-22 (70), Little Murders (71), The Last of the Red Hot Lovers (72), Freebie and The Bean (74), Hearts of the West

(75), Rafferty and the Gold Dust Twins (75), The Seven Percent Solution (76), The In-Laws (79), Simon (80).

ARLISS, DIMITRA: A Perfect Couple (79).

ARMSTRONG, PETER: Natural Enemies (79).

ARNAZ, DESI, Jr.: Red Sky at Morning (70), Marco (73), Joyride (77), A Wedding (78).

ARNOTT, MARK: Return Of The Secaucus Seven (80).

ASHLEY, ELIZABETH: The Carpetbaggers (64), Ship of Fools (65), The Third Day (65), The Marriage of a Young Stockbroker (71), Paperback Hero (73), Golden Needles (74), Rancho De Luxe (74), 92 in the Shade (76), The Great Scout & Cathouse Thursday (76), Coma (78), Windows (80).

ASKEW, LUKE: Wanda Nevada (79).

ASSANTE, ARMAND: Prophecy (79), Little Darlings (80), Private Benjamin (80).

ASTIN, PATTY DUKE: The Miracle Worker (62), Billie (65), Valley of the Dolls (67), Me, Natalie (68), My Sweet Charlie (70), You'll Like My Mother (72), The Swarm (78).

ATHERTON, WILLIAM: Class of '44 (73), The Sugarland Express (73), The Day of the Locust (75), The Hindenburg (75), Looking for Mr. Goodbar (77).

ATKIN, HARVEY: Meatballs (79).

ATKINS, CHRISTOPHER: Blue Lagoon (80).

ATKINSON, ROWAN: The Secret Policeman's Ball (79).

ATTAWAY, RUTH: Being There (79).

ATTENBOROUGH, RICHARD: The Human Factor (79).

AUBERJONOIS, RENE: Brewster McCloud (70), MASH (70), McCabe and Mrs. Miller (71), Images (72), Pete 'n Tillie (72), The Hindenburg (75), King Kong (76), The Big Bus (76), Eyes of Laura Mars (78), Where The Buffalo Roam (80).

AUDRAN, STEPHANE: Eagle's Wing (79), The Big Red One (80).

AUGER, CLAUDINE: Travels With Anita (79).

AUMONT, JEAN-PIERRE: Something Short Of Paradise (79).

AUSTIN, STEVE: Natural Enemies (79).

AVALOF, LOUIS: Hot Stuff (79).

AVERY, MARGARET: The Fish That Saved Pittsburgh (79).

AVERY, VAL: The Amityville Horror (79), The Wanderers (79), Brubaker (80).

AXTON, HOYT: The Black Stallion (79).

AYKROYD, DAN: 1941 (79), Mr. Mike's Mondo Video (79), The Blues Brothers (80).

AZZARA, CANDICE: Fatso (80).

BABCOCK, BARBARA: The Black Marble (80).

BACALL, LAUREN: Harper (66), Murder on the Orient Express (74), The Shootist (76), Health (80).

Anne Archer.

Rosalind Cash.

BACH, BARBARA: Up The Academy (80).

BACKUS, JIM: There Goes the Bride (80).

BADEL, ALAN: Nijinsky (80).

BAER, MAX, Jr.: Macon County Line (73), The McCulloughs (75).

BAFF, REGINA: Below The Belt (80).

BAIO, SCOTT: Skatetown USA (79), Foxes (80).

BAKER, BLANCHE: French Postcards (79).

BAKER, CARROLL: The Watcher In The Woods (80).

BAKER, GEORGE: ffolkes (80).

BAKER, JOE DON: Cool Hand Luke (67), Guns of the Magnificent Seven (69), Wild Rovers (71), Charley Varrick (72), Junior Bonner (72), The Outfit (73), Walking Tall (73), Golden Needles (74), Mitchell (74), Framed (75).

BAKER, KEN: Dressed To Kill (80).

BAKER, KENNY: The Empire Strikes Back (80).

BAKER, LENNY: Next Stop, Greenwich Village (76).

BALABAN, BOB: Report to the Commissioner (75), Close Encounters of the Third Kind (77), Girl Friends (78), Altered States (80).

BALDING, REBECCA: Silent Scream (80).

BALDWIN, ADAM: My Bodyguard (80), Ordinary People (80).

BALLARD, KAYE: Falling In Love Again (80).

BALSAM, MARTIN: The Carpetbaggers (63), Seven Days in May (64), Youngblood Hawke (64), A Thousand Clowns (65), After the Fox (66), Hombre (67), Me, Natalie (68), The Good Guys and the Bad Guys (69), Catch-22 (70), Little Big Man (70), Tora! Tora! Tora! (70), The Anderson Tapes (71), Summer Wishes, Winter Dreams (73), The Stone Killer (73), Mitchell (74), Murder on the Orient Express (74), The Taking of Pelham 1-2-3 (74), All the President's

Men (76), Two-Minute Warning (76), The Sentinel (77), Silver Bears (78), Cuba (79), There Goes the Bride (80).

BALSAM, TALIA: Sunnyside (79).

BANCROFT, ANNE: The Miracle Worker (62), The Pumpkin Eater (64), Seven Women (65), The Slender Thread (65), The Graduate (67), Young Winston (72), The Hindenburg (75), The Prisoner of Second Avenue (75), Lipstick (76), Silent Movie (76), The Turning Point (77), Fatso (80), The Elephant Man (80).

BANHAM, RUSS: Meatballs (79).

BANKS, SETH: The Main Event (79).

BANNEN, IAN: The Watcher In The Woods (80).

BARBEAU, ADRIENNE: The Fog (80).

BARBER, ELLEN: Natural Enemies (79).

BARKETT, BEEGE: The Onion Field (79).

BARNES, PRISCILLA: The Last Married Couple In America (80).

BARON, GERALDINE: Time After Time (79).

BARRAULT, MARIE-CHRISTINE: Stardust Memories (80).

BARRETT, MAJEL: Star Trek (79).

BARRIE, BARBARA: Breaking Away (79), The Bell Jar (79), Private Benjamin (80).

BARRINGTON, DIANA: Lost And Found (79).

BARRY, GENE: Guyana: Cult Of The Damned (80).

BARRY, MATTHEW: Luna (79).

BARTH, EDDIE: Fame (80).

BARTRAM, LAURIE: Friday the 13th (80).

BASEHART, RICHARD: Being There (79).

BATES, ALAN: The Fixer (68), Women in Love (69), The Go-Between (71), Royal Flash (75), An Unmarried Woman (78), The Shout (78), The Rose (79), Nijinsky (80).

BATT, SHELLY: Loving Couples (80).

BATTAGLIA, ANTHONY: Serial (80).

BAUER, BELINDA: The American Success Company (79), Winter Kills (79).

BAXTER, ANNE: Jane Austen In Manhattan (80).

BAXTER, PHYLLIS: Superman (78).

BAXTER, TERESA: It's My Turn (80).

BEATTY, NED: Deliverance (72), The Last American Hero (73), Nashville (75), W.W. and the Dixie Dancekings (75), Network (76), The Big Bus (76), Exorcist II-The Heretic (77), Silver Streak (77), Superman (78), 1941 (79), Promises In The Dark (79), The American Success Company (79), Wise Blood (79), Hopscotch (80), Superman II (80).

BEATTY, WARREN: Splendor in the Grass (61), The Roman Spring of Mrs. Stone (61), All Fall Down (62), Lilith (65), Mickey One (65), Kaleidoscope (66), Promise Her Anything (66), Bonnie and Clyde

(67), The Only Game in Town (69), $ (71), McCabe and Mrs. Miller (71), The Parallax View (74), Shampoo (75), Heaven Can Wait (78).

BEAUCHAMP, RICHARD: Sunnyside (79).

BECHER, JOHN C.: Below The Belt (80).

BECK, JOHN: Lawman (71), Mrs. Pollifax-Spy (71), Pat Garrett and Billy The Kid (73), Sleeper (73), Rollerball (75), The Big Bus (76), Audrey Rose (77), The Other Side of Midnight (77).

BECK, MICHAEL: The Warriors (79), Xanadu (80).

BECKLEY, TONY: When A Stranger Calls (79).

BEDELIA, BONNIE: Lovers and Other Strangers (69), The Gypsy Moths (69), They Shoot Horses, Don't They? (69), The Strange Vengeance of Rosalie (72), The Big Fix (78).

BEGLEY, ED, Jr.: The In-Laws (79).

BEGLEY, ELIZABETH: The Outsider (79).

BEHLING, ROBERT: Northern Lights (79).

BELLAFONTE, HARRY: The Angel Levine (70), Buck and The Preacher (71).

BELLAVER, HARRY: Hero At Large (80).

BELLER, KATHLEEN: Movie Movie Dynamite Hands (78), Promises In The Dark (79).

BELUSHI, JOHN: Goin' South (78), National Lampoon's Animal House (78), 1941 (79), Old Boyfriends (79), The Blues Brothers (80).

BENEDICT, PAUL: Billy In The Lowlands (79).

BENJAMIN, PAUL: Escape From Alcatraz (79).

BENJAMIN, RICHARD: Goodbye Columbus (69), Catch-22 (70), Diary of a Mad Housewife (70), The Marriage of a Young Stockbroker (71), The Steagle (71), Portnoy's Complaint (72), The Last of Sheila (73), Westworld (73), The Sunshine Boys (75), House Calls (78), Scavenger Hunt (79), First Family (80), How To Beat The High Cost of Living (80), The Last Married Couple In America (80).

BENSON, ROBBY: Jory (72), Jeremy (73), Lucky Lady (75), Ode to Billie Joe (76), One on One (77), Ice Castles (78), The End (79), Walk Proud (79), Die Laughing (80), Tribute (80).

BENTON, EDDIE: Prom Night (80).

BERENGER, TOM: Butch And Sundance (79).

BERENSON, BERRY: Remember My Name (78).

BERGEN, CANDICE: The Group (66), The Sand Pebbles (66), The Day the Fish Came Out (67), Vivre pour Vivre (67), The Magus (68), Getting Straight (70), Soldier Blue (70), The Adventurers (70), Carnal Knowledge (71), The Hunting Party (71), T.R. Baskin (72), 11 Harrowhouse (74), Bite the Bullet (75), The Wind and the Lion (75), The Domino Principle (77), Oliver's Story (78), Starting Over (79).

BERGEN, EDGAR: The Muppet Movie (79).

BERGHOF, HERBERT: Those Lips Those Eyes (80), Times Square (80).

BERLE, MILTON: The Muppet Movie (79).

BERLIN, JEANNIE: A Night of Rain (70), Getting Straight (70), Move (70), On a Clear Day You Can See Forever (70), The Baby Maker (70), The Strawberry Statement (70), Bone (72), Portnoy's Complaint (72), The Heartbreak Kid (72), Why (72), Sheila Levine Is Dead and Living in New York (75).

BERNARD, THELONIOUS: A Little Romance (79).

BERRIDGE, BETH: Natural Enemies (79).

BIERI, RAMON: The Frisco Kid (79).

BILL, TONY: Heart Beat (79), The Little Dragons (80).

BINNS, EDWARD: Oliver's Story (78).

BIRNEY, DAVID: Oh, God! Book II (80).

BISHOP, ED: Brass Target (78), Saturn 3 (80).

BISOGLIO, VAL: The Frisco Kid (79).

BISSET, JACQUELINE: Bullitt (68), The Detective (68), The First Time (68), Airport (69), The Grasshopper (69), Believe in Me (71), Secrets (71), Stand Up and Be Counted (71), The Mephisto Waltz (71), The Life and Times of Judge Roy Bean (72), La Nuit Americaine (73), St. Ives (73), The Thief Who Came to Dinner (73), Murder on the Orient Express (74), End of the Game (76), The Sunday Woman (76), The Deep (77), The Greek Tycoon (78), Who Is Killing the Great Chef's of Europe (78), When Time Ran Out (80).

BJORN, ANNA: More American Graffiti (79).

BLACK, KAREN: You're a Big Boy Now (67), Hard Contract (68), Easy Rider (69), A Gunfight (70), Drive, He Said (70), Five Easy Pieces (70), Born to Win (71), Cisco Pike (71), Portnoy's Complaint (72), Rhinoceros (73), The Outfit (73), The Pyx (73), Law and Disorder (74), The Great Gatsby (74), Airport 75 (75), Nashville (75), The Day of the Locust (75), Burnt Offerings (76), Family Plot (76), Capricorn One (78), The Squeeze (78), The Last Word (79), Valentine (79), Miss Right (80).

BLAIR, LINDA: The Exorcist (73), Airport 75 (75), Exorcist II-The Heretic (77), Roller Boogie (79).

BLAKE, ROBERT: The Greatest Story Ever Told (65), In Cold Blood (67), Tell Them Willie Boy Is Here (69), Corky (72), Electra Glide in Blue (73), Coast To Coast (80), Second-Hand Hearts (80).

BLAKE, SONDRA: Second-Hand Hearts (80).

BLAKELY, COLIN: Nijinsky (80).

BLAKELY, DON: Defiance (80).

BLAKELY, SUSAN: Savages (72), Capone (73), The Way We Were (73), Report to the Commissioner (74), The Lords of Flatbush (74), The Towering Inferno (74), Shampoo (75), Dreamer (79), The Concorde-Airport '79 (79).

BLAKLEY, RONEE: Nashville (75), Renaldo and Clara (78), The Driver (78), The Baltimore Bullet (80).

Lindsay Crouse, Gwen Welles.   Trini Alvarado, Kathryn Walker.

BLESSED, BRIAN: Flash Gordon (80).

BLISS, IMOGENE: Chapter Two (79).

BLOOM, LINDSAY: The Main Event (79).

BLOOM, VERNA: Medium Cool (69), The Hired Hand (71), High Plains Drifter (72), Badge 373 (73), National Lampoon's Animal House (78).

BLOSSOM, ROBERTS: Escape From Alcatraz (79), Resurrection (80).

BLUESTONE, ABBY: Night Of The Juggler (80).

BLUM, JACK: Meatballs (79).

BOCHNER, HART: Breaking Away (79), Terror Train (80).

BOEN, EARL: The Main Event (79).

BOLGER, RAY: Just You And Me, Kid (79), The Runner Stumbles (79).

BOLOGNA, JOSEPH: Made for Each Other (71), Cops and Robbers (73), Mixed Company (74), The Big Bus (76), Chapter Two (79).

BOND, RALEIGH: The Onion Field (79).

BONERZ, PETER: Serial (80).

BONO, SONNY: Escape To Athena (79).

BOONE, RICHARD: Winter Kills (79).

BORGNINE, ERNEST: The Adventurers (70), The Black Hole (79), The Double Mcguffin (79), When Time Ran Out (80).

BOSTWICK, BARRY: Movie Movie Baxter's Beauties (78), Movie Movie Dynamite Hands (78).

BOTTOMS, JOHN: The Long Riders (80).

BOTTOMS, JOSEPH: The Black Hole (79), Cloud Dancer (80).

BOTTOMS, SAM: Apocalypse Now (79), Bronco Billy (80).

BOTTOMS, TIMOTHY: Johnny Got His Gun (71), The Last Picture Show (71), Love, Pain and the Whole Damn Thing (72), The Paper Chase (73), The Crazy World of Julius Vrooder (74), The White Dawn (74), Operation Daybreak (75), A Small Town in Texas (76), Rollercoaster (77), Hurricane (79).

BOVASSO, JULIE: Willie & Phil (80).

BOVENS, PHYLLIS: Coal Miner's Daughter (80).

BOWEN, ROGER: The Main Event (79), Foxes (80).

BOWER, ANTOINETTE: Prom Night (80).

BOYAR, SULLY: Oliver's Story (78), Night Of The Juggler (80).

BOYLE, PETER: Joe (70), T.R. Baskin (71), Dime Box (72), Slither (72), Steelyard Blues (72), The Candidate (72), Kid Blue (73), The Friends of Eddie Coyle (73), Crazy Joe (74), Young Frankenstein (74), Swashbuckler (76), Taxi Driver (76), F.I.S.T. (78), Beyond The Poseidon Adventure (79), Brinks (79), Hardcore (79), In God We Trust (80), Where The Buffalo Roam (80).

BRADFORD, RICHARD: More American Graffiti (79).

BRAND, NEVILLE: The Ninth Configuration (80), Without Warning (80).

BRANDO, JOCELYN: Movie Movie Baxter's Beauties (78), Why Would I Lie? (80).

BRANDO, MARLON: The Chase (65), A Countess from Hong Kong (67), Reflections in a Golden Eye (67), Burn! (68), Candy (68), The Night of the Following Day (68), The Night Comers (71), Last Tango in Paris (72), The Godfather (72), The Missouri Breaks (76), Superman (78), Apocalypse Now (79), The Formula (80).

BRANDON, MICHAEL: Promises In The Dark (79), A Change of Seasons (80).

BRAVERMAN, BART: Alligator (80).

BRAY, JIM: Roller Boogie (79).

BRENNAN, EILEEN: The Last Picture Show (71), Scarecrow (73), The Sting (73), Daisy Miller (74), At Long Last Love (75), Hustle (75), Murder by Death (76), FM (78), The Cheap Detective (78), Private Benjamin (80).

BRENNAN, TOM: Willie & Phil (80).

BRESSLAW, BERNARD: Hawk the Slayer (80).

BRIDGES, BEAU: The Incident (67), For Love of Ivy (68), Gaily, Gaily (69), Adam's Woman (70), The Landlord (70), The Christian Licorice Store (71), Child's Play (72), Hammersmith Is Out (72), Lovin' Molly (73), The Other Side of the Mountain (75), Dragonfly (76), Swashbuckler (76), Two-Minute Warning (76), Greased Lightning (77), Norma Rae (79), The Runner Stumbles (79), Honky Tonk Freeway (80).

BRIDGES, JEFF: Halls of Anger (68), The Last Picture Show (71), Bad Company (72), Fat City (72), Lolly Madonna XXX (73), The Iceman Cometh (73), The Last American Hero (73), Rancho De Luxe (74), Thunderbolt and Lightfoot (74), Hearts of the West (75), King Kong (76), Stay Hungry (76), Somebody Killed Her Husband (78), The American Success Company (79), Tilt (79), Winter Kills (79), Heaven's Gate (80).

BRIDGES, LLOYD: Airplane (80).

BRIGHT, RICHARD: On The Yard (79).

BRODERICK, JAMES: The Group (66), Alice's Restaurant (69), The

Taking of Pelham 1-2-3 (74), Dog Day Afternoon (75).

BROLIN, JAMES: Skyjacked (72), Westworld (73), Gable and Lombard (76), The Car (77), Capricorn One (78), The Amityville Horror (79), Night Of The Juggler (80).

BRON, ELEANOR: The Secret Policeman's Ball (79).

BRONSON, CHARLES: The Magnificent Seven (60), The Dirty Dozen (67), Guns for San Sebastian (68), Villa Rides (68), Once Upon a Time in the West (69), Rider in the Rain (69), Twinky (69), You Can't Win Them All (70), Chato's Land (71), Cold Sweat (71), The Family (71), The Mechanic (72), The Valachi Papers (72), St. Ives (73), The Stone Killer (73), Wild Horses (73), Death Wish (74), Mr. Majestyk (74), Breakheart Pass (75), Breakout (75), Hard Times (75), From Noon to Three (76), Telefon (77), Borderline (80).

BROOK, CLAUDIO: The Bees (78).

BROOK, FAITH: ffolkes (80), The Sea Wolves (80).

BROOKE, PAUL: Agatha (79).

BROOKS, ALBERT: Taxi Driver (76), Real Life (79).

BROOKS, ALBERTA: Private Benjamin (80).

BROOKS, FOSTER: The Villain (79).

BROOKS, JOSEPH: If Ever I See You Again (78).

BROOKS, MEL: The Twelve Chairs (70), Blazing Saddles (74), Silent Movie (76), The Muppet Movie (79).

BROOKS, PATTI: The Fifth Floor (80).

BROPHY, KEVIN: The Long Riders (80).

BROWN, BLAIR: Altered States (80), One Trick Pony (80).

BROWN, DARREN: Clarence And Angel (80).

BROWN, GEORGE STANFORD: Stir Crazy (80).

BROWN, JAMES: The Blues Brothers (80).

BROWN, JIM: Rio Conchos (64), The Dirty Dozen (67), Dark of the Sun (68), Ice Station Zebra (68), Riot (68), The Split (68), 100 Rifles (69), The Grasshopper (69), Tick, Tick, Tick... (69), Kenner (71), Black Gun (72), Slaughter (72), I Escaped from Devil's Island (73), Slaughter's Big Rip-Off (73), The Slams (74), Three the Hard Way (74), Take a Hard Ride (75), Fingers (78).

BROWN, WENDELL: Up The Academy (80).

BROWNE, LESLIE: Nijinsky (80).

BROWNE, ROSCOE LEE: Topaz (69), The Liberation of L.B. Jones (70), Cisco Pike (71), The Cowboys (72), Superfly Two (73), The World's Greatest Athlete (73), Uptown Saturday Night (74), Logan's Run (76), Twilight's Last Gleaming (77), Nothing Personal (80).

BRYNNER, YUL: The Magnificent Seven (60), Invitation to a Gunfighter (64), The Poppy Is Also a Flower (68), Villa Rides (68), The Madwoman of Chaillot (69), Romance of a Horse Thief (71), The Light at the End of the World (71), Fuzz (72), Westworld (73), The Serpent (74), The Ultimate Warrior (74), Futureworld (76).

George Burns, Lee Strasberg, Art Carney.

BUCHHOLZ, HORST: Avalanche Express (79).

BUJOLD, GENEVIEVE: Isabel (67), King of Hearts (67), Act of the Heart (70), Anne of the Thousand Days (70), The Trojan Women (71), Earthquake (74), Alex and the Gypsy (76), Obsession (76), Swashbuckler (76), Coma (78), Murder By Decree (79), Final Assignment (80).

BUONO, VICTOR: The Man With Bogart's Face (80).

BURKE, MILDRED: Below The Belt (80).

BURNETT, CAROL: Pete 'n Tillie (72), The Front Page (74), A Wedding (78), Health (80).

BURNS, GEORGE: The Sunshine Boys (75), Oh, God! (77), Sergeant Pepper's Lonely Hearts Club Band (78), Going In Style (79), Just You And Me, Kid (79), Two of a Kind (79), Oh, God! Book II (80).

BURNS, STEPHAN W.: Herbie Goes Bananas (80).

BURR, RAYMOND: Out Of The Blue (80).

BURSTYN, ELLEN: Goodbye Charlie (64), For Those Who Think Young (65), Pit Stop (69), Tropic of Cancer (69), Alex in Wonderland (70), The Last Picture Show (71), The King of Marvin Gardens (72), The Exorcist (73), Alice Doesn't Live Here Anymore (74), Harry and Tonto (74), Providence (77), A Dream of Passion (78), Same Time Next Year (78), Resurrection (80).

BURTON, LEVAR: The Hunter (80).

BURTON, RICHARD: Who's Afraid of Virginia Woolf (66), Candy (68), Staircase (69), Where Eagles Dare (69), Anne of the Thousand Days

(70), Bluebeard (72), Hammersmith Is Out (72), The Assassination of Trotsky (72), The Klansman (74), Equus (77), Exorcist II-The Heretic (77), Breakthrough (79), Circle Of Two (80).

BURTON, TONY: Rocky II (79), The Shining (80).

BUSEY, GARY: A Star is Born (76), The Gumball Rally (76), Big Wednesday (78), Straight Time (78), The Buddy Holly Story (78), Carny (80), Foolin' Around (80).

BUSH, BILLY GREEN: Tom Horn (80).

BUTTONS, RED: Movie Movie Baxter's Beauties (78), Movie Movie Dynamite Hands (78), When Time Ran Out (80).

BUZBY, ZANE: Americathon (79).

BUZZI, RUTH: Skatetown Usa (79), The Villain (79).

BYRNE, ANNE: Manhattan (79), Why Would I Lie? (80).

CAAN, JAMES: Lady in a Cage (64), El Dorado (67), Countdown (68), Journey to Shilo (68), Submarine XI (68), Man Without Mercy (69), The Rain People (69), Rabbit Run (70), Brian's Song (71), T.R. Baskin (71), Slither (72), The Godfather (72), Cinderella Liberty (74), Freebie and The Bean (74), Funny Lady (75), Rollerball (75), The Gambler (75), The Killer Elite (75), Harry and Walter Go to New York (76), A Bridge Too Far (77), Another Chance (78), Another Man (78), Comes a Horseman (78), Chapter Two (79), Hide In Plain Sight (80).

CAESAR, SID: It's a Mad, Mad, Mad, Mad World (63), A Guide For The Married Man (67), The Busy Body (67), Ten From Your Show of Shows (74), Airport 75 (75), Silent Movie (76), The Cheap Detective (78), The Fiendish Plot Of Dr. Fu Manchu (80).

CAINE, MICHAEL: The Ipcress File (65), Alfie (66), Hurry Sundown (67), Too Late the Hero (69), Zee and Co. (71), Pulp (72), Sleuth (72), The Black Windmill (74), Peeper (75), The Man Who Would Be King (75), The Romantic Englishwoman (75), The Wilby Conspiracy (75), Harry and Walter Go to New York (76), A Bridge Too Far (77), The Eagle Has Landed (77), California Suite (78), Silver Bears (78), The Swarm (78), Ashanti (79), Beyond The Poseidon Adventure (79), Dressed To Kill (80), The Island (80).

CALHOUN, RORY: The Main Event (79), Motel Hell (80).

CALI, JOSEPH: The Competition (80).

CALLAN, K.: The Onion Field (79).

CALLOWAY, CAB: The Blues Brothers (80).

CALVIN, JOHN: Foolin' Around (80).

CAMBRIDGE, GODFREY: The President's Analyst (67), Bye Bye Braverman (68), The Biggest Bundle of Them All (68), Watermelon Man (69), Cotton Comes to Harlem (70), Come Back Charleston Blue (72), The Biscuit Eater (72).

CAMERON, KIMBERLY: H.O.T.S. (79).

CAMP, COLLEEN: Cloud Dancer (80).

CAMPANELLA, JOSEPH: The St. Valentine's Day Massacre (67), Ben (72), Meteor (79), Hangar 18 (80).

CANDY, JOHN: The Blues Brothers (80).

CANNON, DYAN: Bob & Carol & Ted & Alice (69), Doctors' Wives (70), Such Good Friends (71), The Anderson Tapes (71), The Love Machine (71), Shamus (72), The Last of Sheila (73), Heaven Can Wait (78), Coast To Coast (80), Honeysuckle Rose (80).

CANNON, J. D.: Raise The Titanic (80).

CARA, IRENE: Fame (80).

CARDOVA, MARK: Clarence And Angel (80).

CAREY, HARRY, Jr.: The Long Riders (80).

CAREY, RON: Fatso (80).

CARIDI, CARMINE: The In-Laws (79).

CARLIN, LYNN: Faces (68), Tick, Tick, Tick... (69), Taking Off (71), Wild Rovers (71), French Postcards (79), Battle Beyond The Stars (80).

CARLSON, KAREN: The Octagon (80).

CARMEN, JULIE: Gloria (80).

CARMICHAEL, IAN: The Lady Vanishes (79).

CARNEY, ART: Harry and Tonto (74), W.W. And the Dixie Dancekings (75), Won Ton Ton, the Dog Who Saved Hollywood (76), The Late Show (77), House Calls (78), Movie Movie Baxter's Beauties (78), Movie Movie Dynamite Hands (78), Going In Style (79), Sunburn (79), Defiance (80), Roadie (80), Steel (80).

CARON, LESLIE: The L-Shaped Room (62), Head of the Family (68), Madron (69), Chandler (72), QB VII (74), Goldengirl (79).

CARRADINE, DAVID: The Violent Ones (67), The Good Guys and the Bad Guys (69), Young Billy Young (69), The McMasters (70), Macho Callahan (71), Boxcar Bertha (72), Mean Streets (73), You And Me (73), Death Race 2000 (75), Bound for Glory (76), Cannonball (76), Thunder and Lightning (76), Circle Of Iron (79), Cloud Dancer (80), The Long Riders (80).

CARRADINE, JOHN: Shock Waves (75), The Bees (78), The Boogey Man (80).

CARRADINE, KEITH: A Gunfight (70), McCabe and Mrs. Miller (71), Emperor of the North Pole (73), Hex (73), Thieves Like Us (74), Nashville (75), Welcome to L.A. (77), Pretty Baby (78), An Almost Perfect Affair (79), Old Boyfriends (79), The Long Riders (80).

CARRADINE, ROBERT: The Cowboys (72), Mean Streets (73), Joyride (77), Orca (77), Coming Home (78), The Pom Pom Girls (78), The Big Red One (80), The Long Riders (80).

CARRERA, BARBARA: When Time Ran Out (80).

CARROLL, DIAHANN: Porgy and Bess (59), Paris Blues (61), Hurry Sundown (67), The Split (68), Claudine (74).

CARSON, JOHN DAVID: The Fifth Floor (80).

CARTER, JACK: Alligator (80).

CARTER, T.K.: Seems Like Old Times (80).

CARTWRIGHT, ANGELA: Beyond The Poseidon Adventure (79).

CARTWRIGHT, VERONICA: Invasion Of The Bodysnatchers (78), Alien (79).

CASADOS, ELOY PHIL: Walk Proud (79).

CASEY, BERNIE: Boxcar Bertha (72), Hit Man (72), Brothers (77).

CASEY, SUE: The Main Event (79).

CASH, ROSALIND: Klute (71), The Omega Man (71), Hickey and Boggs (72), Melinda (72), The New Centurions (72), Amazing Grace (74), Uptown Saturday Night (74), Hit the Open Man (75).

CASSAVETES, JOHN: Taxi (53), The Night Holds Terror (55), Crime in the Streets (56), A Man is Ten Feet Tall (57), Affair in Havana (57), Edge of the City (57), Saddle the Wind (58), Virgin Island (58), The Webster Boy (62), The Killers (64), The Devil's Angles (67), The Dirty Dozen (67), Bandits in Rome (68), Machine Gun McCain (68), Rosemary's Baby (68), If It's Tuesday This Must Be Belgium (69), Husbands (70), Minnie and Moskowitz (71), Capone (75), Mikey and Nicky (76), Two-Minute Warning (76), Opening Night (77), Brass Target (78), The Fury (78).

CASSEL, SEYMOUR: Faces (68), Minnie and Moskowitz (71), The Killing of a Chinese Bookie (76), California Dreaming (78), Convoy (78), Sunburn (79), The Mountain Men (80).

CASTELLANO, RICHARD: Night Of The Juggler (80).

CASTLE, JOHN: Eagle's Wing (79).

CATTRALL, KIM: Tribute (80).

CAVANAUGH, MICHAEL: Any Which Way You Can (80).

CAVETT, DICK: Health (80).

CAZALE, JOHN: The Godfather (72), The Conversation (74), The Godfather, Part II (74), Dog Day Afternoon (75), The Deerhunter (78).

CERVANTES, GARY: Walk Proud (79).

CHAMBERLAIN, RICHARD: Joy In The Morning (65), Petulia (68), The Madwoman of Chaillot (69), Julius Caesar (70), The Music Lovers (70), Lady Caroline Lamb (72), The Three Musketeers (73), The Four Musketeers (74), The Towering Inferno (74), The Slipper and the Rose (76), The Swarm (78).

CHAN, JACKIE: The Big Brawl (80).

CHANNING, STOCKARD: The Fortune (75), The Big Bus (76), Sweet Revenge (77), Grease (78), The Cheap Detective (78), The Fish That Saved Pittsburgh (79).

CHAPIN, MILES: French Postcards (79).

CHAPLIN, GERALDINE: Doctor Zhivago (65), The Hawaiians (70), Zero Population Growth (71), Innocent Bystanders (72), The Three Musketeers (73), The Four Musketeers (74), Nashville (75), Buffalo

Bill and the Indians (76), A Wedding (78), Remember My Name (78), The Mirror Crack'd (80).

CHAPMAN, GRAHAM: Life Of Brian (79).

CHARLES, RAY: The Blues Brothers (80).

CHARLESON, RAY: Hawk the Slayer (80).

CHARO: The Concorde-Airport '79 (79).

CHASE, CHEVY: Foul Play (78), Oh Heavenly Dog (80), Seems Like Old Times (80).

CHASE, CHRIS: All That Jazz (79).

CHESHIRE, ELIZABETH: Melvin and Howard (80).

CHIANESE, DOMINIC: ...And Justice For All (79), On The Yard (79).

CHILDRESS, ALVIN: The Main Event (79).

CHILES, LOIS: The Way We Were (73), The Great Gatsby (74), Coma (78), Death on the Nile (78), Moonraker (79).

CHONG, THOMAS: Up In Smoke (78), Cheech And Chong's Next Movie (80).

CHRISTIAN, ROBERT: ...And Justice For All (79).

CHRISTIE, JULIE: Doctor Zhivago (65), Petulia (68), In Search of Gregory (69), McCabe and Mrs. Miller (71), The Go-Between (71), Don't Look Now (73), Nashville (75), Shampoo (75), Demon Seed (77), Heaven Can Wait (78).

CHRISTOPHER, DENNIS: Breaking Away (79), The Last Word (79), Fade to Black (80).

CIOFFI, CHARLES: Klute (71), Shaft (71), The Don is Dead (73), The Thief Who Came to Dinner (73), Crazy Joe (74), The Next Man (76), The Other Side of Midnight (77), Time After Time (79).

CLAPP, GORDON: Return Of The Secaucus Seven (80).

CLARK, CANDY: American Graffiti (73), The Man Who Fell to Earth (76), Citizen's Band (Handle With Care) (77), The Big Sleep (78), More American Graffiti (79).

CLARK, MATT: Brubaker (80).

CLARK, SUSAN: Banning (67), Coogan's Bluff (68), Madigan (68), Skullduggery (69), Tell Them Willie Boy Is Here (69), The Forbin Project (69), Valdez is Coming (70), The Skin Game (71), Showdown (72), The Midnight Man (74), Airport 75 (75), The Apple Dumpling Gang (75), Murder By Decree (79), Promises In The Dark (79), The North Avenue Irregulars (79), Double Negative (80).

CLARKE, ROBIN: Sunburn (79), The Prize Fighter (79), The Formula (80).

CLAYBURGH, JILL: Portnoy's Complaint (72), The Thief Who Came to Dinner (73), The Terminal Man (74), Hustling (75), Gable and Lombard (76), Semi-Tough (77), The Silver Streak (77), An Unmarried Woman (78), Luna (79), Starting Over (79), It's My Turn (80).

Jill Clayburgh, Burt Reynolds.   Anne Ditchburn, Paul Sorvino.

CLEESE, JOHN: Life Of Brian (79), The Secret Policeman's Ball (79).

CLENNON, DAVID: Billy In The Lowlands (79).

CLINGER, DEBRA: Midnight Madness (80).

CLYDE, JEREMY: ffolkes (80).

COBURN, JAMES: The Magnificent Seven (60), Charade (63), The Great Escape (63), The Americanization of Emily (64), Our Man Flint (66), In Like Flint (67), The President's Analyst (67), Dead Heat on a Merry-Go-Round (68), Duffy (68), Hard Contract (68), Blood Kin (69), A Fistful of Dynamite (71), The Honkers (71), The Carey Treatment (72), Harry in Your Pocket (73), Pat Garrett and Billy The Kid (73), The Last of Sheila (73), Bite the Bullet (75), Hard Times (75), Midway (76), Sky Riders (76), The Last Hard Men (76), Cross of Iron (77), Firepower (79), Goldengirl (79), The Muppet Movie (79), Loving Couples (80), The Baltimore Bullet (80).

COCO, JAMES: Tell Me That You Love Me, Junie Moon (69), A New Leaf (71), Such Good Friends (71), Man of La Mancha (72), The Wild Party (74), Murder by Death (76), The Cheap Detective (78), Scavenger Hunt (79), Wholly Moses! (80).

COE, DAVID ALLEN: Lady Grey (80).

COE, GEORGE: French Postcards (79), Kramer vs Kramer (79), First Deadly Sin (80).

COFFIELD, PETER: Times Square (80).

COLEMAN, DABNEY: How To Beat The High Cost of Living (80), Melvin and Howard (80), Nine To Five (80), Nothing Personal (80).

COLICOS, JOHN: Phobia (80), The Changeling (80).

COLLINS, GARY: Hangar 18 (80).

COLLINS, JOAN: Sunburn (79).

COLLINS, PATRICIA: Circle Of Two (80).

COLLINS, STEPHEN: Star Trek (79), The Promise (79), Loving Couples (80).

COLOSANTO, NICHOLAS: Raging Bull (80).

CONGREGATION, MIKE CURB: The Magic Of Lassie (78).

CONNERY, SEAN: Dr. No (62), From Russia with Love (63), Goldfinger (64), Marnie (64), The Hill (65), Thunderball (65), A Fine Madness (66), You Only Live Twice (67), The Molly Maguires (68), Diamonds Are Forever (71), The Anderson Tapes (71), The Offence (72), Zardoz (73), Murder on the Orient Express (74), Ransom (74), The Man Who Would Be King (75), The Wind and the Lion (75), Robin and Marian (76), The Next Man (76), A Bridge Too Far (77), Meteor (78), Cuba (79), The Great Train Robbery (79).

CONNORS, MIKE: Avalanche Express (79).

CONREID, HANS: Oh, God! Book II (80).

CONSIDINE, JOHN: Buffalo Bill and the Indians (76), Welcome to L.A. (77), A Wedding (78), When Time Ran Out (80).

CONVY, BERT: Hero At Large (80).

CONWAY, KEVIN: F.I.S.T. (78), Brinks (79).

CONWAY, TIM: The Prize Fighter (79), The Private Eyes (80).

COOK, ELISHA, Jr.: The Maltese Falcon (40), The Big Sleep (46), The Killing (56), Welcome to Hard Times (67), The Great Bank Robbery (69), The Great Northfield Minnesota Raid (71), St. Ives (73), The Emperor of the North Pole (73), The Outfit (73), The Black Bird (75), The Champ (79), Carny (80).

COOK, PETER: The Secret Policeman's Ball (79).

COOPER, JACKIE: Superman (78), Superman II (80).

COOPER, JEFF: Circle Of Iron (79).

COPPERFIELD, DAVID: Terror Train (80).

CORBIN, BARRY: Any Which Way You Can (80).

COREY, JEFF: Butch And Sundance (79), Battle Beyond The Stars (80).

CORLEY, PAT: The Onion Field (79).

CORT, BUD: The Traveling Executioner (69), Brewster McCloud (70), Gas-s-s (70), MASH (70), The Strawberry Statement (70), Harold and Maude (71), Hitler's Son (78), Die Laughing (80).

CORTESA, VALENTINA: When Time Ran Out (80).

CORTESE, JOSEPH: Windows (80).

COSBY, BILL: Hickey and Boggs (72), Uptown Saturday Night (74), Let's Do It Again (75), Mother, Jugs and Speed (76), California Suite (78).

COSTANZO, ROBERT: Fatso (80).

COSTELLO, MARICLARE: Ordinary People (80).

COSTER, NICHOLAS: Stir Crazy (80), Why Would I Lie? (80).

COTTEN, JOSEPH: Guyana: Cult Of The Damned (80), Heaven's Gate (80), The Hearse (80).

COULOURIS, GEORGE: It's Not The Size That Counts (79).

COUSINEAU, MAGGIE: Return Of The Secaucus Seven (80).

COX, RICHARD: Cruising (80).

COX, RONNY: The Onion Field (79).

COX, RUTH: Swap Meet (79).

CRANDALL, BRAD: In Search Of Historic Jesus (80).

CRAWFORD, BRODERICK: There Goes the Bride (80).

CRITTENDEN, DIANNE: Sunday Lovers (80).

CROSBY, HARRY: Friday the 13th (80).

CROTHERS, SCATMAN: Hello Dolly! (69), The Great White Hope (70), Lady Sings The Blues (72), The King Of Marvin Gardens (72), One Flew Over The Cuckoo's Nest (75), The Fortune (75), The Shootist (76), Silver Streak (77), Scavenger Hunt (79), Bronco Billy (80), The Shining (80).

CROUSE, LINDSAY: All the President's Men (76), Between the Lines (77), Slapshot (77).

CULP, ROBERT: Sunday in New York (64), Bob & Carol & Ted & Alice (69), Hannie Caulder (71), Hickey and Boggs (72), The Castaway Cowboy (74), Breaking Point (76), Sky Riders (76), The Great Scout & Cathouse Thursday (76), Goldengirl (79).

CUMBUKA, HESHIMU: Sunnyside (79).

CUMBUKA, JITU: Walk Proud (79).

CUMMINGS, QUINN: The Goodbye Girl (78).

CUNNINGHAM, JOHN: Lost And Found (79).

CURRERI, LEE: Fame (80).

CURRIE, SANDEE: Terror Train (80).

CURRY, TIM: Times Square (80).

CURTIN, JANE: Mr. Mike's Mondo Video (79), How To Beat The High Cost of Living (80).

CURTIN, VALERIE: Why Would I Lie? (80).

CURTIS, JAMIE LEE: Prom Night (80), Terror Train (80), The Fog (80).

CURTIS, TONY: Little Miss Marker (80), The Mirror Crack'd (80).

CUSHING, PETER: Shock Waves (75).

D'ANGELO, BEVERLY: Every Which Way But Loose (78), Hair (79), Coal Miner's Daughter (80).

D'ARBANVILLE, PATTI: L'Amour, La Maison, La Saignee, Rancho Deluxe, The Crazy American Girl (75), The Main Event (79), Time After Time (79), Hog Wild (80), The Fifth Floor (80).

DALLESANDRO, JOE: Heat (72), Warhol's Dracula (74).

DALTON, TIMOTHY: Agatha (79), Flash Gordon (80).

DALTREY, ROGER: The Legacy (79).

DAMON, CATHRYN: How To Beat The High Cost of Living (80).

DANA, BILL: The Nude Bomb (80).

DANE, LAWRENCE: Running (79), Nothing Personal (80).

DANIELS, ANTHONY: The Empire Strikes Back (80).

DANIELS, WILLIAM: The Graduate (67), Two for the Road (67), Marlowe (69), 1776 (72), The Parallax View (74), Sunburn (79),

Blue Lagoon (80).

DANNER, BLYTHE: To Kill a Clown (71), 1776 (72), Lovin' Molly (73), Hearts of the West (75), Futureworld (76), The Great Santini (80).

DANNING, SYBIL: Battle Beyond The Stars (80).

DANSLER, ANITA: Hero At Large (80).

DANSON, TED: The Onion Field (79).

DARBY, KIM: A Time for Living (69), Generation (69), Norwood (69), True Grit (69), The Strawberry Statement (70), The Grissom Gang (71), The One and Only (77).

DARDEN, SEVERN: Wanda Nevada (79), In God We Trust (80), Why Would I Lie? (80).

DARLING, JOAN: Sunnyside (79).

DARROW, HENRY: Walk Proud (79).

DAVENPORT, MARY: Home Movies (79).

DAVID, CLIFFORD: Resurrection (80).

DAVIDSON, JOHN: The Concorde-Airport '79 (79).

DAVIES, BRIAN: American Gigolo (80).

DAVIS, BETTE: The Watcher In The Woods (80).

DAVIS, BRAD: A Small Circle Of Friends (80).

DAVIS, JIM: The Day Time Ended (80).

DAVIS, MAC: North Dallas Forty (79), Cheaper to Keep Her (80).

DAVIS, OSSIE: The Hill (65), The Scalp Hunters (68), Sam Whiskey (69), Slaves (69), Malcolm X (72), Let's Do It Again (75), Hot Stuff (79).

DAVIS, STEVE: Battle Beyond The Stars (80).

DAVISON, BRUCE: Last Summer (69), The Strawberry Statement (70), The Jerusalem File (71), Willard (71), Ulzana's Raid (72), Mame (74), Mother, Jugs and Speed (76), Short Eyes (77), Brass Target (78).

DE BELL, KRISTINE: Meatballs (79), The Main Event (79).

DE CARLO, YVONNE: Guyana: Cult Of The Damned (80), Silent Scream (80), The Man With Bogart's Face (80).

DE HETRE, KATHERINE: Joni (80).

De JEUDE, ERLAND Van LIDTH: The Wanderers (79), Stir Crazy (80).

DE LA PAZ, DANNY: Boulevard Nights (79), Cuba (79).

DE LUISE, DOM: Hot Stuff (79), The Muppet Movie (79), Fatso (80), Smokey And The Bandit II (80), The Last Married Couple In America (80), Wholly Moses! (80).

DE NIRO, ROBERT: A Wedding Party (69), Bloody Mama (70), Hi, Mom! (70), The Gang That Couldn't Shoot Straight (71), Bang the Drum Slowly (73), Mean Streets (73), The Godfather, Part II (74), Taxi Driver (76), The Last Tycoon (76), 1900 (77), New York, New York (77), The Deerhunter (78), Raging Bull (80).

DEACON, BRIAN: Jesus (79).

DEAN, LAURA: Fame (80).

Goldie Hawn.

Amy Irving.

DEBELL, KRISTINE: The Big Brawl (80).

DEE, RUBY: A Raisin in the Sun (61), The Balcony (62), Buck and The Preacher (71), Black Girl (72).

DEEZEN, EDDIE: 1941 (79), Midnight Madness (80).

DELAPENA, GEORGE: Nijinsky (80).

DELON, ALAIN: The Concorde-Airport'79 (79).

DEMUNN, JEFFREY: Resurrection (80).

DENAVA, AL: The Main Event (79).

DENNEHY, BRIAN: 10 (79), Butch And Sundance (79), Little Miss Marker (80).

DENNIS, SANDY: Splendor in the Grass (61), Up the Down Staircase (67), Sweet November (68), The Fox (68), A Touch of Love (69), That Cold Day in the Park (69), The Out of Towners (70), Million Dollar Duck (71), The Only Way Out Is Dead (72), Nasty Habits (77).

DENOS, JOHN: Wanda Nevada (79).

DENSMORE, GENE: Gal Young Un (79).

DEREK, BO: 10 (79), A Change of Seasons (80).

DERN, BRUCE: Castle Keep (68), Will Penny (68), Number One (69), They Shoot Horses, Don't They? (69), Bloody Mama (70), Drive, He Said (70), The Incredible Two-Headed Transplant (70), Silent Running (71), The Cowboys (72), The King of Marvin Gardens (72), The Laughing Policeman (73), The Great Gatsby (74), Posse (75), Smile (75), Black Sunday (77), Coming Home (78), The Driver (78), Middle Age Crazy (80), Tattoo (81).

DESALVO, ANNE: Stardust Memories (80).

DEVANE, WILLIAM: Family Plot (76), Rolling Thunder (77), The Bad

News Bears in Breaking Training (77), Yanks (79), Honky Tonk Freeway (80).

DEWHURST, COLLEEN: The Cowboys (72), Annie Hall (77), Ice Castles (78), When A Stranger Calls (79), Final Assignment (80), Tribute (80).

DI CICCO, BOBBY: 1941 (79), The Big Red One (80).

DICKINSON, ANGIE: The Chase (65), Cast a Giant Shadow (66), Point Blank (68), Sam Whiskey (69), Young Billy Young (69), Pretty Maids All in a Row (71), Big Bad Mama (74), Dressed To Kill (80).

DILLMAN, BRADFORD: Piranha (78), Guyana: Cult Of The Damned (80).

DILLON, MATT: Over The Edge (79), Little Darlings (80), My Bodyguard (80).

DILLON, MELINDA: Bound for Glory (76), Close Encounters of the Third Kind (77), Slapshot (77), F.I.S.T. (78).

DISHY, BOB: First Family (80), The Last Married Couple In America (80).

DITCHBURN, ANNE: Slow Dancing In The Big City (78).

DIXON, MACINTYRE: Popeye (80).

DJOLA, BADJA MEDU: The Main Event (79).

DOOHAN, JAMES: Star Trek (79).

DOOLEY, PAUL: A Wedding (78), A Perfect Couple (79), A Romance (79), Breaking Away (79), Rich Kids (79), Health (80), Popeye (80).

DOQUI, ROBERT: Nashville (75), Buffalo Bill and the Indians (76).

DORN, DOLORES: Tell Me a Riddle (80).

DOUGLAS, GORDON: Chuka (67), In Like Flint (67), Tony Rome (67), Lady in Cement (68), The Detective (68), Skullduggery (69).

DOUGLAS, JAMES: The Changeling (80).

DOUGLAS, KIRK: A Lovely Way to Die (68), The Brotherhood (68), A Gunfight (70), There Was a Crooked Man (70), Catch Me a Spy (71), The Light at the End of the World (71), Scalawag (73), Once is Not Enough (75), Posse (75), The Fury (78), Home Movies (79), The Helper (79), The Villain (79), Saturn 3 (80), The Final Countdown (80).

DOUGLAS, MELVYN: I Never Sang for My Father (69), One Is a Lonely Number (72), The Candidate (72), Twilight's Last Gleaming (77), Being There (79), The Seduction Of Joe Tynan (79), Tell Me a Riddle (80), The Changeling (80).

DOUGLAS, MICHAEL: Hail Hero (70), Summertree (71), Napoleon and Samantha (72), One Is a Lonely Number (72), Coma (78), The China Syndrome (79), Running (79), It's My Turn (80).

DOUGLAS, SARAH: Superman (78), Superman II (80).

DOUGLASS, ROBYN: Breaking Away (79).

DOURIF, BRAD: Wise Blood (79), Heaven's Gate (80).

DOWN, LESLEY-ANNE: The Pink Panther Strikes Again, A Little Night
Music (77), The Betsy (77), Hanover Street (79), The Great Train
Robbery (79), Rough Cut (80).

DRESCHER, FRAN: The Hollywood Knights (80).

DREYFUSS, RICHARD: Hello Down There (68), The Young Runaways
(69), American Graffiti (73), Dillinger (73), The Apprenticeship of
Duddy Kravitz (74), Jaws (75), Inserts (76), Close Encounters of the
Third Kind (77), The Big Fix (78), The Goodbye Girl (78), The
Competition (80).

DRURY, PATRICK: The Awakening (80).

DU BOIS, MARTA: Boulevard Nights (79).

DUFF, HOWARD: The Late Show (77), A Wedding (78), Kramer vs.
Kramer (79), Double Negative (80), Oh, God! Book II (80).

DUKE, BILL: American Gigolo (80).

DUKES, DAVID: A Little Romance (79), First Deadly Sin (80).

DULLEA, KEIR: David and Lisa (62), Bunny Lake Is Missing (65),
Madame X (66), 2001: A Space Odyssey (68), The Fox (68), De Sade
(69), Pope Joan (72), Paperback Hero (73), The Last of The Big
Guns (73), Paul and Michelle (74), Black Christmas (75).

DUNAWAY, FAYE: Bonnie and Clyde (67), Hurry Sundown (67), The
Happening (67), The Thomas Crown Affair (68), A Place for Lovers
(69), The Arrangement (69), The Extraordinary Seaman (69), Little
Big Man (70), Puzzle of a Downfall Child (70), Doc (71), The
Deadly Trap (71), Oklahoma Crude (73), The Three Musketeers
(73), Chinatown (74), The Four Musketeers (74), The Towering
Inferno (74), Three Days of the Condor (75), Network (76), Voyage
of the Damned (76), Eyes of Laura Mars (78), The Champ (79), First
Deadly Sin (80).

DUNCAN, ANDREW: A Little Romance (79), Used Cars (80).

DUNCAN, SANDY: Million Dollar Duck (71), Star Spangled Girl (71).

DUNNE, GRIFFIN: Head Over Heels (79).

DUNNE, MURPHY: The Blues Brothers (80).

DURNING, CHARLES: The Sting (73), The Front Page (74), Breakheart
Pass (75), Dog Day Afternoon (75), The Hindenburg (75), An Enemy
of the People (76), Harry and Walter Go to New York (76),
Twilight's Last Gleaming (76), F.I.S.T. (78), The Fury (78), The
Greek Tycoon (78), North Dallas Forty (79), Starting Over (79), The
Muppet Movie (79), Tilt (79), When A Stranger Calls (79), Die
Laughing (80), The Final Countdown (80).

DUSENBERRY, ANNE: Heart Beat (79).

DUSSAULT, NANCY: The In-Laws (79).

DUVALL, ROBERT: The Chase (65), Bullitt (68), The Countdown (68),
The Rain People (69), True Grit (69), Lawman (70), MASH (70),
The Revolutionary (70), THX 1138 (70), The Great Northfield
Minnesota Raid (71), Joe Kidd (72), The Godfather (72), Lady Ice

(73), The Outfit (73), The Godfather, Part II (74), Breakout (75), The Killer Elite (75), Network (76), The Seven Percent Solution (76), The Betsy (77), The Eagle Has Landed (77), Apocalypse Now (79), The Great Santini (80).

DUVALL, SHELLEY: Brewster McCloud (70), McCabe and Mrs. Miller (71), Thieves Like Us (74), Nashville (75), Buffalo Bill and the Indians (76), Annie Hall (77), Three Women (77), Popeye (80), The Shining (80).

DYSART, RICHARD: An Enemy Of The People (76), Being There (79), Meteor (79), Prophecy (79).

EARECKSON, JONI: Joni (80).

EAST, JEFF: Superman (78).

EASTWOOD, CLINT: Coogan's Bluff (68), Hang 'Em High (68), Paint Your Wagon (69), Two Mules for Sister Sara (69), Where Eagles Dare (69), Kelly's Heroes (70), Dirty Harry (71), Play Misty for Me (71), The Beguiled (71), High Plains Drifter (72), Joe Kidd (72), Magnum Force (73), Thunderbolt and Lightfoot (74), The Eiger Sanction (75), The Enforcer (76), The Outlaw Josey Wales (76), The Gauntlet (77), Every Which Way But Loose (78), Escape From Alcatraz (79), Any Which Way You Can (80), Bronco Billy (80).

EDELMAN, HERBERT: California Suite (78).

EGAN, RICHARD: The Sweet Creek County War (79).

EICHHORN, LISA: Yanks (79), Why Would I Lie? (80).

EIKENBERRY, JILL: Butch And Sundance (79), Hide In Plain Sight (80).

ELAM, JACK: The Villain (79).

ELCAR, DANA: The Nude Bomb (80).

ELIZONDO, HECTOR: Cuba (79), American Gigolo (80).

ELLIOTT, DENHOLM: Cuba (79), It's Not The Size That Counts (79), Bad Timing (80), Sunday Lovers (80).

ELLIOTT, PATRICIA: Natural Enemies (79).

ELLIOTT, SAM: The Legacy (79).

ELPHICK, MICHAEL: The Elephant Man (80).

EMIL, MICHAEL: Sitting Ducks (79).

ENCINIAS, ALLCIA: The Bees (78).

ENGLISH, BRAD: The Onion Field (79).

ERRICKSON, KRISTA: Little Darlings (80).

ERVING, JULIUS: The Fish That Saved Pittsburgh (79).

ERWIN, BILL: Somewhere In Time (80).

EVANS, LINDA: Avalanche Express (79), Tom Horn (80).

FAIRCHILD, MARGARET: Heart Beat (79).

FAITH, ADAM: Foxes (80).

FALK, PETER: Anzio (68), Castle Keep (68), Husbands (70), Machine Gun McCain (70), A Woman Under the Influence (74), Mikey and Nicky (76), Murder by Death (76), The Cheap Detective (78), Brinks (79), The In-Laws (79).

Lauren Hutton, Richard Gere.   John Heard, Mary Beth Hurt.

FARACY, STEPHANIE: Scavenger Hunt (79).

FARALDO, DANIEL: Walk Proud (79).

FARENTINO, JAMES: The Final Countdown (80).

FARGAS, ANTONIO: Carwash (76), Next Stop Greenwich Village (76), Pretty Baby (78).

FARNSWORTH, RICHARD: The Duchess And The Dirtwater Fox (76), Comes A Horseman (78), Resurrection (80), Tom Horn (80).

FARRELL, JUDY: Chapter Two (79).

FARRELL, SHARON: Out Of The Blue (80), The Fifth Floor (80), The Stunt Man (80).

FARROW, MIA: A Dandy in Aspic (67), Rosemary's Baby (68), Secret Ceremony (68), John and Mary (69), See No Evil (71), Follow Me (72), Scoundrel in White (72), The Great Gatsby (74), A Wedding (78), Death on the Nile (78).

FAWCETT, FARRAH: Logan's Run (76), Somebody Killed Her Husband (78), Sunburn (78), Strictly Business (79), The Helper (79), Saturn 3 (80).

FAYE, ALICE: The Magic Of Lassie (78).

FELDMAN, MARTY: Every Home Should Have One (69), Young Frankenstein (74), The Adventure of Sherlock Holmes (75), Silent Movie (76), The Last Remake of Beau Geste (77), High Anxiety (78), In God We Trust (80).

FELDSHUH, TOVAH: Cheaper to Keep Her (80), The Idolmaker (80).

FERGUS, TOM: Over The Edge (79).

FERNANDES, MIGUEL: The Kidnapping Of The President (80).

FERRELL, CONCHATA: Heartland (80).

FERRER, JOSE: Natural Enemies (79), The Big Brawl (80).

FERRER, MEL: The Fifth Floor (80).

FIELD, SALLY: The Way West (67), Stay Hungry (76), Heroes (77), Smokey and the Bandit (77), Hooper (78), The End (78), Beyond The Poseidon Adventure (79), Norma Rae (79), Smokey And The Bandit II (80).

FINLAY, FRANK: Murder By Decree (79).

FINLEY, WILLIAM: Simon (80).

FISHBURNE, LARRY: Apocalypse Now (79), Willie & Phil (80).

FISHER, CARRIE: Shampoo (75), Star Wars (77), Mr. Mike's Mondo Video (79), The Blues Brothers (80), The Empire Strikes Back (80).

FIX, PAUL: Wanda Nevada (79).

FLANDERS, ED: The Ninth Configuration (80).

FLEMING, RHONDA: The Nude Bomb (80).

FLETCHER, LOUISE: Thieves Like Us (74), One Flew Over the Cuckoo's Nest (75), Russian Roulette (75), Exorcist II-The Heretic (77), The Cheap Detective (78), Natural Enemies (79), The Lucky Star (80).

FLEUGEL, DARLANNE: Battle Beyond The Stars (80).

FOLDI, ERZSEBET: All That Jazz (79).

FOLSOM, MEGAN: Heartland (80).

FONDA, HENRY: Madigan (68), Yours, Mine and Ours (68), Once Upon a Time in the West (69), Too Late the Hero (69), The Cheyenne Social Club (70), There Was a Crooked Man (70), Sometimes a Great Notion (71), The Serpent (74), Midway (76), Rollercoaster (77), The Swarm (78), Meteor (79), The Journey of Simon McKeever (79), Wanda Nevada (79).

FONDA, JANE: Cat Ballou (65), The Chase (65), Any Wednesday (66), Barefoot in the Park (67), Hurry Sundown (67), Barbarella (68), They Shoot Horses, Don't They? (69), Klute (71), Steelyard Blues (72), A Doll's House (73), The Blue Bird (76), Fun with Dick and Jane (77), Julia (77), California Suite (78), Comes a Horseman (78), Coming Home (78), The China Syndrome (79), The Electric Horseman (79), The Journey of Simon McKeever (79), Nine To Five (80).

FONDA, PETER: Easy Rider (69), The Hired Hand (71), The Last Movie (71), Two People (73), Dirty Mary, Crazy Larry (74), Open Season (74), Race with the Devil (75), Fighting Mad (76), Futureworld (76), Outlaw Blues (77), Wanda Nevada (79).

FONG, BENSON: Oliver's Story (78).

FORD, GLENN: Superman (78).

FORD, HARRISON: The Conversation (74), Heroes (77), Star Wars (77), Force 10 from Navarone (78), Apocalypse Now (79), Hanover Street (79), The Frisco Kid (79), The Empire Strikes Back (80).

FORREST, FREDERIC: The Conversation (74), Apocalypse Now (79), The Rose (79).

FORREST, IRENE: Sitting Ducks (79).

FORREST, STEVE: North Dallas Forty (79).

FORSTER, ROBERT: Reflections in a Golden Eye (67), The Stalking Moon (68), Justine (69), Medium Cool (69), Pieces of Dreams (70), Cover Me Babe (72), The Don is Dead (73), The Black Hole (79), Alligator (80).

FORSYTHE, JOHN: ...And Justice For All (79).

FOSTER, JODIE: One Little Indian (73), Tom Sawyer (73), Alice Doesn't Live Here Anymore (74), Bugsy Malone (76), Taxi Driver (76), Candleshoe (77), Freaky Friday (77), The Little Girl Who Lives Down Lane (77), Carny (80), Foxes (80).

FOSTER, MEG: Carny (80).

FOX, BERNARD: The Private Eyes (80).

FOX, EDWARD: The Mirror Crack'd (80).

FOXWORTH, ROBERT: Prophecy (79), The Black Marble (80).

FRANCESCHI, ANTONIA: Fame (80).

FRANCISCUS, JAMES: When Time Ran Out (80).

FRANK, JEFFREY: The Island (80).

FRANKEN, STEVE: The North Avenue Irregulars (79), The Fiendish Plot Of Dr. Fu Manchu (80), There Goes the Bride (80).

FRANKLIN, ARETHA: The Blues Brothers (80).

FRANZ, DENNIS: Dressed To Kill (80).

FRAZIER, SHEILA: California Suite (78).

FREDERICK, LYNNE: The Prisoner Of Zenda (79).

FREEMAN, AL, Jr.: Black Like Me (64), The Dutchman (67), Castle Keep (68), Finian's Rainbow (68), The Detective (68), The Lost Man (69), A Fable (71).

FREEMAN, MORGAN: Brubaker (80).

FRENCH, LEIGH: The Hollywood Knights (80).

FRENCH, SUSAN: Somewhere In Time (80).

FREY, LEONARD: Tell Me That You Love Me, Junie Moon (69), The Boys in the Band (70), The Magic Christian (70), Fiddler on the Roof (71), Up The Academy (80), Where The Buffalo Roam (80).

FRIEDRICH, JOHN: The Wanderers (79).

FROBE, GERT: Bloodline (79).

FUCHS, LEO: The Frisco Kid (79).

FURST, STEPHEN: Take Down (79), Midnight Madness (80).

GABEL, MARTIN: First Deadly Sin (80).

GABOURIE, RICHARD: Final Assignment (80).

GAINES, BOYD: Fame (80).

GAINES, LEONARD: Hardcore (79), Where The Buffalo Roam (80).

GALLAGHER, PETER: The Idolmaker (80).

GARDENIA, VINCENT: Cold Turkey (70), Little Murders (71), Bang the Drum Slowly (73), Death Wish (74), The Front Page (74), Greased Lightning (77), Heaven Can Wait (78), Home Movies (79).

GARDNER, AVA: Mayerling (69), The Life and Times of Judge Roy Bean

(72), Earthquake (74), The Blue Bird (76), The Cassandra Crossing (77), The Sentinel (77), The Kidnapping Of The President (80).

GARFIELD (GOORWITZ), ALLEN: The Owl and the Pussycat (70), Get to Know Your Rabbit (72), Slither (72), The Candidate (72), Busting (74), The Conversation (74), The Front Page (74), Nashville (75), Mother, Jugs and Speed (76), Brinks (79), One Trick Pony (80), The Stunt Man (80).

GARFUNKEL, ART: Catch-22 (70), Carnal Knowledge (71), Bad Timing (80).

GARLAND, BEVERLY: Roller Boogie (79), It's My Turn (80).

GARNER, JAMES: The Great Escape (63), The Thrill of It All (63), The Americanization of Emily (64), Thirty Six Hours (64), Hour of the Gun (67), How Sweet It Is (68), Support Your Local Sheriff (68), The Pink Jungle (68), Marlowe (69), Support Your Local Gunfighter (71), The Skin Game (71), They Only Kill Their Masters (72), One Little Indian (73), Health (80).

GARNETT, GALE: Tribute (80).

GARR, TERI: The Conversation (74), Close Encounters of the Third Kind (77), Mr. Mike's Mondo Video (79), The Black Stallion (79).

GARY, LORRAINE: Jaws (75), I Never Promised You a Rose Garden (77), Jaws 2 (78), 1941 (79), Just You And Me, Kid (79).

GASSMAN, VITTORIO: The Nude Bomb (80).

GAUTREAUX, DAVID: The Hearse (80).

GAZZARA, BEN: The Bridge at Remegen (69), Husbands (70), Capone (73), The Neptune Factor (73), High Velocity (76), The Killing of a Chinese Bookie (76), Voyage of the Damned (76), Opening Night (77), Bloodline (79), Saint Jack (79), They All Laughed (81).

GAZZO, MICHAEL V.: King Of The Gypsies (78), The Fish That Saved Pittsburgh (79), Alligator (80).

GEER, ELLEN: Harold and Maude (71), Over The Edge (79).

GEER, WILL: Seconds (66), In Cold Blood (67), Bandolero (68), The Reivers (69), Brother John (70), The Moonshine War (70), Jeremiah Johnson (72), Napoleon and Samantha (72), Executive Action (73), Moving Violation (76), The Blue Bird (76).

GEESON, JUDY: It's Not The Size That Counts (79).

GEORGE, CHIEF DAN: Little Big Man (70), Alien Thunder (73), Harry and Tonto (74), The Bears and I (74), The Outlaw Josey Wales (76), Americathon (79).

GEORGE, SUSAN: The Looking Glass War (69), Straw Dogs (71), Dirty Mary, Crazy Larry (74), Mandingo (75), Out of Season (75), A Small Town in Texas (76).

GERARD, GIL: Buck Rogers (79).

GERE, RICHARD: Report to the Commissioner (74), Baby Blue Marine (76), Looking for Mr. Goodbar (77), Bloodbrothers (78), Days of Heaven (78), Yanks (79), American Gigolo (80).

Albert Hall.

Terry Kiser.

GIANNINI, GIANCARLO: Travels With Anita (79).

GIBSON, HENRY: The Long Goodbye (73), Nashville (75), A Perfect Couple (79), Health (80), The Blues Brothers (80).

GIELGUD, JOHN: Caligula (79), Murder By Decree (79), The Human Factor (79), The Elephant Man (80), The Formula (80).

GIFFORD, GLORIA: California Suite (78).

GILAN, YVONNE: Agatha (79).

GILFORD, JACK: A Funny Thing Happened on the Way... (66), Catch-22 (70), They Might Be Giants (71), Save the Tiger (72), Harry and Walter Go to New York (76), Cheaper to Keep Her (80), Wholly Moses! (80).

GILLIAM, TERRY: Life Of Brian (79).

GIRLING, CINDY: The Kidnapping Of The President (80).

GLASER, PAUL MICHAEL: Phobia (80).

GLEASON, JACKIE: Smokey And The Bandit II (80).

GLEASON, REDMOND: Steel (80).

GLENN, SCOTT: The Baby Maker (69), Nashville (75), Apocalypse Now (79), More American Graffiti (79), Urban Cowboy (80).

GLOVER, JOHN: The American Success Company (79), Melvin and Howard (80), The Mountain Men (80).

GOLD, AMBER ROSE: Second-Hand Hearts (80).

GOLDBLUM, JEFF: California Split (74), Death Wish (74), Nashville (75), Next Stop, Greenwich Village (76), Between the Lines (77), Invasion Of The Bodysnatchers (78), Remember My Name (78), Thank God It's Friday (78), Escape to Athena (79).

GOLDEN, ANNIE: Hair (79).

GOLDEN, LARRY: Wanda Nevada (79).

GOLDMAN, DANNY: Swap Meet (79), Where The Buffalo Roam (80).

Larry Fishburne.   John Lithgow.

GOLDONI, LELIA: Invasion Of The Bodysnatchers (78).
GOLONKA, ARLENE: The In-Laws (79), The Last Married Couple In
America (80).
GOMEZ, PANCHITO: Walk Proud (79).
GONZALEZ, PANCHO: Players (79).
GOODFELLOW, JOAN: Sunburn (79).
GOORWITZ, ALLEN: see Garfield, Allen.
GORDON, DON: Out Of The Blue (80).
GORDON, HANNAH: The Elephant Man (80).
GORDON, KEITH: All That Jazz (79), Home Movies (79), Dressed To
Kill (80).
GORDON, RUTH: Inside Daisy Clover (66), Lord Love a Duck (66),
Rosemary's Baby (68), Harold and Maude (71), The Big Bus (76),
Every Which Way But Loose (78), Boardwalk (79), Any Which Way
You Can (80), My Bodyguard (80).
GORMAN, CLIFF: Justine (69), The Boys in the Band (70), Cops and
Robbers (73), Rosebud (75), An Unmarried Woman (78), All That
Jazz (79), Night Of The Juggler (80).
GORNEL, RANDY: The Hollywood Knights (80).
GORNEY, KAREN LYNN: Saturday Night Fever (77).
GOULD, ELLIOTT: The Confession (66), The Night They Raided
Minsky's (68), Bob & Carol & Ted & Alice (69), Getting Straight
(70), I Love My Wife (70), MASH (70), Move (70), Little Murders
(71), The Long Goodbye (73), Busting (74), California Split (74),
SPYS (74), Who? (74), Nashville (75), Harry and Walter Go to New
York (76), I Will, I Will...For Now (76), Whiffs (76), A Bridge Too
Far (77), Capricorn One (78), Matilda (78), The Lady Vanishes (79),
The Muppet Movie (79), Falling In Love Again (80).

GOULD, HAROLD: Seems Like Old Times (80).

GOULET, ROBERT: Atlantic City U S A (80).

GRAHAM, GARY: The Hollywood Knights (80).

GRAHAM, GERRIT: Home Movies (79), Old Boyfriends (79), Used Cars (80).

GRAHAME, GLORIA: Head Over Heels (79), Melvin and Howard (80).

GRANT, DAVID MARSHALL: French Postcards (79), Happy Birthday, Gemini (80).

GRANT, LEE: In the Heat of the Night (67), Valley of the Dolls (67), Marooned (69), The Big Bounce (69), The Landlord (70), There Was a Crooked Man (70), Plaza Suite (71), Portnoy's Complaint (72), Shampoo (75), Voyage of the Damned (76), Airport 77 (77), Damien-Omen II (78), The Swarm (78), Little Miss Marker (80).

GRAUBART, JUDY: Simon (80).

GRAVES, PETER: Airplane (80).

GRAY, CHARLES: The Legacy (79).

GRAY, ERIN: Buck Rogers (79).

GREEN, ADOLPH: Simon (80).

GREER, MICHAEL: The Rose (79).

GREGORY, CELIA: Agatha (79).

GREGORY, JAMES: The Main Event (79).

GREY, JOEL: Cabaret (72), Man on a Swing (73), Buffalo Bill and the Indians (76), The Seven Percent Solution (76).

GRIER, PAM: Beyond the Valley of the Dolls (70), Blacula (72), Hit Man (72), Twilight People (72), Black Mama (74), Coffy (74), White Mama (74), The Arena (75), Greased Lightning (77).

GRIES, JONATHAN: Sunnyside (79), Swap Meet (79).

GRIFASI, JOE: Hide In Plain Sight (80).

GRIFFITH, MELANIE: Smile (76), Joyride (77), One on One (77).

GRIMES, GARY: The Summer of '42 (71), The Culpepper Cattle Company (72), Cahill (73), Class of '44 (73), The Spikes Gang (74), Gus (76).

GRIMES, TAMMY: The Runner Stumbles (79), Can't Stop The Music (80).

GRIZZARD, GEORGE: Comes A Horseman (78), Seems Like Old Times (80).

GRODIN, CHARLES: Rosemary's Baby (68), The Heartbreak Kid (72), King Kong (76), Thieves (77), Heaven Can Wait (78), Real Life (79), Sunburn (79), It's My Turn (80), Seems Like Old Times (80).

GRODY, KATHRYN: My Bodyguard (80).

GROSSO, SONNY: Cruising (80).

GROVER, STANLEY: The Onion Field (79).

GUARDINO, HARRY: Madigan (68), The Hell with Heroes (68), Lovers and Other Strangers (69), Red Sky at Morning (70), Dirty Harry (71), St. Ives (73), The Enforcer (76), Rollercoaster (77), Matilda (78),

Goldengirl (79), Any Which Way You Can (80).

GUEST, CHRISTOPHER: The Last Word (79), The Long Riders (80).

GUEST, NICHOLAS: The Long Riders (80).

GUILLAUME, ROBERT: Seems Like Old Times (80).

GUINNESS, ALEC: Scrooge (70), Murder by Death (76), Star Wars (77), Raise The Titanic (80), The Empire Strikes Back (80).

GULAGER, CLU: Winning (69), The Last Picture Show (71), McQ (74), The Other Side of Midnight (77), Touched By Love (80).

GUNN, BILL: Ganja and Hess (73).

GUNN, MOSES: The Great White Hope (70), Shaft (71), Wild Rovers (71), Shaft's Big Score (72), The Hot Rock (72), Rollerball (75), Remember My Name (78), The Ninth Configuration (80).

GUTTENBERG, STEVE: Players (79), Can't Stop The Music (80).

GWYNNE, FRED: Luna (79), Simon (80).

GWYNNE, MICHAEL C.: Butch And Sundance (79).

HACKETT, JOAN: The Group (66), Will Penny (67), Support Your Local Sheriff (68), Assignment to Kill (69), The Rivals (72), The Last of Sheila (73), Treasure of Matecumbe (76), Mr. Mikes Mondo Video (79), The North Avenue Irregulars (79), One Trick Pony (80).

HACKETT, JONATHAN: The Lady Vanishes (79).

HACKMAN, GENE: Bonnie and Clyde (67), Riot (68), The Split (68), Downhill Racer (69), I Never Sang for My Father (69), Marooned (69), The Gypsy Moths (69), Doctors' Wives (70), Cisco Pike (71), The French Connection (71), The Hunting Party (71), Prime Cut (72), The Poseidon Adventure (72), Scarecrow (73), The Conversation (74), Young Frankenstein (74), Zandy's Bride (74), Bite the Bullet (75), French Connection II (75), Lucky Lady (75), Night Moves (75), A Bridge Too Far (77), March or Die (77), The Domino Principle (77), Superman (78), Superman II (80).

HACKMAN, ROBERT: Falling In Love Again (80).

HADDOCK, JULIE ANNE: The Great Santini (80).

HADDON, DAYLE: North Dallas Forty (79).

HAGERTY, JULIE: Airplane (80).

HAGMAN, LARRY: The Group (66), Up in the Cellar (70), Harry and Tonto (74), Stardust (74), Mother, Jugs and Speed (76), The Big Bus (76), The Eagle Has Landed (77).

HAGUE, ALBERT: Fame (80).

HAID, CHARLES: Oliver's Story (78), Altered States (80).

HALE, GEORGINA: The Watcher In The Woods (80).

HALEY, JACKIE EARLE: The Bad News Bears (76), The Bad News Bears in Breaking Training (77), Breaking Away (79).

HALL, ALBERT: Apocalypse Now (79).

HALLAHAN, CHARLES: Going In Style (79).

HALPRIN, LUKE: Shock Waves (75).

HAMEL, VERONICA: Beyond The Poseidon Adventure (79), When Time

Jack Lemmon, Genevieve Bujold.   Tatum O'Neal, Kristy McNichol.

Ran Out (80).

HAMILL, MARK: Star Wars (77), The Big Red One (79), The Empire Strikes Back (80).

HAMILTON, GEORGE: Act One (63), Evil Knievel (71), The Man Who Loved Cat Dancing (73), Once is Not Enough (75), Love at First Bite (79).

HAMILTON, MURRAY: The Graduate (67), The Way We Were (73), Jaws (75), Jaws 2 (78), 1941 (79), The Amityville Horror (79), Brubaker (80).

HAMILTON, RICHARD: Resurrection (80).

HAMLIN, HARRY: Movie Movie Dynamite Hands (78).

HANCOCK, JOHN: First Family (80), The Black Marble (80).

HANFT, HELEN: Stardust Memories (80), Willie & Phil (80).

HARDING, JACKI: The Lady Vanishes (79).

HARGREAVES, DAVID: Agatha (79).

HARMON, DEBORAH: Used Cars (80).

HARMON, MARK: Beyond The Poseidon Adventure (79).

HARPER, GERALD: The Lady Vanishes (79).

HARPER, JESSICA: Stardust Memories (80).

HARPER, VALERIE: Chapter Two (79), The Last Married Couple In America (80).

HARRIS, BARBARA: A Thousand Clowns (65), Oh Dad... (66), Plaza Suite (71), Who is Harry Kellerman .... (71), The War Between Men and Women (72), Mixed Company (74), Nashville (75), Freaky Friday (77), Movie Movie Baxter's Beauties (78), The Seduction Of Joe Tynan (79), Second-Hand Hearts (80).

HARRIS, DAVID: The Warriors (79).

HARRIS, EMMYLOU: Honeysuckle Rose (80).

HARRIS, JULIE: The Bell Jar (79).

HARRIS, JULIUS: First Family (80).

HARRIS, LEONARD: Hero At Large (80).

HARRIS, RICHARD: The Molly Maguires (68), A Man Called Horse (70), Man in the Wilderness (71), 99 44/100 Percent Dead (74), Juggernaut (74), Robin and Marian (76), The Return of a Man Called Horse (76), Orca (77), The Cassandra Crossing (77), The Last Word (79).

HARRISON, CATHRYN: Images (72), Black Moon (75).

HARRISON, GEORGE: Life Of Brian (79).

HARROLD, KATHRYN: Nightwing (79), The Hunter (80).

HARRY, DEBORAH: Mr. Mikes Mondo Video (79), Roadie (80), Union City (80).

HARTMAN, ELIZABETH: A Patch of Blue (66), The Group (66), You're a Big Boy Now (67), The Fixer (68), The Beguiled (71), Walking Tall (73).

HASSETT, MARILYN: Two-Minute Warning (76), The Other Side of the Mountain (78), The Bell Jar (79).

HAVOC, JUNE: Can't Stop The Music (80).

HAWKINS, RONNIE: Heaven's Gate (80).

HAWN, GOLDIE: The One and Only Genuine Original... (68), Cactus Flower (69), There's a Girl in my Soup (70), $ (71), Butterflies Are Free (72), The Sugarland Express (73), The Girl from Petrovka (74), Shampoo (75), The Duchess and the Dirtwater Fox (76), Foul Play (78), Travels With Anita (79), Private Benjamin (80), Seems Like Old Times (80).

HAYDEN, STERLING: Loving (70), The Godfather (72), The Long Goodbye (73), 1900 (77), King of the Gypsies (78), The Outsider (79), Winter Kills (79), Nine To Five (80).

HAYES, HELEN: Airport (69), Herbie Rides Again (73), One of Our Dinosaurs Is Missing (75), Candleshoe (77).

HAYS, ROBERT: Airplane (80).

HEARD, JOHN: Between the Lines (77), Head Over Heels (79), Heart Beat (79), On The Yard (79).

HEDIN, SERENE: Windwalker (80).

HEDISON, DAVID: ffolkes (80).

HEFLIN, MARTA: A Star is Born (76), A Wedding (78), A Perfect Couple (79), A Romance (79).

HEFLIN, NORA: Head Over Heels (79).

HELM, LEVON: Coal Miner's Daughter (80).

HELPER, TODD: Falling In Love Again (80).

HEMINGWAY, MARGAUX: Lipstick (76).

HEMINGWAY, MARIEL: Manhattan (79).

HEMMINGS, DAVID: Murder By Decree (79).

HENDERSON, TY: The Competition (80).

HENDRICKSON, NANCY: Mother's Day (80).

HENRY, BUCK: The Graduate (67), Catch-22 (70), Taking Off (71), The Man Who Fell to Earth (76), Heaven Can Wait (78), Old Boyfriends (79), First Family (80), Gloria (80).

HENRY, JUSTIN: Kramer vs Kramer (79).

HENSLEY, PAMELA: Buck Rogers (79).

HEPBURN, AUDREY: Two for the Road (67), Wait Until Dark (67), Robin and Marian (76), Bloodline (79), They All Laughed (81).

HEPBURN, KATHARINE: The Lion in Winter (68), The Madwoman of Chaillot (69), The Trojan Women (71), A Delicate Balance (73), Love Among the Ruins (75), Rooster Cogburn (75).

HERD, RICHARD: The Onion Field (79), Schizoid (80).

HERRMANN, EDWARD: The Day of the Dolphin (73), The Paper Chase (73), The Great Gatsby (74), The Great Waldo Pepper (75), Eleanor and Franklin (76), The Betsy (77), Brass Target (78), Take Down (79), The North Avenue Irregulars (79).

HERSHEY, BARBARA: see Seagull, Barbara.

HESTON, CHARLTON: Will Penny (67), The Planet of the Apes (68), Beneath the Planet of the Apes (69), Number One (69), Julius Caesar (70), The Hawaiians (70), Anthony and Cleopatra (71), The Omega Man (71), Skyjacked (72), Soylent Green (72), The Three Musketeers (73), Earthquake (74), The Four Musketeers (74), Airport 75 (75), Midway (76), The Last Hard Men (76), Two-Minute Warning (76), The Awakening (80), The Mountain Men (80).

HICKS, WILLIAM T.: Living Legend (80).

HIGGINS, MICHAEL: An Enemy Of The People (76), The Black Stallion (79).

HILL, ARTHUR: Harper (66), Petulia (68), The Chairman (69), Rabbit Run (70), The Andromeda Strain (70), The Pursuit of Happiness (70), The Killer Elite (75), Futureworld (76), A Bridge Too Far (77), A Little Romance (79), Butch And Sundance (79).

HILL, MARIANA: Schizoid (80).

HILL, STEVEN: It's My Turn (80).

HILL, THOMAS: Hide In Plain Sight (80).

HILLER, WENDY: The Elephant Man (80).

HILLERMAN, JOHN: Sunburn (79).

HINDLE, ART: Invasion Of The Body Snatchers (78), The Octagon (80).

HINGLE, PAT: Hang 'Em High (68), Norwood (69), Bloody Mama (70), W.U.S.A (70), The Carey Treatment (72), One Little Indian (73), Run Wild (73), Norma Rae (79).

HINTON, JAMES DAVID: Galaxina (80).

HIRSCH, JUDD: King Of The Gypsies (78), Ordinary People (80).

HOFFMAN, BASIL: Ordinary People (80).

HOFFMAN, DUSTIN: Madigan's Millions (66), The Graduate (67), The

Tiger Makes Out (67), Un Dollaro Per Sette Vigliachi (67), John and
Mary (69), Midnight Cowboy (69), Little Big Man (70), Straw Dogs
(71), Who Is Harry Kellerman .... (71), Alfredo (72), Papillon (73),
Lenny (74), All the President's Men (76), Marathon Man (76),
Straight Time (78), Agatha (79), Kramer vs. Kramer (79).

HOGAN, SUSAN: Phobia (80).

HOGG, IAN: The Legacy (79).

HOLBROOK, HAL: The Group (66), Wild in the Streets (68), The Great
White Hope (70), The People Next Door (70), They Only Kill Their
Masters (72), Magnum Force (73), All the President's Men (76),
Midway (76), Julia (77), Capricorn One (78), Natural Enemies (79),
The Fog (80), The Kidnapping Of The President (80).

HOLCOMB, SARAH: Walk Proud (79), Happy Birthday, Gemini (80).

HOLDEN, WILLIAM: The Devil's Brigade (68), The Christmas Tree (69),
The Wild Bunch (69), Wild Rovers (71), The Revengers (72), Breezy
(73), Open Season (74), The Towering Inferno (74), Network (76),
Damien-Omen II (78), Ashanti (79), The Earthling (80), When Time
Ran Out (80), S.O.B. (81).

HOLLAND, ANTHONY: All That Jazz (79).

HOLLY, ELLEN: Cops and Robbers (73).

HOLM, IAN: Alien (79).

HONG, JAMES: The In-Laws (79).

HOOKS, KEVIN: Take Down (79).

HOPE, BOB: The Muppet Movie (79).

HOPKINS, ANTHONY: Magic (78), A Change of Seasons (80), The
Elephant Man (80).

HOPKINS, BO: The Wild Bunch (69), Monte Walsh (70), The
Culpepper Cattle Company (72), The Getaway (72), American
Graffiti (73), The Man Who Loved Cat Dancing (73), White
Lightning (73), The Nickel Ride (74), Posse (75), The Day of the
Locust (75), The Killer Elite (75), Breaking Point (76), More
American Graffiti (79), The Fifth Floor (80).

HOPPER, DENNIS: Cool Hand Luke (67), Easy Rider (69), True Grit
(69), The Last Movie (71), Kid Blue (73), An American Friend (77),
Apocalypse Now (79), Out Of The Blue (80).

HORSFORD, ANNA MARIA: Times Square (80).

HOTCHKIS, JOAN: Old Boyfriends (79).

HOTTON, DONALD: The Hearse (80).

HOUGHTON, JAMES: More American Graffiti (79).

HOUSEMAN, JOHN: St. Ives (73), The Paper Chase (73), Rollerball
(75), Three Days of the Condor (75), The Cheap Detective (78),
Old Boyfriends (79), My Bodyguard (80), The Fog (80), Wholly
Moses! (80).

HOUSER, JERRY: Magic (78).

HOWARD, ANDREA: The Nude Bomb (80).

Linda Manz.

HOWARD, KAREN: The Bell Jar (79).

HOWARD, RON: Smoke (69), The Wild Country (70), American Graffiti (73), The Spikes Gang (74), The Shootist (76), More American Graffiti (79).

HOWARD, TREVOR: Superman (78), Hurricane (79), Meteor (79), The Sea Wolves (80), Windwalker (80).

HUBBARD, ELIZABETH: The Bell Jar (79), Ordinary People (80).

HUBLEY, SEASON: Hardcore (79).

HUCKABEE, COOPER: Joni (80).

HUDDLE, ELIZABETH: Pilgrim, Farewell (80).

HUDDLESTON, DAVID: Smokey And The Bandit II (80).

HUDSON, ROCK: Tobruk (67), Ice Station Zebra (68), A Fine Pair (69), Darling Lili (69), Generation (69), Hornet's Nest (69), The Undefeated (69), Pretty Maids All in a Row (71), Showdown (72), Two-Minute Warning (76), The Mirror Crack'd (80).

HUFFMAN, DAVID: Ice Castles (78), The Onion Field (79).

HUGHES, BARNARD: The Hospital (71), Rage (72), Sisters (73).

HUGHES, HELEN: Middle Age Crazy (80), The Lucky Star (80).

HUGHES, TRESA: Fame (80).

HULCE, THOMAS: Those Lips Those Eyes (80).

HULL, DIANE: The Onion Field (79), The Fifth Floor (80), You Better Watch Out (80).

HUNTER, KAKI: Roadie (80).

HUPPERT, ISABELLE: Heaven's Gate (80).

HURT, JOHN: Alien (79), Heaven's Gate (80), The Elephant Man (80).

HURT, MARY BETH: Head Over Heels (79), A Change of Seasons (80).

HURT, WESLEY IVAN: Popeye (80).

HURT, WILLIAM: Altered States (80).

HUSSEY, OLIVIA: Romeo and Juliet (68), All the Right Noises (69), Summertime Killer (72), Lost Horizon (73), Black Christmas (75), The Cat and The Canary (77), Death on the Nile (78), The Man With Bogart's Face (80).

HUSTON, ANGELICA: A Walk with Love and Death (69), Sinful Davey (69), The Last Tycoon (76).

HUSTON, JOHN: Winter Kills (79), Wise Blood (79), Head On (80).

HUTTON, LAUREN: Paper Lion (68), Little Fauss and Big Halsey (70), The Gambler (75), Gator (76), Viva Knievel! (77), Welcome to L.A. (77), A Wedding (78), American Gigolo (80).

HUTTON, TIMOTHY: Ordinary People (80).

HYDE-WHITE, WILFRID: In God We Trust (80), Oh, God! Book II (80).

IDLE, ERIC: Life Of Brian (79).

IMAN: The Human Factor (79).

IMHOFF, GARY: The Nude Bomb (80).

INWOOD, STEVE: Fame (80).

IRELAND, JOHN: The Shape Of Things To Come (79), Guyana:Cult Of The Damned (80).

IRVING, AMY: Carrie (76), The Fury (78), Honeysuckle Rose (80), The Competition (80).

ISACKSEN, PETER: The Fish That Saved Pittsburgh (79).

IVES, BURL: Just You And Me, Kid (79).

JACK, WOLFMAN: Motel Hell (80).

JACKSON, ANNE: The Secret Life of an American Wife (68), Lovers and Other Strangers (69), Dirty Dingus Magee (70), The Angel Levine (70), ZigZag (70), Nasty Habits (77), The Bell Jar (79), The Shining (80).

JACKSON, GLENDA: Marat/Sade (66), Negatives (68), Women in Love (69), The Music Lovers (70), Sunday, Bloody Sunday (71), Mary, Queen of Scots (71), The Boyfriend (71), The Triple Echo (72), A Bequest to the Nation (73), A Touch of Class (73), The Maids (74), The Romantic Englishwoman (75), Hedda (76), The Incredible Sarah (76), Nasty Habits (77), House Calls (78), Lost And Found (79), Health (80), Hopscotch (80).

JACOBI, DEREK: The Human Factor (79).

JACOBI, LOU: The Lucky Star (80).

JACOBS, JAMES H.: Love in a Taxi (80).

JACOBS, JOE D.: Walk Proud (79).

JAECKEL, RICHARD: Herbie Goes Bananas (80).

JAFFE, SAM: Battle Beyond The Stars (80).

JAGGER, BIANCA: The American Success Company (79).

JAGGER, DEAN: Alligator (80).
JAGLOM, HENRY: Sitting Ducks (79).
JAMES, CLIFTON: Superman II (80).
JAMES, CLIVE: The Secret Policeman's Ball (79).
JAMES, RON: The Boogey Man (80).
JAMISON, RICHARD: Over The Edge (79).
JANIS, CONRAD: Oh, God! Book II (80).
JANSSEN, DAVID: The Green Berets (68), Generation (69), Marooned (69), Where It's At (69), Once is Not Enough (75).
JARVIS, GRAHAM: Middle Age Crazy (80).
JEFFRIES, LIONEL: The Prisoner Of Zenda (79).
JENKINS, TIMOTHY: Happy Birthday, Gemini (80).
JENNER, BRUCE: Can't Stop The Music (80).
JENS, SALOME: Cloud Dancer (80).
JENSON, ROY: Any Which Way You Can (80).
JOHNSON, BEN: Will Penny (67), Hang 'Em High (68), The Undefeated (69), The Wild Bunch (69), Chisum (70), The Last Picture Show (71), Junior Bonner (72), The Getaway (72), Dillinger (73), Kid Blue (73), The Sugarland Express (73), The Train Robbers (73), Bite the Bullet (75), Breakheart Pass (75), Hustle (75), The Town That Dreaded Sundown (77), Terror Train (80), The Hunter (80).
JOHNSON, LAMONT: Sunnyside (79), Foxes (80).
JOHNSON, LYNN HOLLY: Ice Castles (78), The Watcher In The Woods (80).
JOHNSON, ROBIN: Times Square (80).
JOHNSON, VAN: The Kidnapping Of The President (80).
JOHNSTON, BRIAN: Return Of The Secaucus Seven (80).
JONES, CHRISTOPHER: Wild in the Streets (68), The Looking Glass War (69), Three in the Attic (69), Ryan's Daughter (71).
JONES, FREDDIE: The Elephant Man (80).
JONES, HENRY: Nine To Five (80).
JONES, JAMES EARL: End of the Road (70), The Great White Hope (70), Claudine (74), Swashbuckler (76), The Bingo Long Traveling All-Stars (76), Exorcist II-The Heretic (77), Star Wars (77), The Last Remake of Beau Geste (77).
JONES, L. Q.: Hang 'Em High (68), The Wild Bunch (69), The Ballad of Cable Hogue (70), The Brotherhood of Satan (70), The Hunting Party (71).
JONES, SAM J.: 10 (79), Flash Gordon (80).
JONES, SHIRLEY: Beyond The Poseidon Adventure (79).
JONES, TERRY: Life Of Brian (79), The Secret Policeman's Ball (79).
JONES, TOMMY LEE: Love Story (70), Jackson County Jail (75), Rolling Thunder (77), The Betsy (77), Eyes of Laura Mars (78), Coal Miner's Daughter (80).
JORDAN, NINA: Old Boyfriends (79).

JORDAN, RICHARD: The Friends of Eddie Coyle (73), Kamouraska (75), Rooster Cogburn (75), The Yakuza (75), Logan's Run (76), Interiors (78), Old Boyfriends (79), Raise The Titanic (80).

JORY, VICTOR: The Mountain Men (80).

JOSEPHSON, ELVA: Blue Lagoon (80).

JOYCE, ELAINE: Motel Hell (80).

JUNG, CALVIN: The Formula (80).

JURGENS, CURT: Breakthrough (79), Goldengirl (79).

JURGENSON, RANDY: Cruising (80).

KA'NE, DAYTON: Hurricane (79).

KAHLER, WOLF: The Lady Vanishes (79).

KAHN, MADELINE: De Duve (68), What's Up, Doc? (72), Paper Moon (73), Blazing Saddles (74), Young Frankenstein (74), At Long Last Love (75), The Adventure of Sherlock Holmes (75), Silent Movie (76), High Anxiety (78), The Cheap Detective (78), The Muppet Movie (79), First Family (80), Happy Birthday, Gemini (80), Simon (80), Wholly Moses! (80).

KALEM, TONI: The Wanderers (79).

KANE, CAROL: The Last Detail (73), Hester Street (74), Annie Hall (77), The Muppet Movie (79), When A Stranger Calls (79).

KANE, SHIRLEY: Foolin' Around (80).

KAPLAN, GABRIEL: Fast Break (79).

KARRAS, ALEX: When Time Ran Out (80).

KASTNER, PETER: You're a Big Boy Now (67), B.S. I Love you (70).

KATT, WILLIAM: Carrie (76), First Love (77), Big Wednesday (78), Butch And Sundance (79).

KAUFMAN, ANDY: In God We Trust (80).

KAY, DIANNE: 1941 (79).

KAYE, JUDY: Just Tell Me What You Want (80).

KEACH, JAMES: Hurricane (79), The Long Riders (80).

KEACH, STACY: The Heart is a Lonely Hunter (68), The Traveling Executioner (69), Brewster McCloud (70), End of the Road (70), Doc (71), Fat City (72), The Life and Times of Judge Roy Bean (72), The New Centurions (72), Luther (73), The Gravy Train (74), The Killer Inside Me (74), Conduct Unbecoming (75), Street People (76), The Squeeze (77), Up in Smoke (78), The Long Riders (80), The Ninth Configuration (80).

KEATON, DIANE: Lovers and Other Strangers (69), Play It Again, Sam (72), The Godfather (72), Sleeper (73), The Godfather, Part II (74), Love and Death (75), Harry and Walter Go to New York (76), I Will, I Will...For Now (76), Annie Hall (77), Looking For Mr. Goodbar (77), Interiors (78), Manhattan (79).

KEATS, STEVEN: The American Success Company (79), Hangar 18 (80).

KEDROVA, LILA: Tell Me a Riddle (80).

KEHOE, JACK: Melvin and Howard (80).

KEITEL, HARVEY: Mean Streets (73), Alice Doesn't Live Here Anymore (74), That's the Way of the World (75), Buffalo Bill and the Indians (76), Mother, Jugs and Speed (76), Taxi Driver (76), The Duelists (77), Welcome to L.A. (77), Blue Collar (78), Fingers (78), Eagle's Wing (79), Bad Timing (80), Saturn 3 (80).

KEITH, BRIAN: Reflections in a Golden Eye (67), Gaily, Gaily (69), The Mackenzie Break (70), The Wind and the Lion (75), The Yakuza (75), Nickelodeon (76), Hooper (78), Meteor (79), The Mountain Men (80).

KEITH, DAVID: The Rose (79), Brubaker (80), The Great Santini (80).

KELLER, MARTHE: Marathon Man (76), Black Sunday (77), Bobby Deerfield (77), Fedora (78), The Formula (80).

KELLERMAN, SALLY: The Boston Strangler (68), The April Fools (69), Brewster McCloud (70), MASH (70), Lost Horizon (72), Slither (72), The Last of the Red Hot Lovers (72), Rafferty and the Gold Dust Twins (75), The Big Bus (76), Welcome to L.A. (77), A Little Romance (79), Foxes (80), Head On (80), Loving Couples (80), Serial (80).

KELLERMAN, SUSAN: Oh Heavenly Dog (80).

KELLERMANN, BARBARA: The Sea Wolves (80).

KELLEY, DE FOREST: Star Trek (79).

KELLIN, MIKE: Riot (68), Freebie and The Bean (74), Next Stop, Greenwich Village (76), Girl Friends (78), Midnight Express (78), On The Yard (79).

KELLY, GENE: Xanadu (80).

KEMP, ELIZABETH: He Knows You're Alone (80).

KEMP, JEREMY: The Prisoner Of Zenda (79).

KENNEDY, GEORGE: Cool Hand Luke (67), Hurry Sundown (67), The Dirty Dozen (67), The Boston Strangler (68), The Legend of Lylah Clare (68), The Pink Panther (68), Airport (69), Gaily, Gaily (69), The Good Guys and the Bad Guys (69), Tick, Tick, Tick... (69), Dirty Dingus Magee (70), Lost Horizon (72), Earthquake (74), Thunderbolt and Lightfoot (74), The Eiger Sanction (75), The Human Factor (75), Airport 77 (77), Brass Target (78), Death on the Nile (78), The Concorde-Airport'79 (79), The Double Mcguffin (79), Steel (80).

KENNEDY, LEON ISAAC: Penitentiary (79).

KENSIT, PATSY: Hanover Street (79).

KERRIDGE, LINDA: Fade to Black (80).

KIDD, MICHAEL: Movie Movie Dynamite Hands (78).

KIDDER, MARGOT: Gaily, Gaily (69), Quackser Fortune Has a Cousin (70), The Gravy Train (74), The Reincarnation of Peter Proud (74), The Great Waldo Pepper (75), 92 in the Shade (76), Superman (78), Mr. Mikes Mondo Video (79), The Amityville Horror (79), Miss Right (80), Superman II (80), Willie & Phil (80).

KIEL, RICHARD: Moonraker (79).

KIGER, SUSAN: H.O.T.S. (79).

KILEY, RICHARD: Pendulum (69), AKA Cassius Clay (70), The Little Prince (74).

KILPATRICK, LINCOLN: Cool Breeze (72), Soul Soldier (72), Soylent Green (73), Chosen Survivors (74), Uptown Saturday Night (74).

KIMBROUGH, CHARLES: The Seduction Of Joe Tynan (79).

KING, ADRIENNE: Friday the 13th (80).

KING, ALAN: Just Tell Me What You Want (80).

KING, MABEL: The Jerk (79).

KING, ZALMAN: Tell Me a Riddle (80).

KINNEAR, ROY: Hawk the Slayer (80).

KINSKI, KLAUS: Schizoid (80).

KIRBY, BRUNO: Borderline (80), Where The Buffalo Roam (80).

KIRKESEY, DEANNE: Rich Kids (79).

KISER, TERRY: Rich Kids (79), Steel (80).

KLEIN, ROBERT: The Bell Jar (79).

KLUGMAN, JACK: The Detective (68), The Split (68), Goodbye Columbus (69), Who Says I Can't Ride a Rainbow (71), Two-Minute Warning (76).

KNIGHT, GLADYS: Pipe Dreams (76).

KNIGHT, ROSALIND: The Lady Vanishes (79).

KNIGHT, SHIRLEY: The Group (66), Dutchman (67), Petulia (68), The Rain People (69), Secrets (71), Juggernaut (74), Beyond The Poseidon Adventure (79).

KNOTTS, DON: The Prize Fighter (79), The Private Eyes (80).

KOENIG, WALTER: Star Trek (79).

KOHAN, GLENN: Blue Lagoon (80).

KOLDEN, SCOTT: The Day Time Ended (80).

KORMAN, HARVEY: Americathon (79), First Family (80), Herbie Goes Bananas (80).

KOTTO, YAPHET: Five Card Stud (68), The Thomas Crown Affair (68), The Liberation of L.B. Jones (70), Across 110th Street (72), Live and Let Die (73), Report to the Commissioner (74), Truck Turner (74), Drum (76), Blue Collar (78), Alien (79), Brubaker (80).

KRAMER, MICHAEL: Over The Edge (79).

KRISTEL, SYLVIA: The Concorde-Airport '79 (79), The Nude Bomb (80).

KRISTOFFERSON, KRIS: Cisco Pike (71), Blume in Love (73), Pat Garrett and Billy The Kid (73), Alice Doesn't Live Here Anymore (74), Bring Me the Head of Alfredo Garcia (74), A Star is Born (76), The Sailor Who Fell from Grace.... (76), Semi-Tough (77), Convoy (78), Heaven's Gate (80).

KRUSCHEN, JACK: Sunburn (79).

KURTZ, SWOOSIE: Oliver's Story (78).

LACK, STEPHEN: Head On (80).

LADD, DIANNE: White Lightning (73), Alice Doesn't Live Here Anymore (74), Chinatown (74).

LAFFERTY, MARCY: The Day Time Ended (80).

LAHTI, CHRISTINE: ...And Justice For All (79).

LAMAS, LORENZO: Take Down (79).

LAMBERT, DOUGLAS: Saturn 3 (80).

LANCASTER, BURT: Castle Keep (68), The Scalp Hunters (68), The Swimmer (68), Airport (69), The Gypsy Moths (69), Lawman (70), Valdez is Coming (70), Scorpio (72), Ulzana's Raid (72), Executive Action (73), The Midnight Man (74), Conversation Piece (75), Buffalo Bill and the Indians (76), Twilight's Last Gleaming (76), 1900 (77), The Cassandra Crossing (77), The Island of Dr. Moreau (77), Go Tell the Spartans (78), Atlantic City U S A (80).

LANCHESTER, ELSA: Die Laughing (80).

LAND, PAUL: The Idolmaker (80).

LANDAU, MARTIN: Meteor (79), The Last Word (79), Without Warning (80).

LANDER, DAVID L.: Used Cars (80), Wholly Moses! (80).

LANE, CHARLES: The Little Dragons (80).

LANE, DIANE: A Little Romance (79), Touched By Love (80).

LANG, JENNINGS: Real Life (79).

LANG, KELLY: Skatetown Usa (79).

LANG, PERRY: Alligator (80).

LANGDON, SUE ANE: Without Warning (80).

LANGE, JESSICA: All That Jazz (79), How To Beat The High Cost of Living (80).

LANGELLA, FRANK: Diary of a Mad Housewife (70), The Twelve Chairs (70), The Wrath of God (72), Dracula (79), Those Lips Those Eyes (80).

LANSBURY, ANGELA: The Lady Vanishes (79), The Mirror Crack'd (80).

LANSING, JOHN: More American Graffiti (79), Sunnyside (79).

LARCH, JOHN: The Amityville Horror (79).

LASSER, LOUISE: Bananas (71), Such Good Friends (71), Everything You Always Wanted to Know About Sex (72), Slither (72), In God We Trust (80).

LASSIE: The Magic Of Lassie (78).

LAUGHLIN, TOM: Born Losers (67), Billy Jack (71), The Trial of Billy Jack (72).

LAUTER, ED: Magic (78).

LAW, JOHN PHILLIP: The Russians Are Coming.... (66), Hurry Sundown (67), Barbarella (68), Danger: Diabolik (68), Skidoo (68), The Sergeant (68), The Hawaiians (70), The Last Movie (71), The Love Machine (71), Sinbad's Golden Voyage (73), Open Season (74), The Cassandra Crossing (77).

LAWSON, LEIGH: It's Not The Size That Counts (79).

LAWSON, RICHARD: The Main Event (79).

LAZAR, VERONICA: Luna (79).

LE GALLIENNE, EVA: Resurrection (80).

LE MAT, PAUL: More American Graffiti (79), Melvin and Howard (80).

LE MESURIER, JOHN: The Fiendish Plot Of Dr. Fu Manchu (80).

LEACHMAN, CLORIS: Butch Cassidy and the Sundance Kid (69), Lovers and Other Strangers (69), The People Next Door (70), The Last Picture Show (71), The Steagle (71), Dillinger (73), Charley and the Angel (74), Daisy Miller (74), Young Frankenstein (74), Crazy Mama (75), High Anxiety (78), Scavenger Hunt (79), The Muppet Movie (79), The North Avenue Irregulars (79), Foolin' Around (80), Herbie Goes Bananas (80).

LEARNED, MICHAEL: Touched By Love (80).

LEE, BERNARD: Moonraker (79).

LEE, CHRISTOPHER: 1941 (79), Circle Of Iron (79), Serial (80).

LEFEVRE, ADAM: Return Of The Secaucus Seven (80).

LEHNE, FREDRIC: Ordinary People (80).

LEIBMAN, RON: Slaughterhouse Five (72), The Hot Rock (72), The Super Cops (74), Your Three Minutes Are Up (74), Won Ton Ton, The Dog Who Saved Hollywood (76), Norma Rae (79), Up The Academy (80).

LEIGH, BARBARA: Seven (79).

LEIGH, JANET: Boardwalk (79), The Fog (80).

LEIGH-HUNT, BARBARA: Oh Heavenly Dog (80).

Vonetta McGee.

Mary Steenburgen.

LEMBECK, MICHAEL: The In-Laws (79).

LEMMON, JACK: The Odd Couple (68), The April Fools (69), The Out of Towners (70), Avanti (72), Save the Tiger (72), The War Between Men and Women (72), The Front Page (74), The Entertainer (75), The Prisoner of Second Avenue (75), Alex and the Gypsy (76), Airport 77 (77), The China Syndrome (79), Tribute (80).

LEMON, MEADOWLARK: The Fish That Saved Pittsburgh (79).

LENARD, MARK: Star Trek (79).

LENZ, KAY: Breezy (73), White Line Fever (75), Great Scout and Cathouse Thursday (76), Moving Violation (76).

LENZ, RICK: Melvin and Howard (80), The Little Dragons (80).

LEONARD, SHELDON: Brinks (79).

LERNER, MICHAEL: Borderline (80), Coast To Coast (80), The Baltimore Bullet (80).

LESLIE, BETHEL: Old Boyfriends (79).

LESTER, LOREN: Swap Meet (79).

LEVENE, SAM: ...And Justice For All (79).

LEVY, EUGENE: Running (79).

LEVY, JEREMY: Rich Kids (79).

LEWIS, FIONA: Wanda Nevada (79).

LEWIS, GEOFFREY: Any Which Way You Can (80), Bronco Billy (80), Heaven's Gate (80).

LIBERTINI, RICHARD: The In-Laws (79), Popeye (80).

LINCOLN, ABBEY: For Love of Ivy (68).

LINDFORS, VIVECA: Puzzle of a Downfall Child (70), The Way We Were (73), Welcome to L.A. (77), A Wedding (78), Girl Friends (78), Natural Enemies (79), Voices (79).

LINKE, PAUL: Motel Hell (80).

LIPSCOMB, DENNIS: Union City (80).

LITHGOW, JOHN: All That Jazz (79), Rich Kids (79).

LITTLE, CLEAVON: What's So Bad About Feeling Good (68), Cotton Comes to Harlem (70), Vanishing Point (71), Blazing Saddles (74), Greased Lightning (77), Scavenger Hunt (79).

LLOYD, CHRISTOPHER: Butch And Sundance (79), The Onion Field (79), Pilgrim, Farewell (80), Schizoid (80).

LLOYD, DANNY: The Shining (80).

LLOYD, KATHLEEN: Take Down (79).

LLOYD, NORMAN: The Nude Bomb (80).

LO BIANCO, TONY: The French Connection (71), The Seven Ups (73), Bloodbrothers (78), F.I.S.T. (78), Valentine (79).

LOCKE, SONDRA: Reflection of Fear (71), Willard (71), The Outlaw Josey Wales (76), The Gauntlet (77), Every Which Way But Loose (78), Any Which Way You Can (80), Bronco Billy (80).

LOCKWOOD, GARY: 2001: A Space Odyssey (68), The Model Shop (69), R.P.M. (70), Stand Up and Be Counted (71).

LOGGIA, ROBERT: The Ninth Configuration (80).

LOM, HERBERT: The Lady Vanishes (79), Hopscotch (80), The Man With Bogart's Face (80).

LOMBARD, MICHAEL: Fatso (80).

LONDON, LISA: H.O.T.S. (79).

LONG, SHELLEY: A Small Circle Of Friends (80).

LOPEZ, FERNANDO: Defiance (80).

LOPEZ, PRISCILLA: Cheaper to Keep Her (80).

LOREN, SOPHIA: Brass Target (78).

LOVE, SUZANNA: The Boogey Man (80).

LOWE, ARTHUR: The Lady Vanishes (79).

LOY, MYRNA: Just Tell Me What You Want (80).

LUCAS, LISA: The Turning Point (77), An Unmarried Woman (78).

LUCE, DEBORAH: Mother's Day (80).

LUCKINBILL, LAURENCE: The Boys In The Band (70), The Promise (79).

LUCKING, BILL: Coast To Coast (80).

LUDWIG, PAMELA: Over The Edge (79).

LUTTER, ALFRED: Alice Doesn't Live Here Anymore (74), The Bad News Bears (76), The Bad News Bears in Breaking Training (77).

LYNCH, KATE: Meatballs (79), Nothing Personal (80).

LYNCH, RICHARD: Steel (80), The Formula (80).

LYNCH, SUSAN: Northern Lights (79).

LYNDE, PAUL: The Villain (79).

LYNLEY, CAROL: Norwood (69), The Maltese Bippy (69), Once you Kiss a Stranger (70), The Poseidon Adventure (72), Cotter (73), The Shape Of Things To Come (79).

MacANALLY, RAY: The Outsider (79).

MacGRAW, ALI: A Lovely Way to Die (68), Goodbye Columbus (69), Love Story (70), The Getaway (72), Convoy (78), Players (78), Just Tell Me What You Want (79).

MACHT, STEPHEN: Nightwing (79), Galaxina (80), The Mountain Men (80).

MacKINNON, DEREK: Terror Train (80).

MacLAINE, SHIRLEY: Woman Times Seven (67), The Bliss of Mrs. Blossom (68), Sweet Charity (69), Two Mules for Sister Sara (69), Desperate Characters (71), The Possession of Joel Delaney (71), The Other Half of the Sky.... (75), The Turning Point (77), Being There (79), A Change of Seasons (80), Loving Couples (80).

MacNEE, PATRICK: The Sea Wolves (80).

MacRAE, HEATHER: A Perfect Couple (79).

MACY, BILL: The Jerk (79), Serial (80).

MAGEE, PATRICK: Rough Cut (80).

MAGGART, BRANDON: You Better Watch Out (80).

MAHER, JOSEPH: Just Tell Me What You Want (80), Those Lips Those Eyes (80).

MAJORS, LEE: Steel (80).

MAKEPEACE, CHRIS: Meatballs (79), My Bodyguard (80).

MAKO: The Big Brawl (80).

MALAVE, CHU CHU: The Main Event (79).

MALDEN, KARL: Blue (68), Hot Millions (68), Cat O'Nine Tails (69), Patton (69), Wild Rovers (71), Meteor (78), Beyond The Poseidon Adventure (79).

MALONE, DOROTHY: Winter Kills (79), The Day Time Ended (80).

MANCUSO, NICK: Nightwing (79).

MANOFF, DINAH: Ordinary People (80).

MANTEE, PAUL: The Great Santini (80).

MANZ, LINDA: Days of Heaven (78), King of the Gypsies (79), The Wanderers (79), Out Of The Blue (80).

MARCOVICCI, ANDREA: The Concorde-Airport'79 (79).

MARGOLIN, JANET: David and Lisa (62), Take the Money and Run (69), Annie Hall (77), The Last Embrace (79).

MARGOLIN, STUART: Kelly's Heroes (70), Limbo (72), Death Wish (74), Futureworld (76), Days of Heaven (78).

MARGULIES, DAVID: All That Jazz (79), Dressed To Kill (80), Hide In Plain Sight (80), Times Square (80).

MARIE, ROSE: Cheaper to Keep Her (80).

MARIN, RICHARD: Up in Smoke (78), Cheech And Chong's Next Movie (80).

MARKHAM, BARBARA: The Lady Vanishes (79).

MARKLAND, TED: Wanda Nevada (79).

MARLEY, BEN: Steel (80).

MARLEY, JOHN: Faces (68), A Man Called Sledge (70), Love Story (70), Jory (72), The Godfather (72), Blade (73), W.C. Fields and Me (76), The Car (77), The Greatest (77), Hooper (78), Oliver's Story (78), Tribute (80).

MARS, KENNETH: The Producers (67), Butch Cassidy and the Sundance Kid (69), Desperate Characters (71), What's Up, Doc? (72), Paper Moon (73), The Parallax View (74), Young Frankenstein (74), Night Moves (75).

MARSH, JEAN: The Changeling (80).

MARSHALL, E.G.: Superman II (80).

MARTIN, DEAN PAUL: Players (79).

MARTIN, NAN: A Small Circle Of Friends (80), Loving Couples (80).

MARTIN, STEVE: The Jerk (79), The Muppet Movie (79).

MARTIN, STROTHER: Butch Cassidy and the Sundance Kid (69), The Wild Bunch (69), True Grit (69), The Ballad of Cable Hogue (70), The Brotherhood of Satan (70), Fool's Parade (71), Pocket Money (72), Sssss (73), Hard Times (75), Rooster Cogburn (75), Slapshot (77), The End (78), Up in Smoke (78), Nightwing (79), The Champ (79), The Villain (79).

MARVIN, LEE: Cat Ballou (65), Point Blank (67), The Dirty Dozen (67), Hell in the Pacific (68), Paint Your Wagon (69), Monte Walsh (70), Pocket Money (72), Prime Cut (72), The Emperor of the North Pole (73), The Iceman Cometh (73), The Klansman (74), The Spikes Gang (74), Great Scout and Cathouse Thursday (76), Shout at the Devil (76), Avalanche Express (79), The Big Red One (79).

MASON, JACKIE: The Jerk (79).

MASON, JAMES: Bloodline (79), Murder By Decree (79), ffolkes (80).

MASON, MARSHA: Blume in Love (73), Cinderella Liberty (74), Audrey Rose (77), The Cheap Detective (78), The Goodbye Girl (78), Chapter Two (79), Promises In The Dark (79).

MASSEY, ANNA: De Sade (69), The Looking Glass War (69), Frenzy (72), A Doll's House (73), Vault of Horror (73).

MASSEY, DANIEL: Fragment of Fear (70), Mary Queen of Scots (71), Vault of Horror (73), The Incredible Sarah (76), Bad Timing (80).

MASUR, RICHARD: Hanover Street (79), Scavenger Hunt (79).

MATHESON, TIM: National Lampoon's Animal House (78), 1941 (79), Dreamer (79).

MATTHAU, DAVID: California Suite (78), FM (78), House Calls (78), The Big Fix (78), Hopscotch (80).

MATTHAU, WALTER: Candy (68), The Odd Couple (68), The Secret Life of an American Wife (68), Cactus Flower (69), Hello Dolly (69), A New Leaf (71), Kotch (71), Plaza Suite (71), Charley Varrick (72), Pete 'n Tillie (72), The Laughing Policeman (73), Earthquake (74), The Front Page (74), The Taking of Pelham 1-2-3 (74), The Sunshine Boys (75), The Bad News Bears (76), Casey's Shadow (77),

Susan Anspach, Kris Kristofferson, George Segal.

California Suite (78), House Calls (78), Hopscotch (80), Little Miss Marker (80).

MAXWELL, LOIS: Moonraker (79).

MAXWELL, ROBERTA: Rich Kids (79), Popeye (80), The Changeling (80).

MAY, ELAINE: Enter Laughing (67), Luv (67), A New Leaf (71), California Suite (78).

MAYER, MELODY: American Odyssey (80).

MAYHEW, PETER: The Empire Strikes Back (80).

MAYO, WHITMAN: The Main Event (79).

MAYRON, MELANIE: Harry and Tonto (74), Girl Friends (78).

McALISTER, JENNIFER: Serial (80).

McCABE, SANDRA: The Rose (79).

McCALLUM, DAVID: The Watcher In The Woods (80).

McCAMBRIDGE, MERCEDES: The Concorde-Airport'79 (79).

McCANN, CHUCK: The Heart is a Lonely Hunter (68), The Projectionist (70).

McCARTHY, KEVIN: Kansas City Bomber (72), Buffalo Bill and the Indians (76), Invasion Of The Body Snatchers (78), Piranha (78), Hero At Large (80), Those Lips Those Eyes (80).

McCLURE, DOUG: Humanoids From The Deep (80).

McCLURE, MARC: Superman (78), Superman II (80).

McCORMICK, MAUREEN: The Idolmaker (80).

McCORMICK, PAT: Smokey And The Bandit II (80).

McCOWEN, ALEC: Hanover Street (79).

Michael Ontkean, Margot Kidder, Ray Sharkey.

McCRANE, PAUL: Fame (80).
McDERMOTT, GARRY: The Lady Vanishes (79).
McDOWALL, RODDY: Circle Of Iron (79), Scavenger Hunt (79).
McDOWELL, MALCOLM: Caligula (79), Time After Time (79).
McGAVIN, DARREN: Hangar 18 (80).
McGEE, VONETTA: Blacula (72), Shaft in Africa (73), The Eiger
    Sanction (75), Brothers (77), Which Way is Up? (77).
McGOOHAN, PATRICK: Brass Target (78), Escape From Alcatraz (79).
McGOVERN, ELIZABETH: Ordinary People (80).
McGOVERN, TERRY: Americathon (79).
McGREEVEY, ANNIE: Below The Belt (80).
McGREGOR, ANGELA PUNCH: The Island (80).
McGUIRE, BIFF: The Last Word (79).
McINTIRE, TIM: The Sterile Cuckoo (69), American Hot Wax (78),
    Brubaker (80).
McKAY, SCOTT: The Bell Jar (79), You Better Watch Out (80).
McKEE, LONETTE: Cuba (79).
McKENNA, T. P.: The Outsider (79).
McKERN, LEO: Blue Lagoon (80).
McKINNEY, BILL: Any Which Way You Can.(80), Bronco Billy (80).
McLAREN, HOLLIS: Lost And Found (79).
McLOUGHLIN, TOMMY: The Black Hole (79).
McMILLAN, KENNETH: Oliver's Story (78), Head Over Heels (79),
    Carny (80), Hide In Plain Sight (80), Little Miss Marker (80).
McNICHOL, KRISTY: Little Darlings (80).

McPEAK, SANDY: The Onion Field (79).

McQUEEN, STEVE: Bullitt (68), The Thomas Crown Affair (68), The Reivers (69), Le Mans (71), Junior Bonner (72), The Getaway (72), Papillon (73), The Towering Inferno (74), An Enemy of the People (76), The Hunter (80), Tom Horn (80).

McSHANE, IAN: Cheaper to Keep Her (80).

MEARA, ANNE: Fame (80).

MEAT LOAF: Americathon (79), Roadie (80).

MEDFORD, KAY: Windows (80).

MEDWIN, MICHAEL: The Sea Wolves (80).

MEEKER, RALPH: Winter Kills (79), Without Warning (80).

MELATO, MARIANGELA: Flash Gordon (80).

MENZIES, HEATHER: Piranha (78).

MERCER, MARIAN: Nine To Five (80).

MEREDITH, BURGESS: Magic (78), Rocky II (79), Final Assignment (80), When Time Ran Out (80).

MERLIN, JOANNA: Fame (80).

MERRILL, DINA: Just Tell Me What You Want (80).

MERRITT, THERESEA: The Great Santini (80).

METCALF, MARK: Head Over Heels (79), Where The Buffalo Roam (80).

METRANO, ART: Cheaper to Keep Her (80), How To Beat The High Cost of Living (80).

MIDDLEMASS, FRANK: The Island (80).

MIDLER, BETTE: The Rose (79), Divine Madness (80).

MIFUNE, TOSHIRO: Hell in the Pacific (68), Red Sun (71), Paper Tiger (75), Midway (76), 1941 (79), Winter Kills (79).

MILES, SARAH: Ryan's Daughter (71), Lady Caroline Lamb (72), The Hireling (73), The Man Who Loved Cat Dancing (73), The Sailor Who Fell from Grace.... (76), The Big Sleep (78).

MILES, SYLVIA: Midnight Cowboy (69), Heat (72), Farewell My Lovely (75), 92 in the Shade (76), Great Scout and Cathouse Thursday (76), The Sentinel (77).

MILFORD, PENELOPE: Man on a Swing (75), Valentino (77), Coming Home (78), The Last Word (79).

MILIAN, TOMAS: Luna (79), Winter Kills (79).

MILLAND, RAY: Love Story (70), Oliver's Story (78).

MILLER, BARRY: Fame (80).

MILLER, DICK: Piranha (78).

MILLER, JASON: The Ninth Configuration (80).

MILLIGAN, SPIKE: Life Of Brian (79).

MIMIEUX, YVETTE: The Black Hole (79).

MINER, JAN: Willie & Phil (80).

MINNELLI, LIZA: Charlie Bubbles (67), Tell Me That You Love Me, Junie Moon (69), The Sterile Cuckoo (69), Cabaret (72), Lucky Lady (75),

A Matter of Time (76), New York, New York (77).

MINTZ, ELI: Boardwalk (79).

MIRREN, HELEN: Caligula (79), The Fiendish Plot Of Dr. Fu Manchu (80).

MITCHELL, CAMERON: Silent Scream (80), Without Warning (80).

MITCHELL, DONNA: The Bell Jar (79).

MITCHUM, CHRISTOPHER: Rio Lobo (70), The Last Hard Men (76), The Day Time Ended (80).

MITCHUM, JAMES: In Harm's Way (65), Ambush Bay (66), The Money Trap (66), The Tramplers (66), Trackdown (76).

MITCHUM, ROBERT: Anzio (68), Five Card Stud (68), Secret Ceremony (68), Villa Rides (68), The Good Guys and the Bad Guys (69), Young Billy Young (69), Going Home (71), Ryan's Daughter (71), The Wrath of God (72), The Friends of Eddie Coyle (73), Farewell My Lovely (75), The Yakuza (75), Midway (76), The Last Tycoon (76), Matilda (78), The Big Sleep (78), Breakthrough (79).

MOFFAT, DONALD: Promises In The Dark (79), On The Nickel (80), Popeye (80).

MONROE, EARL: Love in a Taxi (80).

MONTAGUE, LEE: Brass Target (78).

MONTANA, LENNY: Defiance (80), The Big Brawl (80).

MOODY, DAVID: Coast To Coast (80).

MOODY, JIM: Fame (80).

MOONEY, DEBRA: Chapter Two (79).

MOORE, DUDLEY: 10 (79), Wholly Moses! (80).

MOORE, MARY TYLER: Thoroughly Modern Millie (67), What's So Bad About Feeling Good (68), Change of Habit (69), Ordinary People (80).

MOORE, ROGER: Escape To Athena (79), Moonraker (79), ffolkes (80), Sunday Lovers (80), The Sea Wolves (80).

MORALES, SANTOS: Defiance (80).

MOREAU, JEANNE: Alex in Wonderland (70), Monte Walsh (70), Louise (72), Mr. Klein (76), The Last Tycoon (76).

MORENO, BELITA: A Perfect Couple (79).

MORENO, RITA: West Side Story (61), The Night of the Following Day (68), Marlowe (69), Popi (69), Carnal Knowledge (71), The Ritz (76), Happy Birthday, Gemini (80).

MORFOGEN, GEORGE: Those Lips Those Eyes (80).

MORGAN, NANCY: Americathon (79).

MORGAN, WENDY: Yanks (79), The Mirror Crack'd (80).

MORIARTY, CATHY: Raging Bull (80).

MORIARTY, MICHAEL: Hickey and Boggs (72), Bang the Drum Slowly (73), The Last Detail (73), Report to the Commissioner (74), Shoot It Black, Shoot It Blue (74), Who'll Stop the Rain (78).

MORITA, PAT: When Time Ran Out (80).

MORITZ, LOUISA: Cuba (79).

MORLEY, ROBERT: Scavenger Hunt (79), The Human Factor (79), Oh Heavenly Dog (80).

MORRIS, GARRETT: How To Beat The High Cost of Living (80).

MORROW, VIC: Humanoids From The Deep (80).

MORSE, BARRY: The Shape Of Things To Come (79), The Changeling (80).

MORSE, HELEN: Agatha (79).

MORTON, DAVID: Billy In The Lowlands (79).

MOSLEY, ROGER: Steel (80).

MOSTEL, ZERO: A Funny Thing Happened on the Way... (66), The Producers (67), Great Catherine (68), The Great Bank Robbery (69), The Angel Levine (70), The Hot Rock (72), Marco (73), Rhinoceros (73), The Front (76).

MULKEY, CHRIS: Sunnyside (79).

MULL, MARTIN: My Bodyguard (80), Serial (80).

MULLIGAN, RICHARD: The Group (66), The Undefeated (69), Little Big Man (70), The Big Bus (76), Scavenger Hunt (79).

MUNCKE, CHRISTOPHER: Saturn 3 (80).

MUNDY, MEG: Oliver's Story (78), The Bell Jar (79), Ordinary People (80).

MURCELO, KARMIN: Borderline (80).

MURPHY, GERARD: Brinks (79).

MURPHY, MICHAEL: Countdown (68), That Cold Day in the Park (69), Brewster McCloud (70), MASH (70), McCabe and Mrs. Miller (71), Nashville (75), The Front (76), An Unmarried Woman (78).

MURRAY, BILL: Meatballs (79), Mr. Mikes Mondo Video (79), Where The Buffalo Roam (80).

MURRAY, MALIK: Love in a Taxi (80).

MUSE, CLARENCE: The Black Stallion (79).

MUTI, ORNELLA: Flash Gordon (80).

MYERS, BRUCE: The Awakening (80).

NAMATH, JOE: Norwood (69), C.C. and Company (70), Avalanche Express (79).

NAPIER, CHARLES: Melvin and Howard (80).

NAUGHTON, DAVID: Midnight Madness (80).

NEAL, PATRICIA: The Subject Was Roses (68), The Night Digger (71), Happy Mother's Day, Love George (73).

NEDEVA, MADLENA: The Lady Vanishes (79).

NEIL, HILDEGARDE: The Legacy (79).

NELKIN, STACY: Serial (80), Up The Academy (80).

NELLIGAN, KATE: Dracula (79).

NELSON, BARRY: Airport (69), Pete 'n Tillie (72), The Shining (80).

NELSON, CHRISTOPHER S.: Without Warning (80).

NELSON, CRAIG RICHARD: A Small Circle Of Friends (80), My

Bodyguard (80).

NELSON, CRAIG T.: ...And Justice For All (79), Stir Crazy (80).

NELSON, MARK: Friday the 13th (80).

NELSON, WILLIE: The Electric Horseman (79), Honeysuckle Rose (80).

NERO, FRANCO: The Man With Bogart's Face (80).

NEWHART, BOB: First Family (80), Little Miss Marker (80).

NEWMAN, BARRY: The Lawyer (69), Vanishing Point (71), Fear is the Key (72), The Salzburg Connection (72).

NEWMAN, LARAINE: Wholly Moses! (80).

NEWMAN, NANETTE: The Raging Moon (70), The Stepford Wives (74), International Velvet (78).

NEWMAN, PAUL: Harper (66), Cool Hand Luke (67), Hombre (67), Butch Cassidy and the Sundance Kid (69), Winning (69), W.U.S.A. (70), Sometimes a Great Notion (71), Pocket Money (72), The Life and Times of Judge Roy Bean (72), The Mackintosh Man (73), The Sting (73), The Towering Inferno (74), The Drowning Pool (75), Buffalo Bill and the Indians (76), Slapshot (77), Quintet (79), Fort Apache (80), When Time Ran Out (80).

NEWMAN, SUSAN KENDALL: A Wedding (78), I Wanna Hold Your Hand (78).

NEWTON-JOHN, OLIVIA: Xanadu (80).

NICHOLLS, ALLAN: A Perfect Couple (79), Popeye (80).

NICHOLS, NICHELLE: Star Trek (79).

NICHOLSON, JACK: Easy Rider (69), Five Easy Pieces (70), On a Clear Day You Can See Forever (70), Carnal Knowledge (71), The King of Marvin Gardens (72), The Last Detail (73), Chinatown (74), The Passenger (74), One Flew Over the Cuckoo's Nest (75), The Fortune (75), Tommy (75), The Last Tycoon (76), The Missouri Breaks (76), Goin' South (78), The Shining (80).

NIELSEN, LESLIE: Airplane (80), Prom Night (80).

NIMOY, LEONARD: Invasion Of The Bodysnatchers (78), Star Trek-The Motion Picture (79).

NITAI, NIKO: Jesus (79).

NIVEN, DAVID: Escape To Athena (79), Rough Cut (80), The Sea Wolves (80).

NOBLE, TRISHA: The Private Eyes (80).

NOIMAN, RIVKA: Jesus (79).

NOLTE, NICK: Return to Macon County (75), The Deep (77), Who'll Stop the Rain (78), Heart Beat (79), North Dallas Forty (79).

NORMAN, MAIDIE: Movie Movie Baxter's Beauties (78).

NORMAN, ZACK: Sitting Ducks (79).

NORRIS, CHUCK: The Octagon (80).

NORTH, ALAN: The Formula (80).

NORTH, SHEREE: Madigan (68), The Gypsy Moths (69), Lawman (70), The Organization (71), Charley Varrick (72), The Outfit (73),

The Carradines, the Guests, the Quaids, the Keaches.

Breakout (75), The Shootist (76).

NORTHUP, HARRY: Over The Edge (79).

NOVAK, KIM: The Mirror Crack'd (80).

NOVELLO, DON: Gilda Live (80).

NUTTER, TARAH: Without Warning (80).

NYE, CARRIE: The Seduction Of Joe Tynan (79).

O'BRIEN, JANE: Below The Belt (80).

O'CONNELL, WILLIAM: Any Which Way You Can (80).

O'CONNOR, CARROLL: For Love of Ivy (68), The Devil's Brigade (68), Death of a Gunfighter (69), Marlowe (69), Doctors' Wives (70), Kelly's Heroes (70), Law and Disorder (74).

O'CONNOR, GLYNNIS: Ode to Billie Joe (76), California Dreaming (78), Those Lips Those Eyes (80).

O'CONNOR, KEVIN: Brinks (79).

O'CONNOR, TIM: Buck Rogers (79).

O'FARRELL, PETER: Hawk the Slayer (80).

O'HALLORAN, JACK: Superman (78), Superman II (80), The Baltimore Bullet (80).

O'HEANEY, CAITLIN: He Knows You're Alone (80).

O'KEEFE, MICHAEL: The Great Santini (80).

O'MALLEY, J. PAT: Cheaper to Keep Her (80).

O'NEAL, RON: Superfly (72), Superfly TNT (73), The Master Gunfighter (75), Brothers (77), When A Stranger Calls (79), The Final Countdown (80).

O'NEAL, RYAN: The Big Bounce (69), Love Story (70), Wild Rovers (71), Paper Moon (73), The Thief Who Came to Dinner (73), Barry Lyndon (75), Nickelodeon (76), A Bridge Too Far (77), Oliver's Story (78), The Driver (78), The Main Event (79).

O'NEAL, TATUM: Paper Moon (73), Nickelodeon (76), The Bad News Bears (76), International Velvet (78), Circle Of Two (80), Little Darlings (80).

O'NEILL, JENNIFER: Rio Lobo (70), Such Good Friends (71), Summer of '42 (71), Glass Houses (72), The Carey Treatment (72), Lady Ice (73), The Reincarnation of Peter Proud (74), Whiffs (75), Caravans (78), Cloud Dancer (80), Steel (80).

O'SHEA, MILO: It's Not The Size That Counts (79).

O'TOOLE, ANNETTE: Smile (75), One on One (77), King of the Gypsies (78), Foolin' Around (80).

O'TOOLE, PETER: Caligula (79), The Stunt Man (80).

OATES, WARREN: In the Heat of the Night (67), The Split (68), The Wild Bunch (69), There Was a Crooked Man (70), The Hired Hand (71), Two-Lane Blacktop (71), Badlands (73), Dillinger (73), Kid Blue (73), The Thief Who Came to Dinner (73), The White Dawn (73), Tom Sawyer (73), Bring Me the Head of Alfredo Garcia (74), Race with the Devil (75), 92 in the Shade (76), Drum (76), 1941 (79), Brinks (79).

OLIVIER, LAURENCE: The Shoes of the Fisherman (68), Three Sisters (70), Nicholas and Alexandra (71), Lady Caroline Lamb (72), Sleuth (72), Love Among the Ruins (75), Marathon Man (76), The Seven Percent Solution (76), A Bridge Too Far (77), The Betsy (77), The Boys from Brazil (78), A Little Romance (79), Dracula (79).

ONTKEAN, MICHAEL: Willie & Phil (80).

ORBACH, JERRY: The Gang That Couldn't Shoot Straight (71), The Sentinel (79).

ORTON, JOE: The Sweet Creek County War (79).

OTT, PAUL: Lady Grey (80).

OWENSBY, EARL: Living Legend (80).

OZ, FRANK: The Blues Brothers (80), The Empire Strikes Back (80).

PACINO, AL: Me, Natalie (68), The Panic in Needle Park (71), The Godfather (72), Scarecrow (73), Serpico (73), The Godfather, Part II (74), Dog Day Afternoon (75), Bobby Deerfield (77), ...And Justice For All (79), Cruising (80).

PAGE, GERALDINE: You're a Big Boy Now (67), Whatever Happened to Aunt Alice (69), J.W. Coop (71), The Beguiled (71), Pete 'n Tillie (72), The Day of the Locust (75), Nasty Habits (77), Interiors (78).

PAGETT, NICOLA: Oliver's Story (78).

PALANCE, JACK: The Shape Of Things To Come (79), Hawk the Slayer (80), Without Warning (80).

PALILLO, RON: Skatetown Usa (79).

PALIN, MICHAEL: Life Of Brian (79), The Secret Policeman's Ball (79).

PALMER, BETSY: Friday the 13th (80).

PALMER, LELAND: All That Jazz (79).

PANTOLIANO, JOE: The Idolmaker (80).

PAPAS, IRENE: Bloodline (79).

PAPPAS, JIM: Natural Enemies (79).

PARKER, ELEANOR: Sunburn (79).

PARKER, JAMESON: The Bell Jar (79), A Small Circle Of Friends (80).

PARKS, MICHAEL: Breakthrough (79), ffolkes (80).

PARSONS, ESTELLE: Bonnie and Clyde (67), Rachel, Rachel (68), Don't Drink the Water (69), I Never Sang for My Father (69), Watermelon Man (69), I Walk the Line (70), Two People (73), For Pete's Sake (74), Foreplay (75).

PARSONS, NANCY: Motel Hell (80).

PARTON, DOLLY: Nine To Five (80).

PASCO, RICHARD: The Watcher In The Woods (80).

PATAKI, MICHAEL: The Onion Field (79).

PATINKIN, MANDY: Night Of The Juggler (80).

PATTERSON, DICK: Can't Stop The Music (80).

PATTERSON, LORNA: Airplane (80).

PAUL, STEVEN: Falling In Love Again (80).

PAUL, STUART: Falling In Love Again (80).

PAXTON, LESLEY: Pilgrim, Farewell (80).

PEARLMAN, MICHAEL: One Trick Pony (80).

PECHEUR, SIERRA: Below The Belt (80).

PECK, DAVID: Gal Young Un (79).

PECK, GREGORY: The Stalking Moon (68), MacKenna's Gold (69), Marooned (69), The Chairman (69), The Most Dangerous Man in the World (69), I Walk the Line (70), Shootout (71), Billy Two Hats (73), The Omen (76), MacArthur (77), The Boys from Brazil (78), The Sea Wolves (80).

PELUSO, CLAUDIA: Brinks (79).

PENDLETON, AUSTIN: Starting Over (79), The Muppet Movie (79), First Family (80), Simon (80).

PEPPARD, GEORGE: P.J. (68), What's So Bad About Feeling Good (68), Pendulum (69), The Executioner (69), Cannon for Cordoba (70), One More Time (71), The Groundstar Conspiracy (72), Newman's Law (74), Damnation Alley (77), Battle Beyond The Stars (80).

PERETZ, SUSAN: Melvin and Howard (80).

PERKINS, ANTHONY: Psycho (60), The Champagne Murders (68), Pretty Poison (69), Catch-22 (70), W.U.S.A (70), Ten Day's Wonder (71), Play It as It Lays (72), The Life and Times of Judge Roy Bean (72), Lovin' Molly (73), Murder on the Orient Express (74), Mahogany (75), Remember My Name (78), The Black Hole (79), Winter Kills (79), Double Negative (80), ffolkes (80).

PERRINE, VALERIE: Slaughterhouse Five (72), The Last American Hero (73), Lenny (74), W.C. Fields and Me (76), Mr. Billion (77), Superman (78), The Electric Horseman (79), Can't Stop The Music (80), Superman II (80).

PERRY, ROGER: Roller Boogie (79).

PERSKY, LISA JANE: Love in a Taxi (80), The Great Santini (80).

PERSOFF, NEHEMIAH: In Search Of Historic Jesus (80).

PESCI, JOE: Raging Bull (80).

PETERS, BERNADETTE: The Jerk (79).

PETERSEN, CHRIS: The Little Dragons (80).

PETERSEN, PAT: The Little Dragons (80).

PETTET, JOANNA: The Group (66), Robbery (67), Blue (68).

PEYSER, PENNY: The Frisco Kid (79), The In-Laws (79).

PFEIFFER, MICHELLE: Falling In Love Again (80).

PHILLIPS, MACKENZIE: American Graffiti (73), More American Graffiti (79).

PHILLIPS, MICHELLE: Bloodline (79), The Man With Bogart's Face (80).

PHILLIPS, SIAN: Nijinsky (80).

PICCOLI, MICHEL: Atlantic City U S A (80).

PICKENS, SLIM: 1941 (79), Beyond The Poseidon Adventure (79), The Sweet Creek County War (79), Honeysuckle Rose (80), Tom Horn (80).

PICKREN, STACEY: Sunnyside (79).

PICKUP, RONALD: Nijinsky (80).

PIERCE, TIANA: Mother's Day (80).

PISIER, MARIE-FRANCE: The Other Side of Midnight (77), French Postcards (79).

PLACE, MARY KAY: More American Graffiti (79), Starting Over (79), Private Benjamin (80).

PLEASENCE, DONALD: Will Penny (67), You Only Live Twice (67), The Madwoman of Chaillot (69), Outback (70), Soldier Blue (70), THX 1138 (70), The Jerusalem File (71), Mutations (74), The Black Windmill (74), Hearts of the West (75), The Last Tycoon (76), Trial by Combat (76), Telefon (77), The Eagle Has Landed (77), Halloween (78), Sergeant Pepper's Lonely Hearts Club Band (78), Dracula (79).

PLESHETTE, JOHN: Rocky II (79).

PLESHETTE, SUZANNE: The Power (68), If It's Tuesday This Must Be Belgium (69), Suppose They Gave a War and Nobody Came (69), Support Your Local Gunfighter (71), The Shaggy D.A (76), Hot Stuff (79), Oh, God! Book II (80).

PLUMMER, CHRISTOPHER: Hanover Street (79), Murder By Decree (79), Somewhere In Time (80).

POGUE, KENNETH: Lost And Found (79).

POINTER, PRISCILLA: The Onion Field (79), Honeysuckle Rose (80),

The Competition (80).

POITIER, SIDNEY: A Patch of Blue (66), In the Heat of the Night (67), To Sir with Love (67), For Love of Ivy (68), The Lost Man (69), Brother John (70), They Call Me Mister Tibbs (70), Buck and The Preacher (71), The Organization (71), A Warm December (72), Uptown Saturday Night (74), Let's Do It Again (75), The Wilby Conspiracy (75).

POLLARD, MICHAEL J.: Bonnie and Clyde (67), Hannibal Brooks (67), Little Fauss and Big Halsey (70), Dirty Little Billy (72), Sunday in the Country (74), Between the Lines (77), Melvin and Howard (80).

POLLARD, THOMMY: Penitentiary (79).

POMEROY, JULIA: Over The Edge (79).

PORTER, DON: The Candidate (72), Forty Carats (73), White Line Fever (75).

POSTON, TOM: Up The Academy (80).

POWELL, ROBERT: Jane Austen In Manhattan (80).

POWERS, STEPHANIE: Warning Shot (67), Herbie Rides Again (73), Escape to Athena (79).

PRANGE, LAURIE: Pilgrim, Farewell (80).

PRENTISS, ANN: Any Wednesday (66), California Split (74).

PRENTISS, PAULA: Catch-22 (70), Born to Win (71), The Last of the Red Hot Lovers (72), Crazy Joe (74), The Parallax View (74), The Stepford Wives (74), The Black Marble (80).

PRESSMAN, LAWRENCE: Walk Proud (79), Nine To Five (80).

PREU, DANA: Gal Young Un (79).

PRICE, VINCENT: It's Not The Size That Counts (79), Scavenger Hunt (79).

PRIMUS, BARRY: Boxcar Bertha (72), The Gravy Train (74), New York, New York (77), The Rose (79), Heartland (80).

PROPHET, MELISSA: Players (79).

PROWSE, DAVID: The Empire Strikes Back (80).

PRYOR, NICHOLAS: Smile (75), The Fish That Saved Pittsburgh (79).

PRYOR, RICHARD: Lady Sings the Blues (72), Hit! Wattstax (73), Some Call It Loving (73), Uptown Saturday Night (74), The Bingo Long Traveling All-Stars (76), Greased Lightning (77), The Silver Streak (77), Blue Collar (78), California Suite (78), The Wiz (78), The Muppet Movie (79), In God We Trust (80), Stir Crazy (80), Wholly Moses! (80).

PYLE, DENVER: Bonnie and Clyde (67), Five Card Stud (68), Something Big (71), Cahill (73), Escape to Witch Mountain (75), Buffalo Bill and the Indians (76), Welcome to L.A. (77).

QUAID, DENNIS: Breaking Away (79), The Long Riders (80).

QUAID, RANDY: The Last Picture Show (71), What's Up, Doc? (72), Lolly Madonna XXX (73), Paper Moon (73), The Last Detail (73), The Apprenticeship of Duddy Kravitz (74), Breakout (75), Bound for

Susan Saint James, Jessica Lange, Jane Curtin.

Glory (76), The Missouri Breaks (76), Midnight Express (78), Foxes (80), The Long Riders (80).

QUANDT, PAUL: My Bodyguard (80).

QUAYLE, ANTHONY: Murder By Decree (79).

QUIGLEY, LEE: Superman (78).

QUINLAN, KATHLEEN: I Never Promised You A Rose Garden (77), The Promise (79), The Runner Stumbles (79), Sunday Lovers (80).

QUINN, ANTHONY: Caravans (78).

QUINN, PAT: Alice's Restaurant (69), An Unmarried Woman (78).

QUINN, PATRICIA: The Outsider (79).

RADER, JACK: The Onion Field (79).

RADNER, GILDA: Mr. Mikes Mondo Video (79), First Family (80), Gilda Live (80).

RAE, BARBARA: Hide In Plain Sight (80).

RAFFIN, DEBORAH: Touched By Love (80).

RAGNO, JOSEPH: Melvin and Howard (80).

RAILSBACK, STEVE: The Stunt Man (80).

RAINES, CRISTINA: Touched By Love (80).

RAMPLING, CHARLOTTE: The Ski Bum (72), Zardoz (73), The Night Porter (74), Foxtrot (76), Orca (77), Stardust Memories (80).

RAMUS, NICK: Windwalker (80).

RANDALL, TONY: Scavenger Hunt (79), Foolin' Around (80).

RANDOLPH, LILLIAN: The Onion Field (79).

RAY, GENE ANTHONY: Fame (80).

RAYE, MARTHA: The Concorde-Airport'79 (79).

REDD, MARY-ROBIN: The Group (66).

REDEKER, QUINN: The Electric Horseman (79), Coast To Coast (80), Ordinary People (80).

REDFORD, ROBERT: Butch Cassidy and the Sundance Kid (69), Downhill Racer (69), Tell Them Willie Boy Is Here (69), Little Fauss and Big Halsey (70), Jeremiah Johnson (72), The Candidate (72), The Hot Rock (72), The Sting (73), The Way We Were (73), The Great Gatsby (74), The Great Waldo Pepper (75), Three Days of the Condor (75), All the President's Men (76), A Bridge Too Far (77), The Electric Horseman (79), The Thorn Birds (79), Brubaker (80).

REDGRAVE, CORIN: The Charge of the Light Brigade (68), David Copperfield (69), Von Richtofen and Brown (71).

REDGRAVE, LYNN: Everything You Always Wanted to Know About Sex (72), The National Health (73), The Happy Hooker (75), The Big Bus (76), Sunday Lovers (80).

REDGRAVE, VANESSA: Isadora (68), The Seagull (68), Oh What a Lovely War (69), Mary, Queen of Scots (71), The Devils (71), The Trojan Women (71), Murder on the Orient Express (74), Out of Season (75), The Seven Percent Solution (76), Julia (77), Agatha (79), Yanks (79).

REED, JERRY: Hot Stuff (79), Smokey And The Bandit II (80).

REED, LOU: One Trick Pony (80).

REED, PAMELA: Melvin and Howard (80), The Long Riders (80).

REEVE, CHRISTOPHER: Superman (78), Somewhere In Time (80), Superman II (80).

REGINA, PAUL: A Change of Seasons (80).

REID, KATE: Atlantic City U S A (80), Circle Of Two (80), Double Negative (80).

REILLY, DIANE: Ice Castles (78).

REINER, CARL: It's a Mad, Mad, Mad, Mad World (64), The Russians Are Coming, The Russians Are Coming (66), A Guide For The Married Man (67), The Comic (69), Oh, God! (77), The End (78), The Jerk (79).

REINKING, ANN: Movie Movie Dynamite Hands (78), All That Jazz (79).

REMAR, JAMES: On the Yard (78), The Warriors (79), The Long Riders (80), Windwalker (80).

REMICK, LEE: The Days of Wine and Roses (63), Hard Contract (68), No Way to Treat a Lady (68), The Detective (68), A Severed Head (70), Loot (70), Sometimes a Great Notion (71), A Delicate Balance (73), Hennessy (75), Hustling (75), The Omen (76), Telefon (77), The Competition (80), Tribute (80).

REMSEN, BERT: Brewster McCloud (70), California Split (74), Thieves Like Us (74), Nashville (75), Buffalo Bill and the Indians (76), A Wedding (78), Uncle Joe Shannon (78), Fast Break (79), Borderline (80), Carny (80), Joni (80), Second-Hand Hearts (80).

RENO, KELLY: The Black Stallion (79).

REY, ALEJANDRO: Cuba (79), Sunburn (79), The Ninth Configuration (80).

REY, FERNANDO: Villa Rides (68), The French Connection (71), The Light at the End of the World (71), French Connection II (75).

REYNOLDS, BURT: Impasse (68), Shark (68), 100 Rifles (69), Sam Whiskey (69), Skullduggery (69), Deliverance (72), Everything You Always Wanted to Know About Sex (72), Fuzz (72), Shamus (72), The Man Who Loved Cat Dancing (73), White Lightning (73), The Longest Yard (74), At Long Last Love (75), Hustle (75), Lucky Lady (75), W.W. And the Dixie Dancekings (75), Nickelodeon (76), Semi-Tough (77), Smokey and the Bandit (77), Hooper (78), Rough Cut (78), The End (78), Starting Over (79), Smokey And The Bandit II (80).

RICHARDS, BEAH: Guess Who's Coming to Dinner? (67), Hurry Sundown (67), In the Heat of the Night (67), Mahogany (75).

RICHARDS, KYLE: The Watcher In The Woods (80).

RICHTER, DEBI: Swap Meet (79).

RIEGERT, PETER: Americathon (79), Head Over Heels (79).

RIGG, DIANA: On Her Majesty's Secret Servic (69), Julius Caesar (70), The Hospital (71), Theatre of Blood (73), A Little Night Music (77).

RIKER, ROBIN: Alligator (80).

RIMMER, SHANE: Hanover Street (79).

RITTER, JOHN: Breakfast In Bed, The Barefoot Executive, The Other, Nickelodeon (76), Americathon (79), Hero At Large (80), Wholly Moses! (80), They All Laughed (81).

RIXON, CHERYL: Swap Meet (79).

ROARKE, ADAM: The Stunt Man (80).

ROBARDS, JASON: A Thousand Clowns (65), Isadora (68), The Night They Raided Minsky's (68), Once Upon a Time in the West (69), Julius Caesar (70), The Ballad of Cable Hogue (70), Tora! Tora! Tora! (70), Johnny Got His Gun (71), Murders in The Rue Morgue (71), Play It as It Lays (72), The War Between Men and Women (72), Pat Garrett and Billy The Kid (73), All The President's Men (76), Julia (77), Comes a Horseman (78), Hurricane (79), Melvin and Howard (80), Raise The Titanic (80).

ROBERTS, ERIC: King Of The Gypsies (78).

ROBERTS, PERNELL: The Magic Of Lassie (78).

ROBERTS, RACHEL: When A Stranger Calls (79), Yanks (79).

ROBERTS, TONY: The Star Spangled Girl (71), Play It Again, Sam (72), Annie Hall (77), Just Tell Me What You Want (80), Stardust Memories (80).

ROBERTSON, CLIFF: Charly (68), Too Late the Hero (69), The Great Northfield Minnesota Raid (71), J.W. Coop (72), Ace Eli and Rodger of the Skies (73), Man on a Swing (73), Out of Season (75), Three

Jody Foster, Gary Busey.   John Savage, Diane Hull.

Days of the Condor (75), Midway (76), Obsession (76), Shoot (76).
ROBERTSON, ROBBIE: Carny (80).
ROBINSON, AMY: Mean Streets (73).
ROBINSON, TOM: The Secret Policeman's Ball (79).
ROCCO, ALEX: Herbie Goes Bananas (80), The Stunt Man (80).
ROGERS, WAYNE: Once In Paris (78).
ROLFING, TOM: He Knows You're Alone (80).
ROMANO, ANDY: Over The Edge (79).
ROMANUS, RICHARD: Sitting Ducks (79).
ROMANUS, ROBERT: Foxes (80).
RONET, MAURICE: Bloodline (79).
ROONEY, MICKEY: The Magic Of Lassie (78), The Black Stallion (79).
ROONEY, MICKEY, Jr.: Honeysuckle Rose (80).
ROSENBERG, ALAN: The Wanderers (79), Happy Birthday, Gemini
   (80).
ROSS, DIANA: Lady Sings the Blues (72), Mahogany (75), The Wiz (78).
ROSS, KATHARINE: The Graduate (67), Butch Cassidy and the Sundance
   Kid (69), Hellfighters (69), Tell Them Willie Boy Is Here (69), Fools
   (70), The Betsy (71), The Swarm (71), Get to Know Your Rabbit
   (72), They Only Kill Their Masters (72), The Stepford Wives (74),
   Voyage of the Damned (76), The Legacy (79), The Final Countdown
   (80).
ROTHMAN, JOHN: Stardust Memories (80).
ROUNDTREE, RICHARD: Shaft (71), Embassy (72), Shaft's Big Score
   (72), Shaft in Africa (73), Earthquake (74), Man Friday (75), Escape
   to Athena (79).
ROWE, MISTY: The Man With Bogart's Face (80).
ROWLANDS, GENA: Tony Rome (67), Faces (68), The Happy Ending
   (69), Minnie and Moskowitz (71), A Woman Under the Influence
   (74), Two-Minute Warning (76), Opening Night (77), Brinks (79),
   Gloria (80).
RUBIN, ANDREW: Sunnyside (79).
RUBINSTEIN, JOHN: In Search Of Historic Jesus (80).

RULE, JANICE: The Swimmer (68), Kid Blue (73), Three Women (77).

RUNACRE, JENNY: The Lady Vanishes (79).

RUSH, BARBARA: Can't Stop The Music (80).

RUSSELL, KURT: Used Cars (80).

RUSSELL, THERESA: Bad Timing (80).

RYAN, MADGE: The Lady Vanishes (79).

RYAN, NATASHA: The Amityville Horror (79), The Day Time Ended (80).

RYERSON, ANN: A Perfect Couple (79).

SACCHI, ROBERT: The Man With Bogart's Face (80).

SACKS, MICHAEL: Hanover Street (79), The Amityville Horror (79).

SAINT, EVA MARIE: On the Waterfront (54), North by Northwest (56), Grand Prix (66), The Russians Are Coming, The Russians Are Coming (66), The Stalking Moon (68), A Talent for Loving (69), Loving (70), Cancel My Reservation (72).

SAINT JAMES, SUSAN: How To Beat The High Cost of Living (80).

SALDANA, THERESA: Defiance (80).

SALMI, ALBERT: The Sweet Creek County War (79), Brubaker (80), Cloud Dancer (80), Steel (80).

SALT, JENNIFER: Brewster McCloud (70), The Revolutionary (70), Sisters (73), It's My Turn (80).

SALVATORI, RENATO: Luna (79).

SANCHEZ, MARCELINO: The Warriors (79).

SAND, PAUL: The Main Event (79), Can't Stop The Music (80), Wholly Moses! (80).

SANTACROCE, MARY NELL: Wise Blood (79), The Private Eyes (80).

SARANDON, CHRIS: Dog Day Afternoon (75), Lipstick (76), The Sentinel (77), Cuba (79).

SARANDON, SUSAN: Joe (70), Lovin' Molly (73), The Front Page (74), The Great Waldo Pepper (75), Dragonfly (76), The Other Side of Midnight (77), King of the Gypsies (78), Pretty Baby (78), Something Short Of Paradise (79), Atlantic City U S A (80), Loving Couples (80).

SARCIONE, RICHARD: Hurricane (79).

SARGENT, DICK: Hardcore (79).

SAROYAN, LUCY: Hopscotch (80).

SARRAZIN, MICHAEL: Gunfight in Abilene (67), Journey to Shilo (67), The Flim Flam Man (67), The Sweet Ride (68), A Man Called Gannon (69), Eye of the Cat (69), They Shoot Horses, Don't They? (69), In Search of Gregory (70), The Pursuit of Happiness (70), Believe in Me (71), Sometimes a Great Notion (71), The Groundstar Conspiracy (72), Harry in Your Pocket (73), For Pete's Sake (74), The Reincarnation of Peter Proud (74), The Gumball Rally (76), Caravans (78), Double Negative (80).

SARTAIN, GAILARD: Roadie (80), The Hollywood Knights (80).

SAVAGE, JOHN: The Deerhunter (78), Hair (79), The Onion Field (79).

SAVALAS, TELLY: Beyond The Poseidon Adventure (79), Escape To Athena (79), The Muppet Movie (79).

SAVOY, TERESA ANN: Caligula (79).

SAXON, JOHN: The Bees (78), The Electric Horseman (79).

SCARDINO, DON: Cruising (80), He Knows You're Alone (80).

SCHALLERT, WILLIAM: Hangar 18 (80).

SCHEIDER, ROY: Puzzle of a Downfall Child (70), Klute (71), The French Connection (71), The Seven Ups (73), Jaws (75), Marathon Man (76), Sorcerer (77), Jaws 2 (78), All That Jazz (79), Last Embrace (79).

SCHELL, CATHERINE: The Prisoner Of Zenda (79).

SCHELL, MARIA: Superman (78).

SCHELL, MAXIMILIAN: The Castle (68), The Passenger (73), The Odessa File (74), The Man in the Glass Booth (75), A Bridge Too Far (77), Cross of Iron (77), Julia (77), Players (78), Avalanche Express (79), The Black Hole (79).

SCHELL, RONNIE: How To Beat The High Cost of Living (80).

SCHIAVELLI, VINCENT: Butch And Sundance (79).

SCHNEIDER, ROMY: Bloodline (79).

SCHREIBER, AVERY: Scavenger Hunt (79), The Concorde-Airport '79 (79), Galaxina (80), Silent Scream (80).

SCHRODER, RICKY: The Champ (79), The Earthling (80).

SCHUCK, JOHN: Brewster McCloud (70), MASH (70), McCabe and Mrs. Miller (71), Hammersmith Is Out (72), Blade (73), Thieves Like Us (74), Butch And Sundance (79), Just You And Me, Kid (79).

SCHWARZENEGGER, ARNOLD: Stay Hungry (76), Pumping Iron (77), The Villain (79).

SCOTT, DONOVAN: Popeye (80).

SCOTT, GEORGE C.: The Flim Flam Man (67), Petulia (68), Patton (69), The Hospital (71), The Last Run (71), They Might Be Giants (71), Rage (72), The New Centurions (72), Oklahoma Crude (73), The Day of the Dolphin (73), The Bank Shot (74), The Savage Is Loose (74), The Hindenburg (75), Islands in the Stream (77), The Prince and the Pauper (77), Movie Movie Baxter's Beauties (78), Movie Movie Dynamite Hands (78), Hardcore (79), The Changeling (80), The Formula (80).

SCOTT, TIMOTHY: The Electric Horseman (79).

SEAGULL, BARBARA HERSHEY: With Six You Get Eggroll (68), Last Summer (69), The Liberation of L.B. Jones (70), The Baby Maker (71), The Pursuit of Happiness (71), Boxcar Bertha (72), The Crazy World of Julius Vrooder (74), Diamonds (75), You And Me (75), The Last Hard Men (76), The Stunt Man (80).

SEALES, FRANKLYN: The Onion Field (79).

SEBERG, JEAN: Saint Joan (57), Breathless (60), The Road to Corinth

(68), Airport (69), Paint Your Wagon (69), Pendulum (69), Macho Callahan (71).

SEGAL, GEORGE: King Rat (65), The Quiller Memorandum (66), Who's Afraid of Virginia Woolf (66), Bye Bye Braverman (68), No Way to Treat a Lady (68), The Bridge at Remegen (69), The Girl Who Couldn't Say No (69), The Southern Star (69), Loving (70), The Owl and the Pussycat (70), Born to Win (71), The Hot Rock (72), A Touch of Class (73), Blume in Love (73), California Split (74), The Terminal Man (74), Russian Roulette (75), The Black Bird (75), Fun with Dick and Jane (76), The Duchess and the Dirtwater Fox (76), Rollercoaster (77), Who Is Killing the Great Chef's of Europe (78), Lost And Found (79), The Last Married Couple In America (80).

SELBY, DAVID: Up the Sandbox (72), The Super Cops (74), Rich Kids (79), Raise The Titanic (80).

SELL, JANIE: Lost And Found (79).

SELLERS, PETER: Being There (79), The Prisoner Of Zenda (79), The Fiendish Plot Of Dr. Fu Manchu (80).

SERNA, PEPE: Walk Proud (79).

SEYMOUR, JANE: Oh Heavenly Dog (80), Somewhere In Time (80).

SHAFFER, PAUL: Gilda Live (80).

SHAMATA, CHARLES: Running (79).

SHARIF, OMAR: Doctor Zhivago (65), Funny Girl (68), MacKenna's Gold (69), The Horsemen (70), The Last Valley (70), Juggernaut (74), Funny Lady (75), Ashanti (79), Bloodline (79), Oh Heavenly Dog (80), The Baltimore Bullet (80).

SHARKEY, RAY: Hot Tomorrows, Who'll Stop The Rain (78), Heart Beat (79), The Idolmaker (80), Willie & Phil (80).

SHARRETT, MICHAEL: The Magic Of Lassie (78).

SHATNER, WILLIAM: Star Trek (79), The Kidnapping Of The President (80).

SHAVER, HELEN: The Amityville Horror (79).

SHAW, ROBERT: Reflection of Fear (71), Young Winston (72), The Hireling (73), The Sting (73), The Taking of Pelham 1-2-3 (74), Diamonds (75), Jaws (75), End of the Game (76), Robin and Marian (76), Swashbuckler (76), Black Sunday (77), The Deep (77), Force 10 from Navarone (78), Avalanche Express (79).

SHAW, STAN: Rocky (76), The Bingo Long Traveling All-Stars (76), The Boys in Company C (78), The Great Santini (80).

SHEARER, HARRY: One Trick Pony (80).

SHEEN, MARTIN: The Incident (67), The Subject Was Roses (68), Catch-22 (70), Rage (72), Badlands (73), The Legend of Earl Durand (75), The Cassandra Crossing (77), The Little Girl Who Lives Down Lane (77), Apocalypse Now (79), Eagle's Wing (79), The Final Countdown (80).

SHEINER, DAVID: The Big Brawl (80).

SHEPARD, SAM: Resurrection (80).

SHEPHERD, CYBILL: The Last Picture Show (71), The Heartbreak Kid (72), Daisy Miller (74), At Long Last Love (75), Special Delivery (76), Taxi Driver (76), Silver Bears (78), The Lady Vanishes (79).

SHEPHERD, ELIZABETH: Double Negative (80).

SHEYBAL, VALDEK: The Lady Vanishes (79).

SHIELDS, BROOKE: King of the Gypsies (78), Pretty Baby (78), Wanda Nevada (78), Just You And Me, Kid (79), Tilt (79), Two of a Kind (79), Blue Lagoon (80).

SHILOAH, YOSSEF: Jesus (79).

SHIMKUS, JOHANNA: Boom (68), The Lost Man (69), The Virgin and the Gypsy (70), The Marriage of a Young Stockbroker (71), Time for Loving (71).

SHIMODA, YUKI: The Octagon (80).

SHIRE, TALIA: Gas-s-s (70), The Christian Licorice Store (70), The Dunwich Horror (70), The Godfather (72), The Outside Man (73), The Godfather, Part II (74), Rocky (76), Old Boyfriends (79), Prophecy (79), Rocky II (79), Windows (80).

SHOR, DANIEL: Wise Blood (79).

SIERRA, GREGORY: The Prisoner Of Zenda (79).

SIKKING, JAMES B.: Ordinary People (80).

SILVA, HENRY: Buck Rogers (79), Alligator (80).

SILVA, TRINIDAD: Walk Proud (79).

SILVER, JOE: Boardwalk (79).

SILVERS, PHIL: There Goes the Bride (80).

SIMON, PAUL: One Trick Pony (80).

SIMPSON, O.J.: The Klansman (74), The Towering Inferno (74), The Cassandra Crossing (77), Capricorn One (78), Firepower (79).

SINATRA, FRANK: First Deadly Sin (80).

SINCLAIR, MADGE: Uncle Joe Shannon (78).

SKALA, LILIA: Heartland (80).

SKERRIT, TOM: MASH (70), Wild Rovers (71), Fuzz (72), Thieves Like Us (74), The Turning Point (77), Up in Smoke (78), Alien (79), Ice Castles (79).

SLOYAN, JAMES: Xanadu (80).

SMALL, MARYA: Fade to Black (80).

SMITH, CHARLES MARTIN: More American Graffiti (79), Herbie Goes Bananas (80).

SMITH, J.: Gal Young Un (79).

SMITH, LANE: Honeysuckle Rose (80).

SMITH, LOIS: Foxes (80), Resurrection (80).

SMITH, MADOLYN: Urban Cowboy (80).

SMITH, MAGGIE: California Suite (78).

SMITH, PAUL LAWRENCE: The In-Laws (79), Popeye (80).

SMITH, SAMMY: The In-Laws (79).

Cindy Williams, Frederic Forrest.   Talia Shire, Richard Jordan.

SMITH, WILLIAM: Seven (79), Any Which Way You Can (80).

SMOLINSKI, AARON: Superman (78).

SMOTHERS, TOM: Serial (80), There Goes the Bride (80).

SNODGRESS, CARRIE: Diary of a Mad Housewife (70), Rabbit Run (70), The Fury (78).

SOKOL, MARILYN: Foul Play (78), Something Short Of Paradise (79), Can't Stop The Music (80), The Last Married Couple In America (80).

SOMACK, JACK: The Frisco Kid (79).

SOMERS, SUZANNE: American Graffiti (73), Nothing Personal (80).

SOMMER, ELKE: It's Not The Size That Counts (79), The Double Mcguffin (79), The Prisoner Of Zenda (79).

SOMMER, JOSEF: Oliver's Story (78).

SOMMERFIELD, DIANE: Love in a Taxi (80).

SORVINO, PAUL: A Touch of Class (73), The Day of the Dolphin (73), The Gambler (75), I Will, I Will...For Now (76), Bloodbrothers (78), Slow Dancing in the Big City (78), Brinks (79), Lost And Found (79), Cruising (80).

SOTHERN, ANN: The Little Dragons (80).

SPACEK, SISSY: Prime Cut (72), Badlands (73), Carrie (76), Three Women (77), Welcome to L.A. (77), Heart Beat (79), Coal Miner's Daughter (80).

SPAETH, MERRI: The World of Henry Orient (64).

SPANO, VINCENT: Over The Edge (79).

SPARV, CAMILLA: Dead Heat on a Merry-Go-Round (66), Murderers' Row (66), The Trouble with Angels (66), Department K (67), The High Commissioner (68), Downhill Racer (69), MacKenna's Gold (69), The Italian Job (69), The Greek Tycoon (78).

SPEARS, HAZEL: Penitentiary (79).

SPECTOR, DAN: Swap Meet (79).

SPIELBERG, DAVID: Real Life (79).

SPIELBERG, STEVEN: The Blues Brothers (80).

SPINELL, JOE: Rocky II (79), Cruising (80), First Deadly Sin (80), The Little Dragons (80), The Ninth Configuration (80).

SPRADLIN, G.D.: North Dallas Forty (79), The Formula (80).

SPRINGER, GARY: Hometown USA (79), A Small Circle Of Friends (80).

ST. JACQUES, RAYMOND: If He Hollers Let Him Go (68), Madigan (68), The Green Berets (68), Uptight (68), Change of Mind (70), Cotton Comes to Harlem (70), Lost in the Stars (73), The Book of Numbers (73).

STACK, ROBERT: 1941 (79), Airplane (80).

STALLONE, SYLVESTER: Bananas (71), Capone (73), The Lords of Flatbush (73), Death Race 2000 (75), The Prisoner of Second Avenue (75), Rocky (76), F.I.S.T. (78), Paradise Alley (78), Rocky II (79).

STAMP, TERENCE: Superman (78), Superman II (80).

STANDER, LIONEL: 1941 (79).

STANDING, JOHN: The Legacy (79), The Sea Wolves (80).

STANTON, HARRY DEAN: Farewell My Lovely (75), Alien (79), The Rose (79), Wise Blood (79), Private Benjamin (80), The Black Marble (80).

STAPLETON, MAUREEN: Airport (69), Plaza Suite (71), Interiors (78), Lost And Found (79).

STEELE, BARBARA: Piranha (78), Silent Scream (80).

STEELSMITH, MARY: H.O.T.S. (79).

STEENBURGEN, MARY: Goin' South (78), Time After Time (79), Melvin and Howard (80).

STEIGER, ROD: In the Heat of the Night (67), No Way to Treat a Lady (68), 3 Into 2 Won't Go (69), The Illustrated Man (69), Waterloo (70), Happy Birthday Wanda June (71), Lolly Madonna XXX (73), F.I.S.T. (78), Breakthrough (79), The Amityville Horror (79), The Lucky Star (80).

STEINBERG, DAVID: Something Short Of Paradise (79).

STEINER, JOHN: Caligula (79).

STERN, ADAM: The Competition (80).

STERN, DANIEL: Breaking Away (79), It's My Turn (80), Stardust Memories (80).

STERNHAGEN, FRANCES: Starting Over (79).

STEVENS, CASEY: Prom Night (80).

STEVENSON, BO: North Dallas Forty (79).

STEWART, ALEXANDRA: Final Assignment (80), Phobia (80).

STEWART, JAMES: Bandolero (68), The Cheyenne Social Club (70), Fool's Parade (71), The Shootist (76), Airport 77 (77), The Big Sleep (78), The Magic Of Lassie (78).

STILLER, JERRY: Those Lips Those Eyes (80).

STILWELL, DIANE: Rich Kids (79).

STIMSON, SARA: Little Miss Marker (80).

STOLER, SHIRLEY: Second-Hand Hearts (80).

STONE, PHILIP: The Shining (80).

STORCH, LARRY: Without Warning (80).

STRAIGHT, BEATRICE: Network (76), Bloodline (79), The Promise (79), The Formula (80).

STRASBERG, LEE: The Godfather, Part II (74), The Cassandra Crossing (77), ...And Justice For All (79), Boardwalk (79), Going In Style (79).

STRATTEN, DOROTHY R.: Galaxina (80).

STRAUSS, PETER: Soldier Blue (71), The Last Tycoon (76).

STREEP, MERYL: Julia (77), The Deerhunter (78), Kramer vs Kramer (79), Manhattan (79), The Seduction Of Joe Tynan (79).

STREISAND, BARBRA: Funny Girl (68), Hello Dolly (69), On a Clear Day You Can See Forever (70), The Owl and the Pussycat (70), Up the Sandbox (72), What's Up, Doc? (72), The Way We Were (73), For Pete's Sake (74), Funny Lady (75), A Star is Born (76), The Main Event (79).

STRICKLAND, GAIL: Norma Rae (79).

STRINGFELLOW, JENNIE: Gal Young Un (79).

STRODE, WOODY: The Man Who Shot Liberty Valance (62), Shalako (68), Che! (69), Once Upon a Time in the West (69), The Gatling Gun (72), The Revengers (72), Winterhawk (76).

STROUD, DON: The Amityville Horror (79).

STRUTHERS, SALLY: The Getaway (72).

STRYKER, AMY: The Long Riders (80).

STUART, MAXINE: Coast To Coast (80).

STUCKER, STEPHEN: Airplane (80).

SUAREZ, MIGUELANGEL: Stir Crazy (80).

SUDROW, IRVING: Divine Madness (80).

SUES, ALAN: Oh Heavenly Dog (80).

SULLIVAN, BRAD: Walk Proud (79).

SUTHERLAND, DONALD: Interlude (68), Joanna (68), Oedipus The King (68), The Split (68), Start the Revolution Without Me (69), Act of the Heart (70), Alex in Wonderland (70), Kelly's Heroes (70), MASH (70), Johnny Got His Gun (71), Klute (71), Little Murders (71), Steelyard Blues (72), Alien Thunder (73), Don't Look Now (73), Lady Ice (73), SPYS (74), The Day of the Locust (75), Casanova (76), 1900 (77), The Eagle Has Landed (77), Invasion Of The Bodysnatchers (78), National Lampoon's Animal House (78), A Man, A Woman, and a Bank (79), Murder By Decree (79), The Great Train Robbery (79), Nothing Personal (80), Ordinary People (80).

SUZMAN, JANET: Nijinsky (80).

SVENSON, BO: Part Two-Walking Tall (75), The Great Waldo Pepper (75), Breaking Point (76), Special Delivery (76).

Tom Berenger, Helen Shaver.

SWANN, GABRIEL: Why Would I Lie? (80).

SWEET, DOLPH: The Wanderers (79).

SWIT, LORETTA: Stand Up and Be Counted (71), Freebie and The Bean (74), Race with the Devil (75).

SYMS, SYLVIA: There Goes the Bride (80).

TAGGART, RITA: Die Laughing (80).

TAKEI, GEORGE: Star Trek (79).

TALBOT, NITA: The Sweet Creek County War (79), Serial (80).

TALBOTT, MICHAEL: Foolin' Around (80).

TAMBOR, JEFFREY: ...And Justice For All (79).

TARI, LE: The Onion Field (79).

TAYLOR, ELIZABETH: Who's Afraid of Virginia Woolf (66), Reflections in a Golden Eye (67), Boom (68), Secret Ceremony (68), The Only Game in Town (69), Under Milkwood (71), Zee and Co. (71), Hammersmith Is Out (72), Ash Wednesday (73), Night Watch (73), The Blue Bird (75), The Driver's Seat (75), A Little Night Music (77), The Mirror Crack'd (80).

TAYLOR, RENEE: The Producers (67), Made for Each Other (71), The Last of the Red Hot Lovers (73).

TAYLOR-YOUNG, LEIGH: I Love You, Alice B. Toklas (68), The Adventurers (69), The Big Bounce (69), The Buttercup Chain (70), The Horsemen (70), The Gang That Couldn't Shoot Straight (71), Soylent Green (72), Can't Stop The Music (80).

TEEFY, MAUREEN: Fame (80).

TERRY, JOHN: Hawk the Slayer (80), There Goes the Bride (80).

TESSLER, ROBERT: Steel (80).

THIBEAU, JACK: Escape From Alcatraz (79).

THOMAS, RICHARD: Last Summer (69), Winning (69), Cactus in the Snow (70), Red Sky at Morning (70), The Todd Killings (70), You Can't Have Everything (70), You'll Like My Mother (72), September 30, 1955 (78), Battle Beyond The Stars (80).

THOMERSON, TIM: Fade to Black (80).

THOMPSON, TIGER: Over The Edge (79).

THORNTON-SHERWOOD, MADELEINE: Resurrection (80), The Changeling (80).

TILLIS, MEL: Smokey And The Bandit II (80).

TODD, ANN: The Human Factor (79).

TOLAN, MICHAEL: All That Jazz (79).

TOMASZEWSKI, HENRY: Billy In The Lowlands (79).

TOMLIN, LILY: Nashville (75), The Late Show (77), Moment By Moment (78), Nine To Five (80).

TOMLINSON, DAVID: The Fiendish Plot Of Dr. Fu Manchu (80).

TOMPKINS, ANGEL: The Bees (78).

TOPOL: Flash Gordon (80).

TORGOV, SARAH: Meatballs (79).

TORN, RIP: You're a Big Boy Now (67), The Rain People (69), Tropic of Cancer (69), Payday (72), Slaughter (72), Crazy Joe (74), Birch Interval (76), The Man Who Fell to Earth (76), Nasty Habits (77), Coma (78), The Seduction Of Joe Tynan (79), First Family (80), Heartland (80), One Trick Pony (80).

TOWNSEND, JILL: The Awakening (80).

TOWNSEND, PATRICE: Sitting Ducks (79).

TOWNSHEND, PETE: The Secret Policeman's Ball (79).

TRAVOLTA, JOEY: Sunnyside (79).

TRAVOLTA, JOHN: Carrie (76), Saturday Night Fever (77), Grease (78), Moment By Moment (80), Urban Cowboy (80).

TRUSLOW, SARA: Just Tell Me What You Want (80).

TUCCI, MICHAEL: Sunnyside (79).

TURKEL, ANN: 99 44/100 Percent Dead (74), The Cassandra Crossing (77), Humanoids From The Deep (80).

TURKEL, JOE: The Shining (80).

TWIGGY: The Boyfriend (71), "W" (74), There Goes the Bride (80).

TYLER, BRIAN: The Warriors (79).

TYRELL, SUSAN: Shootout (71), The Steagle (71), Fat City (72), Catch My Soul (74), Andy Warhol's Bad (77), I Never Promised You a Rose Garden (77), Islands in the Stream (77), September 30, 1955 (78).

TYSON, CICELY: A Man Called Adam (66), The Comedians (67), The Heart is a Lonely Hunter (68), Sounder (72), The Autobiography of Ms. Jane Pitman (74), The Blue Bird (76), Roots (77), The Concorde-Airport'79 (79).

TYZACK, MARGARET: The Legacy (79).

ULLMANN, LIV: The Night Visitor (70), Pope Joan (72), The Emigrants

Danny Aiello, Jill Eikenberry,
James Caan.

Annette O'Toole.

(72), Forty Carats (73), Lost Horizon (73), The New Land (73), The Abdication (74), Zandy's Bride (74), A Bridge Too Far (77).

VACCARO, BRENDA: Midnight Cowboy (67), Where It's At (69), I Love My Wife (70), Summertree (71), Honor Thy Father (73), Once is Not Enough (75), Airport 77 (77), House by the Lake (77), Capricorn One (78), First Deadly Sin (80).

VALENTINE, KAREN: The North Avenue Irregulars (79).

VALENTY, LILI: Tell Me a Riddle (80).

VAN CLEEF, LEE: The Good, the Bad and the Ugly (67), Sabata (69), Barquero (70), El Condor (70), Bad Man's River (71), Captain Apache (71), The Magnificent Seven Ride (72), Take a Hard Ride (75), The Octagon (80).

VAN CLIEF, RON: Fist of Fear Touch of Death (80).

VAN DEVERE, TRISH: The Last Run (71), One Is a Lonely Number (72), Day of the Dolphin (73), Harry in Your Pocket (73), The Savage Is Loose (74), Movie Movie Baxter's Beauties (78), Movie Movie Dynamite Hands (78), The Changeling (80), The Hearse (80).

VAN DREELEN, JOHN: The Formula (80).

VAN DYKE, DICK: Bye Bye Birdie (63), Mary Poppins (64), Divorce American Style (67), Fitzwilly (67), Never a Dull Moment (67), Chitty Chitty Bang Bang (68), Some Kind of Nut (69), The Comic (69), Cold Turkey (70), The Runner Stumbles (79).

VAN FLEET, JO: Cool Hand Luke (67), I Love You, Alice B. Toklas (68), The Gang That Couldn't Shoot Straight (71), The Tenant (76).

VAN PALLANDT, NINA: American Gigolo (80), Cloud Dancer (80).

VAN PATTEN, JIMMY: Roller Boogie (79).

VAN VALKENBURGH, DEBORAH: The Warriors (79).

VAN ZANDT, BILLY: Star Trek (79).

VANDIS, TITOS: A Perfect Couple (79).

VANS, GENE: The Magic Of Lassie (78).

VARGAS, ANTONIO: Up The Academy (80).

VARSI, DIANE: Wild in the Streets (68), Killers Three (69), Bloody

Mama (70), Johnny Got His Gun (71), I Never Promised You a Rose Garden (77).

VAUGHN, ROBERT: The Magnificent Seven (60), The Venetian Affair (67), Bullitt (68), The Helicopter Spies (68), The Bridge at Remegen (69), The Mind of Mr. Soames (69), Julius Caesar (70), The Statue (70), The Towering Inferno (70), Brass Target (78), Battle Beyond The Stars (80), Hangar 18 (80).

VELA, ROSEANNE: Heaven's Gate (80).

VENNERA, CHICK: Yanks (79).

VENTURE, RICHARD: The Onion Field (79), The Hunter (80).

VEREEN, BEN: All That Jazz (79).

VERNON, JOHN: Topaz (69), The Outlaw Josey Wales (76), National Lampoon's Animal House (78), Herbie Goes Bananas (80).

VERNON, RICHARD: The Human Factor (79).

VICIOUS, SID: Mr. Mikes Mondo Video (79).

VICTOR, JAMES: Boulevard Nights (79).

VIHARO, ROBERT: Happy Birthday, Gemini (80), Hide In Plain Sight (80).

VINCENT, FRANK: Raging Bull (80).

VINCENT, JAN MICHAEL: The Undefeated (68), The Mechanic (72), The World's Greatest Athlete (73), Buster and Billie (74), Bite the Bullet (75), White Line Fever (75), Baby Blue Marine (76), Damnation Alley (77), Big Wednesday (78), Hooper (78), Defiance (80).

VOIGHT, JON: The Hour of the Gun (67), Fearless Frank (68), Midnight Cowboy (69), Out of It (69), Catch-22 (70), The Revolutionary (70), Deliverance (72), The All-American Boy (73), Conrack (74), The Odessa File (74), End of the Game (76), Coming Home (78), The Champ (79).

VON LEER, HUNTER: Steel (80).

VON SYDOW, MAX: The Greatest Story Ever Told (65), Hawaii (66), The Quiller Memorandum (66), The Kremlin Letter (70), The Emigrants (72), The Exorcist (73), Foxtrot (75), The New Land (75), Three Days of the Condor (75), Voyage of the Damned (76), Exorcist II-The Heretic (77), March or Die (77), Brass Target (78), Hurricane (79), Flash Gordon (80).

VOSKOVEC, GEORGE: Somewhere In Time (80).

WAGNER, LINDSAY: The Paper Chase (73), Two People (73).

WAGNER, ROBERT: Harper (66), Don't Just Stand There (68), Winning (69), The Towering Inferno (74), Midway (76), The Concorde-Airport '79 (79).

WAHL, KEN: The Wanderers (79).

WAITE, RALPH: On The Nickel (80).

WAITES, THOMAS: On the Yard (78), ...And Justice For All (79), The Warriors (79).

WALKEN, CHRISTOPHER: The Anderson Tapes (71), Annie Hall (77), Roseland (77), The Sentinel (77), The Deerhunter (78), Last Embrace (79), Heaven's Gate (80).

WALKER, JIMMIE: The Concorde-Airport'79 (79).

WALKER, KATHRYN: Rich Kids (79).

WALKER, SCOTT: The Muppet Movie (79).

WALKER, TIPPI: The World of Henry Orient (64).

WALL, MAX: Hanover Street (79).

WALLACE, DEE: 10 (79).

WALLACH, ELI: Act One (63), The Good, the Bad and the Ugly (67), The Tiger Makes Out (67), A Lovely Way to Die (68), How to Save a Marriage (68), MacKenna's Gold (69), The Brain (69), The Angel Levine (70), The People Next Door (70), Romance of a Horse Thief (71), Cinderella Liberty (74), Crazy Joe (74), Nasty Habits (77), The Deep (77), The Domino Principle (77), The Sentinel (77), Girl Friends (78), Movie Movie Baxter's Beauties (78), Movie Movie Dynamite Hands (78), Circle Of Iron (79), Winter Kills (79), The Hunter (80).

WALSH, M. EMMET: The Fish That Saved Pittsburgh (79), The Jerk (79), Brubaker (80), Ordinary People (80), Raise The Titanic (80).

WALSH, RICHARD: Brubaker (80).

WALSTON, RAY: Popeye (80).

WALTER, JESSICA: Lilith (64), Grand Prix (66), The Group (66), Bye Bye Braverman (68), Number One (69), Play Misty for Me (71).

WANAMAKER, SAM: Private Benjamin (80), The Competition (80).

WARD, FRED: Escape From Alcatraz (79).

WARD, KELLY: The Big Red One (80).

WARD, RICHARD: The Jerk (79).

WARDEN, JACK: Welcome to the Club (70), Summertree (71), Billy Two Hats (73), The Man Who Loved Cat Dancing (73), The Apprenticeship of Duddy Kravitz (74), Shampoo (75), All the President's Men (76), The White Buffalo (77), Death on the Nile (78), Heaven Can Wait (78), ...And Justice For All (79), Being There (79), Beyond The Poseidon Adventure (79), Dreamer (79), The Champ (79), Used Cars (80).

WARNER, DAVID: Morgan (66), The Bofors Gun (68), The Fixer (68), The Seagull (68), Michael Kohlhaas (69), Perfect Friday (70), The Ballad of Cable Hogue (70), Straw Dogs (71), A Doll's House (73), Tales From the Crypt (73), Little Malcolm (75), The Omen (76), Cross of Iron (77), Providence (77), Nightwing (78), The Concorde-Airport'79 (79), Time After Time (79), The Island (80).

WARREN, JENNIFER: Night Moves (75), Another Chance (77), Another Man (77), Slapshot (77), Ice Castles (78).

WASSON, CRAIG: The Outsider (79), Schizoid (80).

WATERSTON, SAM: A Time for Giving (69), A Delicate Balance (73),

Antonio Fargas,
Christopher Walken.

Rancho De Luxe (74), The Great Gatsby (74), Sweet Revenge (77),
Capricorn One (78), Interiors (78), Eagle's Wing (79), Heaven's
Gate (80), Hopscotch (80).

WATSON, JACK: ffolkes (80).

WATSON, JAMES A., Jr.: Goldengirl (79).

WAYNE, DAVID: The Prize Fighter (79).

WAYNE, JOHN: The Green Berets (68), Hellfighters (69), The
Undefeated (69), True Grit (69), Chisum (70), Rio Lobo (70), Big
Jake (71), The Cowboys (72), Cahill (73), The Train Robbers (73),
McQ (74), Brannigan (75), Rooster Cogburn (75), The Shootist
(76).

WAYNE, PATRICK: McLintock (63), The Green Berets (68), Big Jake
(71), The Bears and I (74), Sinbad and the Eye of the Tiger (79),
The People That Time Forgot (79).

WEATHERS, CARL: Force 10 from Navarone (78), Rocky II (79).

WEAVER, FRITZ: The Maltese Bippy (69), A Walk in the Spring Rain
(70), The Day of the Dolphin (73), Marathon Man (76), Black
Sunday (77), The Demon Seed (77), The Big Fix (78).

WEAVER, LEE: The Onion Field (79).

WEAVER, SIGOURNEY: Alien (79).

WEBBER, ROBERT: 10 (79), Private Benjamin (80).

WEBBER, TIMOTHY: Terror Train (80).

WEINTRAUB, CINDY: Humanoids From The Deep (80).

WELCH, RACQUEL: Bandolero (68), Bedazzled (68), Lady in Cement
(68), The Beloved (68), The Oldest Profession (68), 100 Rifles (69),

Flare Up (69), Myra Breckinridge (70), The Magic Christian (70), Hannie Caulder (71), Bluebeard (72), Fuzz (72), Kansas City Bomber (72), The Last of Sheila (73), The Three Musketeers (73), The Four Musketeers (74), The Wild Party (74), Mother, Jugs and Speed (76), The Prince and the Pauper (77).

WELD, TUESDAY: The Cincinnati Kid (65), Lord Love a Duck (66), Pretty Poison (69), I Walk the Line (70), A Safe Place (71), Play It as It Lays (72), Looking for Mr. Goodbar (77), Serial (80).

WELLER, MARY LOUISE: The Bell Jar (79).

WELLER, PETER: Butch And Sundance (79), Just Tell Me What You Want (80).

WELLES, GWEN: California Split (74), Nashville (75), Between the Lines (77).

WELLES, ORSON: The Muppet Movie (79).

WEST, TIMOTHY: Rough Cut (80).

WESTON, JACK: Cuba (79), Can't Stop The Music (80).

WHITING, RICHARD: Ordinary People (80).

WHITMAN, STUART: Guyana:Cult Of The Damned (80).

WHITMORE, JAMES: First Deadly Sin (80).

WHITMORE, JAMES, Jr.: The Long Riders (80).

WIDDOES, KATHLEEN: The Group (66), Petulia (68), The Seagull (68), The Mephisto Waltz (71).

WIDMARK, RICHARD: The Bedford Incident (65), Madigan (68), A Talent for Loving (69), Death of a Gunfighter (69), The Moonshine War (70), When the Legends Die (72), Murder on the Orient Express (74), The Sellout (76), Rollercoaster (77), The Domino Principle (77), Twilight's Last Gleaming (77), Coma (78), The Swarm (78).

WILDER, GENE: Bonnie and Clyde (67), The Producers (67), Start the Revolution Without Me (69), Quackser Fortune Has a Cousin (70), Willy Wonka and the Chocolate Factory (71), Everything You Always Wanted to Know About Sex (72), Rhinoceros (73), Blazing Saddles (74), The Little Prince (74), Young Frankenstein (74), The Adventure of Sherlock Holmes (75), The Silver Streak (77), No Knife (79), The Frisco Kid (79), Stir Crazy (80), Sunday Lovers (80).

WILDER, YVONNE: Seems Like Old Times (80).

WILKES, DONNA: Schizoid (80).

WILKIN, BRAD: Midnight Madness (80).

WILLARD, FRED: Americathon (79), First Family (80), How To Beat The High Cost of Living (80).

WILLIAMS, BERT: Wanda Nevada (79).

WILLIAMS, BILLY DEE: Lady Sings the Blues (72), The Take (74), Mahogany (75), The Bingo Long Traveling All-Stars (76), The Empire Strikes Back (80).

WILLIAMS, CINDY: Drive, He Said (70), Travels with My Aunt (72),

Michael Beck, Deborah Van Valkenburgh.

American Graffiti (73), The Conversation (74), Mr. Ricco (75), More American Graffiti (79).

WILLIAMS, DICK ANTHONY: The Jerk (79).

WILLIAMS, FRANK: Oh Heavenly Dog (80).

WILLIAMS, HAL: On The Nickel (80).

WILLIAMS, JOBETH: Kramer vs Kramer (79), Stir Crazy (80).

WILLIAMS, PAUL: Phantom of The Paradise (74), Smokey and the Bandit (77), The Cheap Detective (78), The Muppet Movie (79), Smokey And The Bandit II (80).

WILLIAMS, ROBIN: Popeye (80).

WILLIAMS, SIMON: The Prisoner Of Zenda (79), The Fiendish Plot Of Dr. Fu Manchu (80).

WILLIAMS, TREAT: 1941 (79), Hair (79), Why Would I Lie? (80).

WILLIAMSON, FRED: Tell Me That You Love Me, Junie Moon (69), MASH (70), Black Caesar (72), Hammer (72), The Legend of Nigger Charlie (72), That Man Bolt (73), Crazy Joe (74), Boss Nigger (75), Darktown (75), Take a Hard Ride (75), Fist of Fear Touch of Death (80).

WILLIAMSON, NICOL: The Human Factor (79).

WILSON, DAVID: Hometown USA (79).

WILSON, ELIZABETH: The Graduate (67), Little Murders (71), The Prisoner of Second Avenue (75), Nine To Five (80).

WILSON, FLIP: Skatetown Usa (79), The Fish That Saved Pittsburgh (79).

Sam Bottoms.   Paul Dooley

WILSON, NED: The Onion Field (79).

WILSON, SCOTT: In Cold Blood (67), The Gypsy Moths (69), The Grissom Gang (71), The New Centurions (72), Lolly Madonna XXX (73), The Great Gatsby (74), The Ninth Configuration (80).

WINFIELD, PAUL: The Lost Man (69), Brother John (70), R.P.M. (70), Sounder (72), Gordon's War (73), Conrack (74), Huckleberry Finn (74), Hustle (75), Damnation Alley (77), Twilight's Last Gleaming (77).

WINGER, DEBRA: French Postcards (79), Urban Cowboy (80).

WINKLER, HENRY: The Lords of Flatbush (73), Heroes (77), The One and Only (78).

WINN, KITTY: The Panic in Needle Park (71), Peeper (75), Exorcist II-The Heretic (77).

WINNINGHAM, MARE: One Trick Pony (80).

WINTER, ED: A Change of Seasons (80).

WINTERS, JONATHAN: The Fish That Saved Pittsburgh (79).

WINTERS, SHELLEY: A Patch of Blue (66), Harper (66), Enter Laughing (67), Buona Sera Mrs. Campbell (68), The Scalp Hunters (68), Wild in the Streets (68), The Mad Room (69), Bloody Mama (70), How Do I Love Thee (70), Something to Hide (72), The Poseidon Adventure (72), Blume in Love (73), Cleopatra Jones (73), Diamonds (75), That Lucky Touch (75), Next Stop, Greenwich Village (76), The Tenant (76), King of the Gypsies (78).

WISEMAN, JOSEPH: Buck Rogers (79).

WOOD, DAVID: ffolkes (80).

WOOD, NATALIE: Splendor in the Grass (61), West Side Story (61), Inside Daisy Clover (66), Penelope (66), This Property is Condemned (66), Bob & Carol & Ted & Alice (69), Peeper (75),

Carl Weathers.

Billy Dee Williams.

Meteor (79), The Last Married Couple In America (80), Willie & Phil (80).

WOODS, JAMES: The Onion Field (79), The Black Marble (80).

WOODWARD, JOANNE: Rachel, Rachel (68), Winning (69), They Might Be Giants (71), The Effect of Gamma Rays (72), Summer Wishes, Winter Dreams (73), The Drowning Pool (75), The End (78).

WOODWARD, MORGAN: Battle Beyond The Stars (80).

WORTH, IRENE: Rich Kids (79).

WRIGHT, AMY: Breaking Away (79), The Amityville Horror (79), Wise Blood (79), Stardust Memories (80).

WRIGHT, DORSEY: The Warriors (79).

WRIGHT, MAX: All That Jazz (79).

WRIGHT, MICHAEL: The Wanderers (79).

WRIGHT, PAMELA PAYTON: Going In Style (79), Resurrection (80).

WRIGHT, TERESA: The Happy Ending (69), Roseland (77), Somewhere In Time (80).

WYNGARDE, PETER: Flash Gordon (80).

WYNN, KEENAN: Finian's Rainbow (68), MacKenna's Gold (69), Once Upon a Time in the West (69), Smith (69), Pretty Maids All in a Row (71), The Mechanic (72), Herbie Rides Again (73), Nashville (75), The Devil's Rain (76), The Shaggy D.A (76), Orca (77), Piranha (78), Sunburn (79), Just Tell Me What You Want (80).

YNIGUEZ, RICHARD: Boulevard Nights (79).

YORK, MICHAEL: Alfred the Great (69), Justine (69), The Guru (69), Something for Everyone (70), Zeppelin (71), Cabaret (72), England Made Me (72), Lost Horizon (73), Murder on the Orient Express (73), The Four Musketeers (73), The Three Musketeers (73),

Conduct Unbecoming (75), Logan's Run (76), The Island of Dr. Moreau (77), The Last Remake of Beau Geste (77), Final Assignment (80).

YORK, REBECCA: Movie Movie Baxter's Beauties (78).

YORK, SUSANNAH: The Killing of Sister George (68), They Shoot Horses, Don't They? (69), Country Dance (70), Happy Birthday Wanda June (71), Zee and Co. (71), Images (72), The Maids (73), Gold (74), Conduct Unbecoming (75), Sky Riders (76), Superman (78), The Shout (78), Falling In Love Again (80), Superman II (80), The Awakening (80).

YOUNG, BURT: The Killer Elite (75), Rocky (76), Twilight's Last Gleaming (77), Convoy (78), Uncle Joe Shannon (78), Rocky II (79).

YOUNG, GIG: Lovers and Other Strangers (69), They Shoot Horses, Don't They? (69), Bring Me the Head of Alfredo Garcia (74), The Hindenburg (75), The Killer Elite (75).

YOUNG, OTIS: The Last Detail (73).

YOUNG, STEPHEN: The Little Dragons (80).

YOUNGS, JIM: The Wanderers (79).

YULIN, HARRIS: End of the Road (70), Doc (71), St. Ives (73), The Midnight Man (74), Night Moves (75), Steel (80).

ZAPATA, CARMEN: Boulevard Nights (79), How To Beat The High Cost of Living (80), There Goes the Bride (80).

ZERBE, ANTHONY: Will Penny (67), The Molly Maguires (68), Cotton Comes to Harlem (70), The Liberation of L.B. Jones (70), They Call Me Mister Tibbs (70), The Omega Man (71), Papillon (73), The Laughing Policeman (73), Farewell My Lovely (75), Rooster Cogburn (75), The Turning Point (77), First Deadly Sin (80).

ZERBE, ARNETTE JENS: Cloud Dancer (80).

ZIMBALIST, STEPHANIE: The Magic Of Lassie (78), The Awakening (80).

Production designers,
Art directors, et cetera

ACHMANN, WERNER: The American Success Company (79)˙.

ACKLAND-SNOW, BRIAN: Dracula (79)˙.

ADAM, KEN: Dr. Strangelove (63), Goldfinger (64), The Ipcress File (65), Thunderball (65), Funeral in Berlin (66), You Only Live Twice (67), Chitty Chitty Bang Bang (68), Goodbye Mr. Chips (69), The Owl and the Pussycat (70), Diamonds Are Forever (71), Sleuth (72), Live and Let Die (73), The Last of Sheila (73), Barry Lyndon (75), The Seven Percent Solution (76), Moonraker (79).

ALDRICH, HANK: Natural Enemies (79).

ALEXANDER, BILL: The Lady Vanishes (79)˙.

ALLEN, GENE: At Long Last Love (75).

ALTADONNA, JOSEPH: Motel Hell (80), The Big Brawl (80)˙.

ALVES, JOE: Jaws (75), Close Encounters of the Third Kind (77)˙.

AMES, PRESTON: Brewster McCloud (70), Lost Horizon (73), Beyond The Poseidon Adventure (79), Oh, God! Book II (80).

ANDERSON, CARL: The Villain (79).

AUSTIN, JOHN: 1941 (79).

AXTELL, KIRK: Raging Bull (80)˙.

BARON, NORMAN: Hero At Large (80)˙.

BARRY, JOHN: Lucky Lady (75), Star Wars (77), Superman (78), Superman II (80)˙.

BENNETT, PHILLIP: Ordinary People (80)˙.

BENTON, BOB: Cheech And Chong's Next Movie (80)˙.

BERGER, RICHARD: Nickelodeon (76), Rocky II (79), Scavenger Hunt (79).

BLEZARD, JOHN: Nijinsky (80).

BLUMENTHAL, HERMAN: The Baltimore Bullet (80)˙, The Formula (80).

BODE, JOHN D.: Coal Miner's Daughter (80).

BONNIERE, CLAUDE: Circle Of Two (80)˙.

BOURNE, MEL: Annie Hall (77), Nunzio (78), Manhattan (79), Windows (80)*.

BOX, JOHN: A Man For All Seasons (66), Nicholas and Alexandra (71), Travels with My Aunt (72), The Great Gatsby (74), Rollerball (75).

BOYLE, ROBERT: Marnie (64), The Thomas Crown Affair (68), The Landlord (70), Mame (74), Winter Kills (79), Private Benjamin (80).

BRENNER, ALBERT: The Other (72), California Suite (78), Coma (78), The Goodbye Girl (78), Divine Madness (80), Hero At Large (80)*.

BROMLEY, KAREN: Middle Age Crazy (80).

BROWN, HILYARD: Coast To Coast (80).

BUMSTEAD, HENRY: High Plains Drifter (72), Slaughterhouse Five (72), The Sting (73), House Calls (78), Same Time Next Year (78), A Little Romance (79)*, The Concorde-Airport'79 (79), Smokey And The Bandit II (80)*.

BURNS, MILLY: Yanks (79)*.

BYDWELL, GLENN: Terror Train (80)*.

CAHILL, KATHY CURTIS: Schizoid (80).

CAIN, SYD: The Sea Wolves (80).

CALLAHAN, GENE: The Friends of Eddie Coyle (73), Bloodbrothers (78), King of the Gypsies (78), Chapter Two (79), Seems Like Old Times (80), The Last Married Couple In America (80)*.

CAMPBELL, STEWART: Urban Cowboy (80)*.

CAMPBELL, WILLIAM L.: Walk Proud (79).

CARFAGNO, EDWARD: The Hindenburg (75), Meteor (79)*, Time After Time (79), Little Miss Marker (80).

CARRERE, FERNANDO: Foolin' Around (80), The Final Countdown (80).

CARTER, RICHARD: Second-Hand Hearts (80)*.

CARTWRIGHT, ROBERT: Hanover Street (79)*, The Elephant Man (80)*.

CASSIDY, WILLIAM J.: Carny (80)*.

CEDER, ELAYNE: Every Which Way But Loose (78), When A Stranger Calls (79).

CHAPMAN, DAVID: The Seduction Of Joe Tynan (79).

CHARLES, DAVID: Meatballs (79).

CHRISTIAN, ROGER: Alien (79)*.

CLATWORTHY, ROBERT: Inside Daisy Clover (66), Cactus Flower (69).

COLLIS, JACK: The Jerk (79)*, The Last Word (79), The Long Riders (80)*.

COMTOIS, GUY: Terror Train (80)*.

CONSTABLE, DAVID: Meteor (79)*.

CORSO, JOHN W.: Xanadu (80).

COUCH, LIONEL: The Awakening (80)*.

CRAIG, STUART: Saturn 3 (80)*, The Elephant Man (80)*.

CREBER, WILLIAM: Any Which Way You Can (80), Hopscotch (80).

CRUGNOLA, AURELIO: The Black Stallion (79)*.

CUTLER, BERNIE: Smokey And The Bandit II (80)*.

DAVERILL, HERBERT SPENCER: The Fish That Saved Pittsburgh (79).

DAVEY, BERT: ffolkes (80).

DE CUIR, JOHN F.: Raise The Titanic (80).

DE GOVIA, JACKSON: Boulevard Nights (79), Butch And Sundance (79)*, It's My Turn (80), My Bodyguard (80).

DE LAMOTHE, FRANCOIS: A Little Romance (79)*.

DE LUCY, FRANCOIS: Circle Of Two (80)*.

DILLEY, LESLIE: Alien (79)*, The Empire Strikes Back (80)*.

DIMITROV, ANTONIN: Head On (80).

DONATI, DANILO: Caligula (79), Hurricane (79), Flash Gordon (80).

DORME, NORMAN: Saturn 3 (80)*.

DOWDING, JON: Blue Lagoon (80).

EATWELL, BRIAN: Butch And Sundance (79)*, The Onion Field (79).

ELLENSHAW, PETER: The Black Hole (79)*.

ERICKSEN, LEON: Medium Cool (69), That Cold Day in the Park (69), The Rain People (69), McCabe and Mrs. Miller (71), Images (72).

ERLER, MICHAEL: Humanoids From The Deep (80).

FELDMAN, RACHEL: Home Movies (79)*.

FIELD, VIRGINIA: Friday the 13th (80).

FISCHER, LEE: The Hollywood Knights (80).

FISK, JACK: Movie Movie Baxter's Beauties (78), Movie Movie Dynamite Hands (78), Heart Beat (79).

FREED, REUBEN: Prom Night (80), The Changeling (80)*, Tribute (80)*.

FRIED, RICHARD: A New Leaf (71).

FUHRMAN, RICHARD: Windows (80)*.

FUMAGALLI, FRANCO: The Outsider (79).

GILLIAM, TERRY: Life Of Brian (79).

GORTOUX, ADRIAN: The Baltimore Bullet (80)*.

GRAHAM, ANGELO: Little Big Man (70)*, The Getaway (72), The Day of the Dolphin (73), The Godfather, Part II (74), F.I.S.T. (78)*, Brinks (79)*, Apocalypse Now (79)*.

GRIMES, STEPHEN: Reflections in a Golden Eye (67), Ryan's Daughter (71), Murder by Death (76), The Electric Horseman (79), Urban Cowboy (80)*.

GUNDLACH, ROBERT: Oliver's Story (78).

GUZMAN, CLAUDIO: Touched By Love (80)*.

GUZMAN, PATO: I Love You, Alice B. Toklas (68), Bob & Carol & Ted & Alice (69), Alex in Wonderland (70), Blume in Love (73), An Unmarried Woman (78), The In-Laws (79), Hide In Plain Sight (80), Willie & Phil (80).

HABER, SHELDON: Raging Bull (80)*.

HALLER, MICHAEL: Being There (79)*.

HARPMAN, FRED: Cheech And Chong's Next Movie (80)*.

HARRIS, LORENZO JODIE: You Better Watch Out (80).

HARRISON, PHILIP: Hanover Street (79).

HAWORTH, TED: Villa Rides (68), The Kremlin Letter (70), The Beguiled (71), Harry and Tonto (74), Telefon (77), Bloodline (79), Rough Cut (80).

HENDRICKSON, STEPHEN: Going In Style (79).

HENNESY, DALE: Everything You Always Wanted to Know About Sex (72), Sleeper (73), Young Frankenstein (74), Logan's Run (76), Norma Rae (79), The Competition (80), The Island (80), Wholly Moses! (80)*.

HENRY, CHRISTOPHER: Silent Scream (80).

HERNDON, WALTER SCOTT: Loving (70), The Last Picture Show (71)*, Sounder (72), Mother, Jugs and Speed (76), Semi-Tough (77), Promises In The Dark (79), Those Lips Those Eyes (80).

HIGGINS, DOUGLAS: The Kidnapping Of The President (80).

HILDITCH, BOB: The Earthling (80).

HINEY, WILLIAM: First Family (80), Little Darlings (80).

HOBBS, RON: Just You And Me, Kid (79)*, The Hunter (80), Tom Horn (80).

HORNER, CHRIS: Movie Movie Baxter's Beauties (78).

HORNER, HARRY: They Shoot Horses, Don't They? (69), Who Is Harry Kellerman .... (71), Up the Sandbox (72), Harry and Walter Go to New York (76), Moment by Moment (78), The Driver (78).

HORRS, RON: The Deerhunter (78)*.

HOWARD, JEFF: Private Benjamin (80).

HUBBARD, JOE: The Jerk (79)*.

HUNDLEY, CRAIG: Roadie (80)*.

HUTCHINSON, TIM: Rough Cut (80).

JAMISON, PETER: Head Over Heels (79), Old Boyfriends (79), The Big Red One (80), Used Cars (80).

JANDA, GERHARD: Breakthrough (79).

JEFFRIES, PHILIP M.: When Time Ran Out (80).

JENKINS, GEORGE: The Angel Levine (70), 1776 (72), Night Moves (75), All the President's Men (76), Comes a Horseman (78), Starting Over (79), The China Syndrome (79).

JOLLEY, STAN: Americathon (79).

JONES, DISLEY: The Legacy (79).

KAUFMAN, SUSAN: He Knows You're Alone (80).

KENNEY, BILL: Uncle Joe Shannon (78), A Change of Seasons (80), The Mountain Men (80).

KERR, MARY: Double Negative (80), Nothing Personal (80).

KIRKLAND, GEOFFREY: Fame (80).

KLATE, SEYMOUR: Somewhere In Time (80).

KOHUT-SVELKO, JEAN-PIERRE: French Postcards (79).

KROEGER, WOLF: Popeye (80).

LANGE, HARRY: The Empire Strikes Back (80)*.

LARRECQ, HENRY: The Blues Brothers (80)*.

LARSEN, JOHANNES: Circle Of Iron (79).

LARSEN, TAMBI: Heaven's Gate (80).

LEE, EUGENE: Mr. Mikes Mondo Video (79)*.

LEE, FRANNE: Mr. Mikes Mondo Video (79)*, Gilda Live (80).

LEVEN, BORIS: Mandingo (75), New York, New York (77), The Last Waltz (78).

LEVESQUE, MICHAEL: Borderline (80), Foxes (80).

LEWIS, GARRETT: Oh Heavenly Dog (80)*.

LITWACK, SYD: Goldengirl (79).

LLOYD, JOHN J.: The Prisoner Of Zenda (79), The Blues Brothers (80)*.

LLOYD, JOHN ROBERT: John and Mary (69), Midnight Cowboy (69), At Long Last Love (75), Swashbuckler (76), National Lampoon's Animal House (78), The Bell Jar (79).

LOMINO, DAN: Close Encounters of the Third Kind (77)*.

LOQUASTO, SANTO: Stardust Memories (80)*.

LOURIE, GENE: Bronco Billy (80).

MacDONALD, RICHARD: Jesus Christ Superstar (73), The Day of the Locust (75), Marathon Man (76), F.I.S.T. (78)*, ...And Justice For All (79), The Rose (79).

MacINTOSH, WOODY: First Deadly Sin (80), One Trick Pony (80)*.

MAINO, MARIA PAOLA: Luna (79)*.

MALLEY, BILL: The Exorcist (73), The Fury (78), Defiance (80), The Ninth Configuration (80)*.

MANSBRIDGE, JOHN B.: The Black Hole (79)*, Herbie Goes Bananas (80)*.

MANSER, ALAN: Raging Bull (80)*.

MARSH, TERENCE: The Frisco Kid (79).

MARTY, JACK: The Big Brawl (80)*.

MAUS, RODGER: 10 (79), Herbie Goes Bananas (80)*.

MAXSTED, JACK: Buffalo Bill and the Indians (76).

MAZEN, ADEL: Penitentiary (79).

McCALL, ROBERT T.: The Black Hole (79)*.

McDONALD, RICHARD: Altered States (80).

MELLIN, BILL: Piranha (78)*.

MELLIN, KERRY: Piranha (78)*.

MENZER, RUSSELL C.: When Time Ran Out (80).

MICHELSON, HAROLD: Star Trek (79), Can't Stop The Music (80).

MIDDLETON, MALCOLM: Hanover Street (79)*.

MIEHL, KEITH: Roller Boogie (79), The Hearse (80).

MITCHELL, DAVID: Rich Kids (79), One Trick Pony (80)*.

MITZNER, DEAN: 1941 (79), Nine To Five (80).

MOLLY, MICHAEL: Stardust Memories (80)*.
MOLYNEAUX, RAY: Touched By Love (80)*.
MOORE, JOHN JAY: Just Tell Me What You Want (80)*.
MORRIS, BRIAN: Yanks (79)*.
MULLINS, PETER: Luther (74), There Goes the Bride (80)*.
MURTON, PETER: Dracula (79)*, Superman II (80)*.
NEWBERRY, NORMAN: Winter Kills (79)*.
NEWPORT, JIM: Over The Edge (79).
O'BRIEN, WILLIAM F.: 1941 (79).
O'DONOVAN, EDWIN: Resurrection (80)*.
ODELL, GARY: Hawaii (66), The Hawaiians (70).
ORR, DENIS GORDON: Cuba (79)*.
PARADISE, LYNDA: Wanda Nevada (79).
PARKER, ART: North Dallas Forty (79).
PARRONDO, GIL: Cuba (79)*.
PAULL, LAWRENCE G.: How To Beat The High Cost of Living (80), In
  God We Trust (80).
PERANIO, VINCENT: The Private Eyes (80).
PETERS, PAUL: Buck Rogers (79)*, Roadie (80)*.
PISONI, EDWARD: Cruising (80)*.
PLATT, POLLY: The Last Picture Show (71)*, What's Up, Doc? (72),
  Paper Moon (73), The Thief Who Came to Dinner (73), A Star is
  Born (76), The Bad News Bears (76).
POPLIN, JACK: The Great Santini (80).
POTTLE, HARRY: Murder By Decree (79).
PRATT, THOMAS: Windwalker (80).
PRESTON, EARL: The Black Stallion (79)*.
PRESTON, WARD: Airplane (80).
QUINN, SPENCER: The Little Dragons (80).
RAFELSON, TOBY CARR: Five Easy Pieces (70), The King of Marvin
  Gardens (72), Alice Doesn't Live Here Anymore (74), Stay Hungry
  (76), Goin' South (78), Melvin and Howard (80)*.
REAMS, RICHARD: Buck Rogers (79)*.
RICHARDSON, ED: The Double Mcguffin (79)*, American Gigolo (80).
RICHARDSON, GEORGE: Oh Heavenly Dog (80)*.
RIVA, J. MICHAEL: Brubaker (80), Ordinary People (80)*.
ROBBINS, SAM: Lady Grey (80).
ROBERTS, JOHN: The Mirror Crack'd (80)*.
ROELOFS, AL: The Black Hole (79)*.
ROMERO, PETER: The Long Riders (80)*.
ROSEN, CHARLES: Taxi Driver (76), Invasion Of The Bodysnatchers
  (78), Last Embrace (79), The Main Event (79).
ROSENBERG, PHILIP: Next Stop, Greenwich Village (76), All That Jazz
  (79).
ROSS, BILL: Joni (80).

RUDOLF, GENE: Raging Bull (80)*.

RUSSELL, SHIRLEY: Agatha (79).

RUSSO, JOSAN F.: Carny (80)*.

RYAN, KEN: The Human Factor (79).

RYMAN, BRIAN: Opening Night (77).

SAMISH, PETER: ...And Justice For All (79).

SANDELL, BILL: Serial (80).

SAWYER, RICHARD: Melvin and Howard (80)*, Where The Buffalo Roam (80).

SCHILLER, JOEL: Kid Blue (73), Lenny (74), Ice Castles (78), The Muppet Movie (79), A Small Circle Of Friends (80), Honeysuckle Rose (80).

SCHOPPE, JAMES: Being There (79)*, The Rose (79), The Octagon (80), The Stunt Man (80).

SCOTT, JAN: The End (78), Loving Couples (80).

SEYMOUR, MICHAEL: Alien (79)*.

SHINGLETON, WILFRED: The Lady Vanishes (79)*.

SHRADY, HENRY: Slow Dancing In The Big City (78).

SIDDALL, JOHN: There Goes the Bride (80)*.

SILVESTRI, GIANNI: Luna (79)*,

SMITH, ALLEN: Escape From Alcatraz (79).

SMITH, PETER: Chapter Two (79), Seems Like Old Times (80), The Last Married Couple In America (80)*.

SMITH, WILLIAM CRAIG: Prophecy (79).

SNYDER, DAVID L.: The Idolmaker (80).

SPENCER, JAMES H.: Die Laughing (80).

SPIER, CAROL: Hog Wild (80).

STAHELI, PAUL: In Search Of Historic Jesus (80).

STAVRINOS, GEORGE: Union City (80).

STOREY, RAY: More American Graffiti (79).

STRINGER, MICHAEL: Robin and Marian (76), The Awakening (80)*, The Mirror Crack'd (80)*.

SURGAL, TOM: Home Movies (79)*.

SWADOS, KIM: The Deerhunter (78)*, The Amityville Horror (79).

SWEENEY, ALFRED: North Dallas Forty (79), Stir Crazy (80), The Black Marble (80).

SYLBERT, PAUL: One Flew Over the Cuckoo's Nest (75), Mikey and Nicky (76), Hardcore (79), Kramer vs Kramer (79), Resurrection (80)*.

SYLBERT, RICHARD: Splendor in the Grass (61), Who's Afraid of Virginia Woolf (66), The Graduate (67), Rosemary's Baby (68), Catch-22 (70), Carnal Knowledge (71), Fat City (72), The Day of the Dolphin (73), Chinatown (74), Shampoo (75), The Fortune (75), Players (79).

TAVOULARIS, DEAN: Bonnie and Clyde (67), Candy (68), Zabriskie

Point (69), Little Big Man (70)*, The Godfather (72), The Conversation (74), The Godfather, Part II (74), Farewell My Lovely (75), Brinks (79)*, Apocalypse Now (79).

TESTER, TED: Sunburn (79).

TINGLOF, SIG: Just You And Me, Kid (79)*.

TOMKINS, ALAN: The Empire Strikes Back (80)*.

TOMKINS, LES: The Shining (80)*.

TRAUNER, ALEXANDER: Uptight (68), The Private Life of Sherlock Holmes (70), The Man Who Would Be King (75), Don Giovanni (79), The Friendish Plot of Dr. Fu Manchu (80).

TUCH, FRED: Avalanche Express (79).

TUNTKE, WILLIAM: The Nude Bomb (80).

TURLLEY, TOM: Galaxina (80).

TYLER, WALTER: Midway (76).

VANCE, JAMES: The Grissom Gang (71), Nightwing (79).

VICKERS, STEVEN: Love in a Taxi (80).

VON BRANDENSTEIN, PATRIZIA: Hester Street (74), Saturday Night Fever (77), Breaking Away (79), Tell Me a Riddle (80), Ragtime (81).

VON KIESERITZKY, GEORGE: The Lady Vanishes (79)*.

WAGER, DIANE: Wholly Moses! (80)*.

WALKER, ROY: The Shining (80)*.

WALLACE, TOMMY: The Fog (80).

WALTON, TONY: The Seagull (68), Murder on the Orient Express (74), The Wiz (78), All That Jazz (79), Just Tell Me What You Want (80)*.

WASHINGTON, J. DENNIS: The Electric Horseman (79), The Ninth Configuration (80)*.

WATKINS, TED: Happy Birthday, Gemini (80).

WEINTRAUB, BRUCE: Cruising (80)*.

WEIST, GARY: Dressed To Kill (80).

WESTBROOK, HERBERT: Eagle's Wing (79).

WHEELER, LYLE: Marooned (69).

WILLIAMS, TREVOR: Lost And Found (79), The Changeling (80)*, Tribute (80)*.

WOOLEY, PETER: High Anxiety (78), Fatso (80), Second-Hand Hearts (80)*, Up The Academy (80).

WRIGHT, HARLAND: The Double Mcguffin (79)*.

WURTZEL, STUART: Between the Lines (77), Night Of The Juggler (80), Simon (80), Times Square (80).

ZEHETBAUER, ROLF: Brass Target (78), The American Success Company (79)*.

Costume designers

ALDREDGE, THEONI V.: No Way To Treat a Lady (67), You're A Big Boy Now (67), Uptight! (68), I Never Sang For My Father (69), Last Summer (69), The Great Gatsby (74), Network (76), The Champ (79), The Rose (79).

BARRETT, ALAN: Nijinsky (80).

BAUER, MONIKA: Brass Target (78).

BAYLESS, LUSTER: Tom Horn (80).

BEAVAN, JENNY: Jane Austen In Manhattan (80).

BIXBY, GAIL: Roadie (80)*.

BLAKE, YVONNE: Charlie Bubbles (66), Judith (66), The Idol (66), The Spy With A Cold Nose (66), Assignment K (67), Duffy (68), Country Dance (69), The Best House In London (69), Puppet On A Chain (70), The Last Valley (70), Nicholas And Alexandra (71), Jesus Christ Superstar (73), The Three Musketeers (73), The Four Musketeers (74), Superman II (80)*.

BLOOMFIELD, JOHN: The Fiendish Plot Of Dr. Fu Manchu (80).

BOXER, JOHN: Starting Over (79).

BRIDGE, JOAN: Hanover Street (79).

BRONSON, TOM: The Long Riders (80).

BROOKS, DONALD: The Bell Jar (79).

BRUNO, RICHARD: Players (79)*.

BRYCE, HOPE: The Human Factor (79).

BUSHNELL, SCOTT: Popeye (80).

CANONERO, MILENA: The Shining (80).

CAPETANOS, GWEN: The Muppet Movie (79)*.

COHEN, ELLIS: Defiance (80).

COLVIG, HELEN: Coogan's Bluff (68), Deadly Roulette (68), Sam Whiskey (68), A Change Of Habit (69), A Man Called Gannon (69), Death of a Gunfighter (69), Two Mules For Sister Sara (69), I Love My Wife (70), The Beguilled (70), Willy Wonka And The Chocolate

Factory (70), Minnie And Moskowitz (71), Play Misty For Me (71),
  The Great Northfield Minnesota Raid (71), Charley Varrick (72).
COX, BETSY: Seems Like Old Times (80).
DALTON, PHYLLIS: The Awakening (80).
DE MORA, ROBERT: The American Success Company (79)*, The
  Wanderers (79), Winter Kills (79), Times Square (80).
DOLAN, JUDY: The Outsider (79).
DONATI, DANILO: Hurricane (79), Flash Gordon (80).
DORLEAC, JEAN-PIERRE: Buck Rogers (79), Blue Lagoon (80).
EDWARDS, PAT: 10 (79).
FASO, TONY: Old Boyfriends (79)*.
FENICHEL, LILLY: Circle Of Iron (79).
FITZGERALD, SALLY: Wise Blood (79).
FLETCHER, ROBERT: Star Trek (79).
GILBERT, SYDNEY: Steel (80)*.
GRACE, SUZANNE: Old Boyfriends (79)*.
GREENWOOD, JANE: Can't Stop The Music (80).
GRENN, JERED EDD: Roadie (80)*.
HARRIS, JULIE: Dracula (79).
HEAD, EDITH: Airport (69), Butch Cassidy and the Sundance Kid (69),
  Skulduggery (69), Tell Them Willie Boy Is Here (69), Topaz (69),
  Myra Breckinridge (70), Red Sky At Morning (70), The Forbin
  Project (70), Sometimes A Great Notion (71), Hammersmith Is Out
  (72), Pete 'N' Tillie (72), A Doll's House (73), Ash Wednesday (73),
  The Don Is Dead (73), The Sting (74), Airport 75 (75), Rooster
  Cogburn (75), The Great Waldo Pepper (75), The Man Who Would
  Be King (75), Gable And Lombard (76).
HENDRICKSON, CALISTA: The Muppet Movie (79)*.
HIGHFILL, ALLEN: Heaven's Gate (80).
HUTCHINSON, TIM: Eagle's Wing (79).
JEAKINS, DOROTHY: The Sound Of Music (64), Any Wednesday (66),
  Hawaii (66), Reflections In A Golden Eye (67), The Flim-Flam Man
  (67), Finian's Rainbow (68), The Fixer (68), The Stalking Moon
  (68), True Grit (68), The Molly Maguires (69), Little Big Man (70),
  Fat City (72), Fuzz (72), The Way We Were (73), The Hindenburg
  (75), Young Frankenstein (75), North Dallas Forty (79).
JOHNSTONE, ANNA HILL: The Group (66), Trilogy (67), Bye Bye
  Braverman (68), The Night They Raided Minsky's (68), The
  Swimmer (68), Alice's Restaurant (69), Cotton Comes to Harlem
  (70), There Was A Crooked Man (70), Who Is Harry Kellerman...?
  (71), Come Back Charleston Blue (72), Play It Again Sam (72), The
  Effect Of Gamma Rays On (72), The Godfather (72), Summer
  Wishes, Winter Dreams (73), The Taking Of Pelham 1-2-3 (75).
JONES, GARY: First Deadly Sin (80).
JONES, JANE: The Prize Fighter (79).

A Bob Mackie costume.

KEMP, LYNDA: Nothing Personal (80).

KLEIN, CALVIN: Players (79)*.

KNODE, CHARLES: Life Of Brian (79)*.

LEVINE, DARRYL: The Hollywood Knights (80).

LOOMIS, STEPHEN: The Fog (80)*.

LOQUASTO, SANTO: Simon (80).

LYNCH, DORIS: Steel (80)*.

MABRY, MOSS: The Detective (68), The Lady In Cement (68), Bob &
    Carol & Ted & Alice (69), Cactus Flower (69), The Great Bank
    Robbery (69), The Maltese Bippy (69), Doctors' Wives (70), How
    Do I Love Thee? (70), The Mephisto Waltz (70), The Love Machine
    (71), Butterflies Are Free (72), Portnoy's Complaint (72), Stand Up
    And Be Counted (72), The Way We Were (73), The Trial Of Billy
    Jack (75), Touched By Love (80).

MACKIE, BOB: Divorce American Style (67), Lady Sings The Blues (72),
    Funny Lady (74).

MANNIX, BOBBIE: The Warriors (79), Xanadu (80).

MARKS, EDDIE: Where The Buffalo Roam (80)*.

McARDLE, NANCY: Die Laughing (80).

MIKON, MARTHE: Don Giovanni (79).

MILLER, BURTON: The Concorde-Airport '79 (79), The Nude Bomb (80).

MOLLO, JOHN: Alien (79), The Empire Strikes Back (80).

MORLEY, RUTH: Kramer vs. Kramer (79), Little Miss Marker (80).

MYERS, RUTH: Altered States (80), In God We Trust (80), It's My Turn (80).

NADOOLMAN, DEBORAH: 1941 (79), The Blues Brothers (80).

NORRIS, PATRICIA: California Suite (78), Movie Movie Baxter's Beauties (78), Movie Movie Dynamite Hands (78), Heart Beat (79), The Fish That Saved Pittsburgh (79), Fatso (80), On The Nickel (80), The Baltimore Bullet (80).

NORTON, ROSANNA: Head Over Heels (79), Airplane (80), The Stunt Man (80).

NOVARESE, VITTORIO NINO: Cromwell (69), Zachariarh (70), Blazing Saddles (74), The Terminal Man (75).

PAREDES, DANIEL: Americathon (79).

PETHIG, HAZEL: Life Of Brian (79)*.

PINNOW, HELGA: The American Success Company (79)*.

POLLACK, BERNIE: Ordinary People (80).

PORTEOUS, EMMA: The Lady Vanishes (79).

RODGERS, AGNES: More American Graffiti (79).

ROSENFELD, HILARY: Rich Kids (79), Heartland (80), One Trick Pony (80).

ROTH, ANN: The World Of Henry Orient (64), A Fine Madness (66), Sweet November (67), Up The Down Staircase (67), Pretty Poison (68), Midnight Cowboy (69), The Owl And The Pussycat (70), They Might Be Giants (70), Klute (71), The Valachi Papers (72), Law And Disorder (75), Murder By Death (76), Hair (79), Promises In The Dark (79), Dressed To Kill (80), Nine To Five (80), The Island (80).

ROUTH, MAY: Being There (79).

RUSSELL, SHIRLEY: French Dressing (64), Billion Dollar Brain (67), Women In Love (69), The Music Lovers (70), The Boy Friend (71), The Devils (71), Savage Messiah (72), Mahler (73), The Little Prince (74), Lisztomania (75), Tommy (75), Valentino (76), Cuba (79), Yanks (79).

SABBATINI, ENRICO: Bloodline (79).

SHIRRARD, MICKEY: Avalanche Express (79).

SYLBERT, ANTHEA: The Tiger Makes Out (67), Rosemary's Baby (68), The Illustrated Man (68), John And Mary (69), Some Kind Of Nut (69), Where It's At (69), A New Leaf (71), Carnal Knowledge (71), The Cowboys (71), Bad Company (72), The Heartbreak Kid (72), Chinatown (74), The Fortune (75).

TALSKY, RON: Such Good Friends (71), Kansas City Bombers (72), Hit (73), The Three Musketeers (73), 99 44/100 Percent Dead (74), The Four Musketeers (74), The Wild Party (75).

TEXTER, GILDA: Where The Buffalo Roam (80)*.

THEISS, WILLIAM: Butch And Sundance (79).

TOMPKINS, JOE: Foolin' Around (80).

VAN RUNKLE, THEADORA: Bonnie and Clyde (67), Bullitt (68), I Love You, Alice B. Toklas (68), The Subject Was Roses (68), The Thomas Crown Affair (68), A Place For Lovers (69), The Arrangement (69), The Reivers (69), Myra Breckinridge (70), Johnny Got His Gun (71), Mame (73), The Godfather Part II (74), The Jerk (79).

VERHILLE, GUY: Wholly Moses! (80).

WALTON, TONY: Mary Poppins (64), A Funny Thing Happened On The Way to the Forum (66), Fahrenheit 451 (66), Petulia (68), The Seagull (69), Murder On The Orient Express (74), The Wiz (78).

WHITTENS, BILL: The Fog (80)*.

WILLIAMS, DIERDRE: You Better Watch Out (80).

WOLSKY, ALBERT: Moment By Moment (78), All That Jazz (79), Manhattan (79).

WOOD, DURINDA RICE: Battle Beyond The Stars (80).

WOOD, YVONNE: The Cheyenne Social Club (69), Dirty Dingus Magee (70), The Life And Times Of Judge Roy Bean (72), The Outfit (73).

WRIGHT, GLENN: Any Which Way You Can (80).

YELLAND, SUSAN: The Prisoner Of Zenda (79), Superman II (80)*.

ZASTUPNEVICH, PAUL: The Poseidon Adventure (72), The Towering Inferno (74), Beyond The Poseidon Adventure (79), When Time Ran Out (80).

ZEA, KRISTI: Fame (80).

Cinematographers

ABRAMS, BARRY: Friday the 13th (80).

ALCOTT, JOHN: Terror Train (80), The Shining (80).

ALMENDROS, NESTOR: Days of Heaven (78), Goin' South (78), Kramer vs Kramer (79), Blue Lagoon (80).

ALONZO, JOHN: Bloody Mama (70), Harold and Maude (71), Vanishing Point (71), Get to Know Your Rabbit (72), Lady Sings the Blues (72), Pete 'n Tillie (72), Sounder (72), Chinatown (74), Conrack (74), Farewell My Lovely (75), Once is Not Enough (75), The Fortune (75), The Bad News Bears (76), Black Sunday (77), Casey's Shadow (77), Close Encounters of the Third Kind (77)*, Which Way Is Up? (77), The Cheap Detective (78), Tom Horn (80).

ANDERSON, JAMIE: Piranha (78).

ARONOVITCH, RICARDO: The Outsider (79), You Better Watch Out (80).

AVILDSEN, JOHN: Turn On to Love (67), Guess What We Learned at School (69), Joe (70), Cry Uncle (71).

BAGGOT, KING: Cheech And Chong's Next Movie (80).

BAILEY, JOHN: Welcome To L.A. (77), Boulevard Nights (79), American Gigolo (80), Ordinary People (80).

BALLARD, LUCIEN: Hour of the Gun (67), Will Penny (67), How Sweet It Is (68), The Party (68), The Wild Bunch (69), True Grit (69), That's the Way It Is (70), The Ballad of Cable Hogue (70), Arruza (71), Junior Bonner (72), The Getaway (72), Lady Ice (73), St. Ives (73), Breakheart Pass (75).

BATKA, FRED: Little Darlings (80).

BEASCOECHEA, FRANK: Buck Rogers (79).

BEESON, PAUL: Hawk the Slayer (80).

BEITENSTEIN, JOCHEN: The Boogey Man (80)*.

BIJOU, LEON: Foxes (80).

BIROC, JOSEPH: Bye Bye Birdie (63), Hush Hush Sweet Charlotte (64), The Russians Are Coming, The Russians Are Coming (66), Lady in

Cement (68), The Detective (68), The Killing of Sister George (68),
The Legend of Lylah Clare (68), Whatever Happened to Aunt Alice
(69), Mrs. Pollifax-Spy (70), The Grissom Gang (71), The
Organization (71), Ulzana's Raid (72), Cahill (73), Emperor of the
North Pole (73), Blazing Saddles (74), The Longest Yard (74), The
Towering Inferno (74), Hustle (75), The Duchess and the Dirtwater
Fox (76), The Choir Boys (77), Beyond The Poseidon Adventure
(79), Airplane (80).

BIZIOU, PETER: Life Of Brian (79).

BODE, RALF: Saturday Night Fever (77), Slow Dancing in the Big City
(78), Rich Kids (79), Coal Miner's Daughter (80), Dressed To Kill
(80).

BOFFETY, JEAN: Thieves Like Us (74).

BRANDT, BYRON: The Prisoner Of Zenda (79)*.

BRENNER, JULES: Johnny Got His Gun (71), Dillinger (73), Posse (75),
The Last Word (79).

BROOKS, RICHARD E.: Natural Enemies (79).

BROWN, ED: The Hot Rock (72), Lovin' Molly (73), The Education of
Sonny Carson (74), Nunzio (78).

BUSH, DICK: The Legacy (79)*, Yanks (79), Falling In Love Again (80)*,
One Trick Pony (80).

BUTLER, BILL: Hickey and Boggs (72), The Conversation (74), Jaws
(75), Alex and the Gypsy (76), Lipstick (76), The Bingo Long
Traveling All-Stars (76), Capricorn One (78), Ice Castles (78), Rocky
II (79), Can't Stop The Music (80), It's My Turn (80).

BUTLER, DAVID: Drive, He Said (70), The Christian Licorice Store (70).

BUTLER, MICHAEL: Dirty Harry (71), Charley Varrick (72), Harry and
Tonto (74), 92 in the Shade (76), The Missouri Breaks (76), Telefon
(77), Wanda Nevada (79), A Small Circle Of Friends (80), Smokey
And The Bandit II (80).

BYRNE, BOBBY: Blue Collar (78), The End (78), The Last Waltz (78),
Head Over Heels (79), The Villain (79), Walk Proud (79), Divine
Madness (80)*, Those Lips Those Eyes (80).

CALLAGHAN, ANDREW: The Scalp Hunters (68), Jeremiah Johnson
(72), The Yakuza (75).

CARDIFF, JACK: Avalanche Express (79), The Awakening (80).

CARTER, JAMES L.: Home Movies (79).

CATHCART, DARRYL: Lady Grey (80), Living Legend (80).

CHALLIS, CHRISTOPHER: Staircase (69), The Private Life of Sherlock
Holmes (70), Mary, Queen of Scots (71), The Little Prince (74),
Mister Quilp (75), The Incredible Sarah (76), Force 10 From
Navarone (78), The Mirror Crack'd (80).

CHAMPION, MARC: Out Of The Blue (80).

CHAPMAN, MICHAEL: The Last Detail (73), White Dawn (73), Taxi
Driver (76), The Front (76), Fingers (78), Invasion Of The

Bodysnatchers (78), The Last Waltz (78), Hardcore (79), The
Wanderers (79), Raging Bull (80).
CHURCHILL, TED: Gilda Live (80)*.
CIUPKA, RICHARD: Atlantic City U S A (80).
CLOQUET, GHISLAIN: Love and Death (75).
CLOTHIER, WILLIAM H.: Hellfighters (69), The Undefeated (69), Rio
Lobo (70), The Train Robbers (73).
CONTNER, JAMES: Cruising (80), Gilda Live (80)*, Times Square (80).
COQUILLON, JOHN: Final Assignment (80), The Changeling (80).
CORRELL, CHARLES: In God We Trust (80).
CRABE, JAMES: ZigZag (70), Save the Tiger (72), W.W. And the Dixie
Dancekings (75), Rocky (76), Players (79), The China Syndrome
(79), How To Beat The High Cost of Living (80), The Baltimore
Bullet (80), The Formula (80).
CRONENWETH, JORDAN: Brewster McCloud (70), Play It as It Lays
(72), The Front Page (74), Zandy's Bride (74), Gable and Lombard
(76), Rolling Thunder (77), Altered States (80).
CUNDEY, DEAN: Roller Boogie (79), Galaxina (80), The Fog (80),
Without Warning (80).
DANIELS, WILLIAM H.: Marlowe (69).
DAVEY, JOHN: Manoeuvre (79).
DAVIS, ANDREW: Over The Edge (79).
DE BESCHE, AUSTIN: Return Of The Secaucus Seven (80).
DE PALMA, BRIAN: Dionysus in 69 (70)*.
DECAE, HENRI: The Island (80).
DEL RUTH, THOMAS: Motel Hell (80).
DESCHANEL, CALEB: Being There (79), More American Graffiti (79),
The Black Stallion (79).
DEVIS, JAMES: There Goes the Bride (80).
FAPP, DANIEL: West Side Story (61), Our Man Flint (66), Ice Station
Zebra (68), Sweet November (68), Marooned (69).
FEIL, GERALD: He Knows You're Alone (80).
FINNERMAN, GERALD PERRY: The Lost Man (69), Brother John (70),
They Call Me Mister Tibbs (70), That Man Bolt (73).
FISHER, GERRY: Secret Ceremony (68), The Seagull (68), Macho
Callahan (70), Man in the Wilderness (71), See No Evil (71), The
Offence (72), Juggernaut (74), SPYS (74), The Adventure of
Sherlock Holmes (75), The Romantic Englishwoman (75), Don
Giovanni (79), Wise Blood (79), The Ninth Configuration (80).
FRAKER, WILLIAM A.: Games (67), The President's Analyst (67), Bullitt
(68), Rosemary's Baby (68), The Fox (68), Paint Your Wagon (69),
Dusty and Sweets McGee (71), The Day of the Dolphin (73), Rancho
De Luxe (74), Aloha Bobby and Rose (75), Coonskin (75), One Flew
Over the Cuckoo's Nest (75), Close Encounters of the Third Kind
(77)*, Looking for Mr. Goodbar (77), American Hot Wax (78),

Heaven Can Wait (78), 1941 (79), Old Boyfriends (79), Divine Madness (80)*, The Hollywood Knights (80).
FRANCIS, FREDDIE: The Elephant Man (80).
FRIEDMAN, BONNIE: The Wobblies (79)*, The Life and Times of Rosie the Riveter (80)*.
FUJIMOTO, TAK: Remember My Name (78), Last Embrace (79), Borderline (80), Melvin and Howard (80), Where The Buffalo Roam (80).
GARNER, GREG: Gal Young Un (79)*.
GENKINS, HARVEY: H.O.T.S. (79).
GEORGE, LASZLO: Running (79), Circle Of Two (80), Nothing Personal (80)*.
GERARD, NORMAN: Mean Streets (73).
GESSNER, PETER: The Wobblies (79)*.
GLENN, PIERRE WILLIAM: A Little Romance (79).
GLICKMAN, PAUL: Sitting Ducks (79).
GLOUNER, RICHARD C.: The Man With Bogart's Face (80).
GRAVER, GARY: Sunnyside (79).
GRAY, ED: The Wizard Of Waukesha (80)*.
GREENBERG, ADAM: The Big Red One (80).
GRIGGS, LOYAL: In Harm's Way (65), In Enemy Country (68), Tick, Tick, Tick... (69).
GUFFEY, BURNETT: King Rat (65), Bonnie and Clyde (67), Halls of Anger (68), The Split (68), Suppose They Gave a War and Nobody Came (69), The Madwoman of Chaillot (69), The Great White Hope (70).
HAITKIN, JACQUES: The Prize Fighter (79), The Private Eyes (80).
HALL, CONRAD: Harper (66), Cool Hand Luke (67), In Cold Blood (67), Hell in the Pacific (68), Butch Cassidy and the Sundance Kid (69), Tell Them Willie Boy Is Here (69), The Happy Ending (69), Fat City (72), Smile (75), The Day of the Locust (75).
HANDLEY, ROBERT: The Life and Times of Rosie the Riveter (80)*.
HARRIS, DOUG: Clarence And Angel (80).
HAUSER, ROBERT: The Odd Couple (68), A Man Called Horse (70), Soldier Blue (70), Willard (71), The Frisco Kid (79).
HAZARD, JOHN: Fist of Fear Touch of Death (80).
HILL, TRAVERS: Cloud Dancer (80).
HIPP, PAUL: Hangar 18 (80), In Search Of Historic Jesus (80).
HIRSCHFELD, GERALD: Goodbye Columbus (69), Last Summer (69), Diary of a Mad Housewife (70), Doc (71), Child's Play (72), Summer Wishes, Winter Dreams (73), Two People (73), Young Frankenstein (74), Two-Minute Warning (76), Americathon (79), The Bell Jar (79), Sunday Lovers (80), Why Would I Lie? (80).
HOLENDER, ADAM: Midnight Cowboy (69), Puzzle of a Downfall Child (70), The Panic in Needle Park (71), Promises In The Dark (79),

The Seduction of Joe Tynan (79), Simon (80), The Idolmaker (80).

HOWE, JAMES WONG: Hombre (67), Seconds (67), The Heart is a Lonely Hunter (68), The Molly Maguires (68), The Last of the Mobile Hotshots (70), Funny Lady (75).

HUGO, MICHEL: One Is a Lonely Number (72), The Mountain Men (80), The Octagon (80).

HUME, ALAN: The Legacy (79)*, The Watcher In The Woods (80).

HURWITZ, LEO: Dialogue With a Woman Departed (80).

IBBETSON, ARTHUR: The Prisoner Of Zenda (79)*, Hopscotch (80), Nothing Personal (80)*.

IMI, TONY: Brass Target (78), Breakthrough (79), It's Not The Size That Counts (79), ffolkes (80), The Sea Wolves (80).

IPPOLITI, SILVANO: Caligula (79).

IROLA, JUDY: The Wobblies (79)*.

JACKMAN, JOE: A Change of Seasons (80)*.

JESSUP, ROBERT: The Big Brawl (80).

KATZ, STEPHEN: The Blues Brothers (80), The Little Dragons (80).

KAWA, MORI: The Hearse (80).

KEATING, KEVIN: On Company Business (80).

KELLY, JAMES B.: Happy Birthday, Gemini (80).

KEMPER, VICTOR J.: Husbands (70), The Hospital (71), They Might Be Giants (71), Who Is Harry Kellerman .... (71), Shamus (72), The Candidate (72), The Last of the Red Hot Lovers (72), Gordon's War (73), The Friends of Eddie Coyle (73), The Reincarnation of Peter Proud (74), Dog Day Afternoon (75), The Gambler (75), Mikey and Nicky (76), Stay Hungry (76), The Last Tycoon (76), Audrey Rose (77), Slapshot (77), Coma (78), ...And Justice For All (79), The Jerk (79), Night Of The Juggler (80), The Final Countdown (80), Xanadu (80).

KLINE, RICHARD: Camelot (67), Hang 'Em High (68), The Boston Strangler (68), A Dream of Kings (69), The Andromeda Strain (70), The Moonshine War (70), Kotch (71), Black Gun (72), Hammersmith Is Out (72), Soylent Green (72), The Mechanic (72), The Harrad Experiment (73), Mr. Majestyk (74), Mandingo (75), King Kong (76), Won Ton Ton, The Dog Who Saved Hollywood (76), The Fury (78), Who'll Stop the Rain (78), Star Trek (79), Tilt (79), The Competition (80), Touched By Love (80).

KNIGHT, NORV: American Odyssey (80)*.

KOENEKAMP, FRED J.: Patton (69), The Great Bank Robbery (69), Beyond the Valley of the Dolls (70), Flap (70), The Skin Game (71), Kansas City Bomber (72), Rage (72), The Magnificent Seven Ride (72), Harry in Your Pocket (73), Papillon (73), The Towering Inferno (74), Uptown Saturday Night (74), Doc Savage (75), Posse (75), Islands in the Stream (77), The Domino Principle (77), The Other Side of Midnight (77), The Amityville Horror (79), The Champ

(79), First Family (80), The Hunter (80), When Time Ran Out (80).

KOONS, EDMOND: A Perfect Couple (79), Health (80).

KOVACS, LASZLO: Targets (68), The Savage Seven (68), Easy Rider (69), That Cold Day in the Park (69), Alex in Wonderland (70), Five Easy Pieces (70), Getting Straight (70), Reflection of Fear (71), The Last Movie (71), The Marriage of a Young Stockbroker (71), Pocket Money (72), Slither (72), Steelyard Blues (72), The King of Marvin Gardens (72), What's Up, Doc? (72), Paper Moon (73), For Pete's Sake (74), Freebie and The Bean (74), Huckleberry Finn (74), At Long Last Love (75), Shampoo (75), Baby Blue Marine (76), Harry and Walter Go to New York (76), Nickelodeon (76), Close Encounters of the Third Kind (77)*, New York, New York (77), F.I.S.T. (78), The Last Waltz (78), Butch And Sundance (79), Heart Beat (79), The Runner Stumbles (79).

KRATINA, RICHARD: Love Story (70), The Angel Levine (70), A Safe Place (71), Born to Win (71), The Pursuit of Happiness (71), The Super Cops (74), The Happy Hooker (75), A Change of Seasons (80)*.

LACAMBRE, DANIEL: Battle Beyond The Stars (80), Humanoids From The Deep (80).

LACHMAN, ED: Union City (80).

LAMKIN, KEN: Scavenger Hunt (79).

LANG, CHARLES: Inside Daisy Clover (66), Hotel (67), The Flim Flam Man (67), A Flea in Her Ear (68), The Stalking Moon (68), A Walk in the Spring Rain (69), Bob & Carol & Ted & Alice (69), Cactus Flower (69), How to Commit Marriage (69), Doctors' Wives (70), The Love Machine (71), Butterflies Are Free (72), Forty Carats (73).

LAPENIEKS, VILIS: If It's Tuesday This Must Be Belgium (69), I Love My Wife (70), Newman's Law (74).

LARNER, STEVAN: Goldengirl (79).

LASSALLY, WALTER: Hullabaloo Over Georgie and Bonnie's Pictures (79), Something Short Of Paradise (79).

LASZLO, ANDREW: You're a Big Boy Now (67), The Night They Raided Minsky's (68), Lovers and Other Strangers (69), The Out of Towners (70), The Owl and the Pussycat (70), The Warriors (79).

LASZLO, ERNEST: Airport (69), Daddy's Gone A-Hunting (69), The First Time (69), Showdown (72), Logan's Run (76).

LATHROP, PHILIP: The Happening (67), Finian's Rainbow (68), I Love You, Alice B. Toklas (68), Point Blank (68), The Gypsy Moths (69), The Illustrated Man (69), The Traveling Executioner (69), They Shoot Horses, Don't They? (69), Rabbit Run (70), The Hawaiians (70), Von Richtofen and Brown (71), Wild Rovers (71), Every Little Crook and Nanny (72), Portnoy's Complaint (72), Lolly Madonna XXX (73), The All-American Boy (73), The Thief Who Came to Dinner (73), Mame (74), Hard Times (75), The Black Bird (75),

Haskell Wexler.

The Killer Elite (75), The Prisoner of Second Avenue (75), Swashbuckler (76), Airport 77 (77), A Different Story (78), Moment By Moment (78), The Driver (78), The Concorde Airport '79 (79), A Change of Seasons (80)*, Foolin' Around (80), Little Miss Marker (80), Loving Couples (80).

LEIGH, A. NORMAN: Brinks (79), Schizoid (80).

LENZER, DON: The Wizard Of Waukesha (80)*.

LEONETTI, MATTHEW F.: Breaking Away (79), Raise The Titanic (80)*.

LERNER, BOB: The War At Home (79)*.

LEVEN, BORIS: Jonathan Livingston Seagull (73).

LOHMANN, PAUL: California Split (74), Nashville (75), Buffalo Bill and the Indians (76), Silent Movie (76), High Anxiety (78), Meteor (79), North Dallas Forty (79), Time After Time (79), Hide In Plain Sight (80).

MANGINE, JOSEPH: Alligator (80), Love in a Taxi (80), Mother's Day (80).

MANKOFSKY, ISIDORE: The Muppet Movie (79), Somewhere In Time (80).

MARCH, RICK: The War At Home (79)*.

MARGULIES, MICHAEL D.: My Bodyguard (80).

MARSH, D'ARCY: Billy In The Lowlands (79).

MARTS, STEVE: American Odyssey (80)*.

McALPINE, DON: The Earthling (80).

McDONOUGH, TOM: Best Boy (79).

MENGES, CHRIS: The Empire Strikes Back (80)*.

METTY, RUSSELL: Madigan (68), The Pink Jungle (68), Eye of the Cat (69), The Omega Man (71), Ben (72).

METZ, REXFORD: Every Which Way But Loose (78), A Change of

Seasons (80)*, Raise The Titanic (80)*, Serial (80).

METZGER, ALAN: Below The Belt (80)*, Gilda Live (80)*.

MILEHAM, MICHAEL: Falling In Love Again (80)*.

MOLLOY, MIKE: The Human Factor (79), The Kidnapping Of The President (80).

MOORE, RICHARD: The Scalp Hunters (68), Wild in the Streets (68), The Reivers (69), Winning (69), W.U.S.A (70), Sometimes a Great Notion (71), The Life and Times of Judge Roy Bean (72), A Complete State of Death (73), The Stone Killer (73).

MORGAN, DONALD M.: Let's Do It Again (75), Skatetown USA (79), Used Cars (80).

MORRILL, JOHN A.: The Day Time Ended (80).

MORRIS, OSWALD: Fiddler on the Roof (71), Sleuth (72), The Mackintosh Man (73), The Man Who Would Be King (75), The Odessa File (75), The Seven Percent Solution (76), The Wiz (78), Just Tell Me What You Want (80).

MORRIS, REGINALD: Murder By Decree (79), Middle Age Crazy (80), Phobia (80), Tribute (80).

MULLER, ROBBY: Saint Jack (79), Honeysuckle Rose (80).

MURPHY, BRIANNE: Fatso (80).

MURPHY, FRED: Heartland (80), Tell Me a Riddle (80).

MURPHY, MICHAEL D.: Silent Scream (80)*.

MYERS, DAVE: THX 1138 (70), Welcome to L.A. (77), The Last Waltz (78), Die Laughing (80), Roadie (80).

NEBBIA, MICHAEL: Alice's Restaurant (69).

NEW, ROBERT: Prom Night (80).

NORMAN, PETER: Gilda Live (80)*.

NUNEZ, VICTOR: Gal Young Un (79)*.

NUYTTEN, BRUNO: French Postcards (79), Brubaker (80).

NYKVIST, SVEN: The Touch (70), One Day in Life of Ivan Denisovich (71), King of the Gypsies (78), Pretty Baby (78), Hurricane (79), Starting Over (79), Willie & Phil (80).

OBENHAUS, MARK: The Wizard Of Waukesha (80)*.

OLLSTEIN, MARTY: Penitentiary (79).

OMORI, EMIKO: The Life and Times of Rosie the Riveter (80)*.

ORNITZ, ARTHUR J.: Act One (63), Charly (68), Me, Natalie (68), The Boys in the Band (70), Minnie and Moskowitz (71), The Anderson Tapes (71), The Possession of Joel Delaney (71), Badge 373 (73), Serpico (73), Death Wish (74), Law and Disorder (74), Next Stop, Greenwich Village (76), An Unmarried Woman (78), Oliver's Story (78).

PAYNTER, ROBERT: Lawman (70), The Nightcomers (71), Scorpio (72), The Big Sleep (78), Superman II (80)*.

PEARL, DAN: The Fifth Floor (80).

PETERMAN, DON: When A Stranger Calls (79).

PHILLIPS, ALEX, Jr.: Sunburn (79), Fade to Black (80).

PHILLIPS, FRANK: The Black Hole (79), Herbie Goes Bananas (80), Midnight Madness (80).

PIZER, LARRY: Phantom of The Paradise (74).

POLITO, GENE: The Forbin Project (69), Prime Cut (72), Five On The Black Hand Side (73), Westworld (73), Futureworld (76), Trackdown (76).

PRIESTLEY, JACK: No Way To Treat A Lady (68), Stiletto (69), Where's Papa? (70), Born to Win (71), First Deadly Sin (80), Rockshow (80).

PROBYN, BRIAN: Downhill Racer (69), The Revolutionary (70), Man At The Top (73), The Satanic Rites Of Dracula (73).

QUAID, DAVID: The Swimmer (68), Pretty Poison (69), Cops And Robbers (73).

RATH, FRANZ: Pilgrim, Farewell (80).

RAYMOND, FRANK: Joni (80).

REBO, BARRY: Mr. Mike's Mondo Video (79).

REDDY, DON: The Double Mcguffin (79), Oh Heavenly Dog (80).

REED, MICHAEL: Von Richthofen And Brown (71), The Groundstar Conspiracy (72).

RESCHER, GAYNE: Rachel Rachel (68), John And Mary (69), A New Leaf (71), Such Good Friends (71), Claudine (74).

RICHMOND, ANTHONY: The Eagle Has Landed (77), The Greek Tycoon (78), The American Success Company (79), Bad Timing (80), Head On (80).

ROIZMAN, OWEN: Stop (70), The French Connection (71), The Gang That Couldn't Shoot Straight (71), Play It Again Sam (72), The Heartbreak Kid (72), The Exorcist (73), The Stepford Wives (74), The Taking Of Pelham 1-2-3 (74), Three Days Of The Condor (75), Network (76), The Return of a Man Called Horse (76), Sergeant Pepper's Lonely Hearts Club Band (78), The Electric Horseman (79), The Black Marble (80).

ROSHER, CHARLES, Jr.: Pretty Maids All In A Row (71), Semi-Tough (77), The Late Show (77), Three Women (77), A Wedding (78), Movie Movie Dynamite Hands (78), Nightwing (79), The Onion Field (79).

ROSSON, EDWARD: Love At First Bite (79).

ROTUNNO, GIUSEPPE: All That Jazz (79), Popeye (80).

RUBAN, AL: Faces (68).

SALMINI, AMBROSE: American Odyssey (80)*.

SALMINI, PETER: American Odyssey (80)*.

SANCHEZ, LEON: The Bees (78).

SCAIFE, EDWARD: The Mercenaries (Dark of the Sun) (68), The Kremlin Letter (70).

SCHULER, FRED: Gloria (80), Stir Crazy (80).

SERESIN, MICHAEL: Fame (80).

SHAMROY, LEON: Planet Of The Apes (68), Skidoo (68), The Secret Life of An American Wife (68), Justine (69).

SHEARMAN, ROGER: Steel (80).

SHORE, DAVID: Silent Scream (80)*.

SILANO, GEORGE: The Last American Hero (73).

SISSEL, SANDI: The Wobblies (79)*.

SLOCOMBE, DOUGLAS: Robbery (67), The Fearless Vampire Killers (67), The Lion In Winter (68), The Buttercup Chain (70), The Music Lovers (70), Murphy's War (71), Travels With My Aunt (72), Jesus Christ Superstar (73), The Great Gatsby (74), The Maids (74), The Marseilles Contract (74), Hedda (76), Rollerball (76), The Sailor Who Fell from Grace With the Sea (76), Close Encounters of the Third Kind (77)*, Julia (77), Caravans (78), Lost And Found (79), The Lady Vanishes (79), Nijinsky (80).

SMITH, JONATHAN: Joe Albany...a Jazz Life (80).

SMITH, ROLAND: Cheaper to Keep Her (80).

SMOKLER, PETER: Today Is For The Championship (80).

SMOOT, REED: Take Down (79), Windwalker (80).

SPERLING, DAVID: The Boogey Man (80)*.

STANLEY, FRANK: J W Coop (71), Magnum Force (73), Thunderbolt And Lightfoot (74), Mr Ricco (75), 10 (79), The Fish That Saved Pittsburgh (79), Wholly Moses! (80).

STINE, HAROLD: MASH (70), The Todd Killings (70).

STORARO, VITTORIO: Last Tango In Paris (72), 1900 (77), Agatha (79), Apocalypse Now (79), Luna (79).

STORZ, WILLIAM: Made For Each Other (71).

STRADLING, HARRY, Jr.: Support Your Local Sherriff (68), The Good Guys And The Bad Guys (69), The Mad Room (69), Young Billy Young (69), Dirty Dingus Magee (70), Little Big Man (70), There Was A Crooked Man (70), Fool's Parade (71), Something Big (71), Support Your Local Gunfighter (71), 1776 (72), Skyjacked (72), The Man Who Loved Cat Dancing (73), The Way We Were (73), McQ (74), The Bank Shot (74), Bite the Bullet (75), Rooster Cogburn (75), Midway (76), Special Delivery (76), The Big Bus (76), Airport 77 (77), Prophecy (79), Carny (80), Up The Academy (80).

SURTEES, BRUCE: Dirty Harry (71), Play Misty For Me (71), The Beguiled (71), The Great Northfield Minnesota Raid (71), High Plains Drifter (72), Joe Kidd (72), Blume in Love (73), The Outfit (73), Lenny (74), Leadbelly (75), Night Moves (75), The Outlaw Josey Wales (76), The Shootist (76), Big Wednesday (78), Movie Movie Baxter's Beauties (78), Dreamer (79), Escape From Alcatraz (79).

SURTEES, ROBERT: The Graduate (67), Sweet Charity (69), The Arrangement (69), The Liberation Of L B Jones (70), Summer Of 42 (71), The Last Picture Show (71), Lost Horizon (72), The Cowboys

(72), The Other (72), Oklahoma Crude (73), The Sting (73), The Great Waldo Pepper (75), The Hindenburg (75), A Star Is Born (76), The Turning Point (77), Bloodbrothers (78), Same Time Next Year (78).

SUSCHITZKY, PETER: The Empire Strikes Back (80)*.

SUSCHITZKY, WOLFGANG: Falling In Love Again (80)*.

SUSLOV, MISHA: Below The Belt (80)*.

TAYLOR, GILBERT: Dr. Strangelove (63), A Hard Day's Night (64), Repulsion (65), Quackser Fortune Has a Cousin.... (70), Macbeth (71), The Omen (76), Star Wars (77), Dracula (79), Flash Gordon (80).

TAYLOR, RONNIE: Circle Of Iron (79).

THACKERY, BUD: The Hell With Angels (68), Nightmare In Chicago (69).

TIDY, FRANK: The Lucky Star (80).

TOSI, MARIO: Some Call It Loving (73), Report To The Commissioner (74), Hearts Of The West (75), Carrie (76), The Main Event (79), Coast To Coast (80), Resurrection (80), The Stunt Man (80).

TOURNIER, JEAN: Moonraker (79), The Fiendish Plot Of Dr. Fu Manchu (80).

TRANE, REUBEN: Shock Waves (75).

TURPIN, GERRY: The Last Of Sheila (73).

UNSWORTH, GEOFFREY: 2001: A Space Odyssey (68), The Assassination Bureau (68), The Reckoning (69), The Magic Christian (70), Three Sisters (70), Cabaret (72), Love, Pain and the Whole Damn Thing (72), Zardoz (73), Murder On The Orient Express (74), Lucky Lady (75), Royal Flash (75), A Matter Of Time (76), Superman (78), The Great Train Robbery (79), Superman II (80)*.

VAN LINT, DEREK: Alien (79).

VAN PEEBLES, MELVIN: Watermelon Man (69).

VAN SICKLE, KENNETH: Hester Street (74), Between the Lines (77).

VERZIER, RENE: Double Negative (80), Hog Wild (80).

VILLALOBOS, RAY: Nine To Five (80), Urban Cowboy (80).

VINCZE, ERNEST: Jane Austen In Manhattan (80).

WAITE, RIC: Defiance (80), On The Nickel (80), The Long Riders (80).

WAKEFORD, KENT L.: Mean Streets (73), Alice Doesn't Live Here Anymore (74), Black Belt Jones (74).

WALSH, DAVID M.: A Gunfight (70), I Walk The Line (70), Monte Walsh (70), Everything You Always Wanted to Know About Sex (72), Sleeper (73), The Laughing Policeman (73), The Other Side Of The Mountain (75), The Sunshine Boys (75), Murder By Death (76), Rollercoaster (77), The Silver Streak (77), California Suite (78), House Calls (78), The Goodbye Girl (78), Chapter Two (79), Just You And Me, Kid (79), The In-Laws (79), Two Of A Kind (79), Hero At Large (80), Private Benjamin (80), Seems Like Old Times (80).

WATKIN, DAVID: Help (65), How I Won The War (67), Catch-22 (70), Mahogany (75), Robin And Marian (76), Cuba (79), Hanover Street (79).

WEXLER, HASKELL: The Loved One (65), Who's Afraid Of Virginia Woolf? (66), In The Heat Of The Night (67), The Thomas Crown Affair (68), Medium Cool (69), American Graffiti (73), The Conversation (74), One Flew Over the Cuckoo's Nest (75), Bound for Glory (76), Coming Home (78), Days Of Heaven (78), No Nukes (80), Second-Hand Hearts (80).

WHEELER, CHARLES F.: Yours, Mine And Ours (68), Che! (69), Cold Turkey (70), Tora, Tora, Tora (70), Silent Running (71), Limbo (72), The War Between Men and Women (72), One Little Indian (73), Slaughter's Big Rip-Off (73).

WILDER, DON: Meatballs (79).

WILLIAMS, BILLY: The Mind Of Mr. Soames (69), Women In Love (69), Kid Blue (73), The Wind And The Lion (75), Boardwalk (79), Eagle's Wing (79), Going In Style (79), Saturn 3 (80).

WILLIAMS, PAUL: Phantom of The Paradise (74).

WILLIS, GORDON: Loving (70), The Landlord (70), The People Next Door (70), Klute (71), Little Murders (71), Bad Company (72), The Godfather (72), Up The Sandbox (72), The Paper Chase (73), The Godfather Part II (74), The Parallax View (74), The Drowning Pool (75), All The President's Men (76), Annie Hall (77), Comes A Horseman (78), Manhattan (79), Stardust Memories (80), Windows (80).

WOLF, HARRY L.: The Nude Bomb (80).

WOOLSEY, RALPH: Little Fauss and Big Halsey (70), The Strawberry Statement (70), The Culpepper Cattle Company (72), The New Centurions (72), The Iceman Cometh (73), The Mackintosh Man (73), 99 44/100 Percent Dead (74), Black Eye (74), Rafferty & The Gold Dust Twins (75), Lifeguard (76), Mother Jugs And Speed (76), The Promise (79), Oh, God! Book II (80), The Great Santini (80), The Last Married Couple In America (80).

WORTH, DAVID: Any Which Way You Can (80), Bronco Billy (80).

YOUNG, FREDDIE: Lawrence Of Arabia (62), Doctor Zhivago (65), The Deadly Affair (67), You Only Live Twice (67), The Battle Of Britain (69), Nicholas and Alexandra (71), Ryan's Daughter (71), Luther (73), The Tamarind Seed (74), Bloodline (79), Rough Cut (80).

ZHEUTIN, CATHY: The Life and Times of Rosie the Riveter (80)*.

ZSIGMOND, VILMOS: Red Sky At Morning (70), McCabe And Mrs. Miller (71), The Hired Hand (71), Deliverance (72), Images (72), Scarecrow (73), The Long Goodbye (73), The Sugarland Express (73), Cinderella Liberty (74), Obsession (76), Close Encounters of the Third Kind (77)*, The Deerhunter (78), The Last Waltz (78), The Rose (79), Winter Kills (79), Heaven's Gate (80).

Sound
(recording and editing)

ADAMS, RICHARD W.: Heaven's Gate (80)*.
ALEXANDER, DICK: First Family (80)*.
ALEXANDER, JIM: The Concorde-Airport '79 (79), Walk Proud (79),
Coal Miner's Daughter (80).
ALEXANDER, LEE: Loving Couples (80), The Great Santini (80).
ALPER, BUD: Breaking Away (79), Why Would I Lie? (80).
ANDERSON, GLENN: Ice Castles (78)*, Stir Crazy (80), The Mountain
Men (80), The Octagon (80).
APPLEBY, DAVE: Terror Train (80)*.
BALL, DEREK: Hopscotch (80)*.
BASSMAN, DON: Oh Heavenly Dog (80)*.
BEGGS, RICHARD: No Nukes (80)*.
BEIL, PETER: Brass Target (78).
BENTLEY, BOB: Hullabaloo Over Georgie and Bonnie's Pictures (79).
BERGER, MARK: No Nukes (80)*.
BISENZ, BRUCE: 10 (79).
BLACK, TREVOR: The Little Dragons (80).
BLONDEAU, HENRI: Final Assignment (80).
BOLGER, MARTIN: When A Stranger Calls (79), Private Benjamin (80),
Up The Academy (80).
BORISEWITZ, RENE: Players (79).
BOXER, NAT: The Wanderers (79), My Bodyguard (80)*.
BRISSEAU, DANIEL: The Fiendish Plot Of Dr. Fu Manchu (80).
BRODIN, JAN: The Hearse (80).
BURTON, WILLIE: Urban Cowboy (80).
BURTT, BEN: The Empire Strikes Back (80)*.
BUSHELMAN, JEFF: It's My Turn (80)*.
CAMPBELL, DAVID: Coast To Coast (80)*.
CANTAMESSA, GENE: 1941 (79), Prophecy (79), Borderline (80),
Coast To Coast (80)*, Hide In Plain Sight (80).

CARPENTER, CHRIS: Oh Heavenly Dog (80)*.
CARTER, JOHN: Buck Rogers (79)*, Little Miss Marker (80).
CHARLES, COLIN: Oh Heavenly Dog (80)*.
CHARMAN, ROY: Cuba (79), Superman II (80).
CLARK, PAUL: Blue Lagoon (80).
CLEARY, KEVIN F.: First Family (80)*.
COGSWELL, RONALD G.: Used Cars (80).
COLLICK, CYRIL: Circle Of Iron (79), The Big Red One (80).
CONNOLLY, DON: The Earthling (80).
CURFMAN, RON: Head Over Heels (79).
CYMOSZINSKI, RAY: My Bodyguard (80)*.
DANEIL, RICHARD: The Shining (80)*.
DARLINGTON, BILL: Divine Madness (80)*.
DAY, BRIAN: Prom Night (80).
DELLINGER, JOHN: Lady Grey (80)*.
DESROIS, MICHEL: A Little Romance (79).
DIETZ, BOB: Without Warning (80).
DRUMMOND, DENNIS: The Changeling (80)*.
DRUMMOND, PATRICK: The Changeling (80)*.
DUCARME, JEAN-LOUIS: Don Giovanni (79)*.
EGAN, PAT: Oh Heavenly Dog (80)*.
ELIOPOULOS, NICHOLAS: Nine To Five (80).
EMERICK, KATHY: American Odyssey (80).
EVERETT, GORDON: Bloodline (79), The American Success Company
    (79).
EVJE, MICHAEL: Cloud Dancer (80), Foolin' Around (80), Raging Bull
    (80)*.
FELBURG, CRAIG: The Fog (80).
FRESHOLTZ, LES: First Family (80)*, The Competition (80)*, Willie &
    Phil (80)*.
GANTON, DOUGLAS: Double Negative (80).
GILMORE, ANDY: Buck Rogers (79)*.
GILMORE, DEAN: Joni (80).
GLASS, ROBERT: A Change of Seasons (80)*, The Idolmaker (80)*.
GOGA, LARRY: Silent Scream (80).
GOODMAN, RICHARD: The Prize Fighter (79), Roadie (80).
GRAGG, RICHARD: A Change of Seasons (80)*.
GRAVENOR, ROBERT: A Perfect Couple (79)*, Boulevard Nights (79)*,
    Health (80), Popeye (80), Xanadu (80).
GREGORY, ROBIN: Dracula (79), Hanover Street (79), The Elephant
    Man (80)*.
GRIEVE, ROBERT: The Changeling (80)*.
GRIFFITH, WILLIAM: Steel (80).
HALLBERG, BERT: Escape From Alcatraz (79), Any Which Way You Can
    (80), Bronco Billy (80).

HARRIS, LOWELL: The Prisoner Of Zenda (79)*, The Nude Bomb (80).
HARRIS, MARK: Humanoids From The Deep (80).
HARWOOD, BO: A Woman Under the Influence (74), Opening Night (77), Terror Train (80)*.
HAYES, JEFFREY: Sitting Ducks (79).
HEMAN, ROGER: Somewhere In Time (80)*.
HENDERSON, ROBERT: ...And Justice For All (79).
HILDYARD, DAVID: Breakthrough (79)*.
HLIDDAL, PETER: The Idolmaker (80)*, Where The Buffalo Roam (80).
HORROCKS, PETER: Breakthrough (79)*.
HUDSON, DAVID: Coast To Coast (80)*.
HUMPHREYS, GERRY: Flash Gordon (80)*.
ISLEY, KENNETH: Boulevard Nights (79)*.
JACOBSEN, JACK: Oliver's Story (78), Apocalypse Now (79), The Warriors (79)*.
JOHNSON, DON: Just You And Me, Kid (79), Scavenger Hunt (79).
JOST, JERRY: Time After Time (79), First Family (80)*, Tom Horn (80)*.
JOST, LARRY: Nightwing (79), North Dallas Forty (79), The In-Laws (79), One Trick Pony (80)*.
KAPLAN, WILLIAM: Heart Beat (79), Old Boyfriends (79), Over the Edge (79), Carny (80), The Blues Brothers (80).
KATZ, STEPHEN: Altered States (80).
KAYE, SIMON: Eagle's Wing (79), Yanks (79).
KEAN, JOHN: Resurrection (80)*.
KIMBALL, DAVID J.: Raging Bull (80)*.
KING, CHARLES L., III: Somewhere In Time (80)*.
KING, KENARD: Schizoid (80).
KITE, JOE: Tom Horn (80)*.
KLIMGER, JAMES J.: The Man With Bogart's Face (80).
KLINE, RICK: Smokey And The Bandit II (80)*.
KNIGHT, DARIN: Promises In The Dark (79).
KNUDSON, BUZZ: The Idolmaker (80)*.
KNUDSON, ROBERT: A Change of Seasons (80)*.
LA RUE, JIM: Americathon (79).
LANGEVIN, OWEN: Circle Of Two (80).
LARGE, CHRIS: Nothing Personal (80).
LAZAROWITZ, LES: Raging Bull (80)*, Times Square (80).
LEATHER, DERRICK: Alien (79).
LEE, DAVID: Middle Age Crazy (80), Tribute (80).
LEWIS, CHARLES: The Muppet Movie (79).
LEWIS, HERMAN: Beyond The Poseidon Adventure (79).
LINDEN, ADRIENNE: Billy In The Lowlands (79).
LITT, BOB: Divine Madness (80)*, The Big Brawl (80)*.
LONDON, ANDREW: The Ninth Configuration (80)*.

LYNCH, DAVID: The Elephant Man (80)*.
MacDOUGALL, DON: A Change of Seasons (80)*, The Idolmaker (80)*.
MADERY, EARL M.: Somewhere In Time (80)*.
MAFFETT, BUD: Hardcore (79), The Fish That Saved Pittsburgh (79).
MAHLER, EDDIE: Cheaper to Keep Her (80), In God We Trust (80).
MAITLAND, DENNIS: Night Of The Juggler (80), Willie & Phil (80)*.
MARKY, BILL: The Last Word (79)*.
MARSHALL, BRIAN: The Prisoner Of Zenda (79)*.
MARSHALL, GARTH: Life Of Brian (79).
MASLOW, STEVE: Divine Madness (80)*.
MATTHEWS, DON: On The Nickel (80).
MAUMONT, JACQUES: Don Giovanni (79)*.
McLAUGHLIN, CHRIS: Nashville (75)*, Buffalo Bill and the Indians
    (76)*, Three Women (77)*, A Wedding (78)*, The Rose (79)*, The
    Long Riders (80)*.
McMILLAN, DAVID: More American Graffiti (79), Die Laughing (80),
    Tell Me a Riddle (80).
MERRITT, DON: A Perfect Couple (79)*.
MIAN, AL: The Warriors (79)*.
MICHAEL, DANNY: The Wizard Of Waukesha (80)*.
MINKLER, MICHAEL: Willie & Phil (80)*.
MITCHELL, DONALD: Raging Bull (80)*, Smokey And The Bandit II
    (80)*.
MITCHELL, JOHN: Lost And Found (79), Rough Cut (80), The Mirror
    Crack'd (80)*.
MITCHELL, P.: Sunday Lovers (80).
MOSS, OLIVER: Hopscotch (80)*.
MURCH, WALTER: The Rain People (69), THX 1138 (70), The
    Godfather (72), American Graffiti (73), The Conversation (74).
NAMES, ART: H.O.T.S. (79).
NELSON, WILLIAM: Defiance (80).
NENY, MICHELE: Don Giovanni (79)*.
NERODA, EMIL: Lady Grey (80)*.
NEWMAN, CHRISTOPHER: Winter Kills (79)*, One Trick Pony (80)*,
    Windows (80).
NICHOLSON, BILL: Raging Bull (80)*, Smokey And The Bandit II (80)*.
NOSCO, JACQUE: The Baltimore Bullet (80).
O'DONOGHUE, ROBIN: Flash Gordon (80)*.
OVERTON, AL: California Suite (78), Skatetown Usa (79), Fatso (80),
    The Formula (80), The Hunter (80).
OVERTON, TOM: Airplane (80), Hero At Large (80).
PARDULA, ROLF: He Knows You're Alone (80).
PIANTADOSI, ARTHUR: Willie & Phil (80)*.
PIGAT, DINO: Terror Train (80)*.
PORTMAN, RICHARD: The Last Word (79)*, Resurrection (80)*.

RAGUSE, RICHARD: Ice Castles (78)*.
RANDALL, BILL: The Hollywood Knights (80).
REITZ, JOHN T.: Coast To Coast (80)*.
RICHARDS, JOHN: The Mirror Crack'd (80)*.
ROCHESTER, ARTHUR: Invasion Of The Bodysnatchers (78),
    Honeysuckle Rose (80).
ROCHIN, AARON: The Competition (80)*.
RONNE, DAVID: Butch And Sundance (79), Melvin and Howard (80),
    Touched By Love (80).
ROWE, BILL: The Mirror Crack'd (80)*.
RUDLOFF, TEX: First Family (80)*, The Competition (80)*.
RUSH, DON: Divine Madness (80)*.
RYDER, WINSTON: Heaven's Gate (80)*.
SABAT, JAMES: Going In Style (79), Starting Over (79), The Double
    Mcguffin (79), The Seduction Of Joe Tynan (79), Just Tell Me What
    You Want (80), Stardust Memories (80).
SANTA CROCE, ANTHONY: Roller Boogie (79).
SCANLON, STEVE: Simon (80).
SHARPLESS, DON: Goldengirl (79), Oh, God! Book II (80), The Last
    Married Couple In America (80).
SHARROCK, IVAN: Flash Gordon (80)*, The Shining (80)*.
SIMMONS, BRIAN: The Awakening (80).
SLINKARD, REX A.: Somewhere In Time (80)*.
SOLOMON, JACK: Meteor (79), The Frisco Kid (79), Serial (80),
    Smokey And The Bandit II (80)*.
SOMERSET, PAT: It's My Turn (80)*.
SORENSON, CLYDE: Buck Rogers (79)*.
SPEAK, JOHN: The Villain (79), Little Darlings (80), The Competition
    (80)*, Wholly Moses! (80).
SPLET, ALAN: The Elephant Man (80)*.
STANDING, JOHN: The Elephant Man (80).
STEVENSON, GEORGE: Avalanche Express (79).
SUTTON, PETER: The Empire Strikes Back (80)*.
TANENBAUM, JIM: The Stunt Man (80).
THOMAS, BARRY: American Gigolo (80).
THOMAS, CHRIS: Rockshow (80).
TYSON, ELLIOT: Divine Madness (80)*.
WADELL, RICK: Home Movies (79).
WALD, BOB: The Big Brawl (80)*.
WALOWITZ, MARVIN: The Ninth Configuration (80)*.
WANGLER, CHRISTIAN: Agatha (79).
WEBB, JIM: Nashville (75)*, Buffalo Bill and the Indians (76)*, Three
    Women (77)*, A Wedding (78)*, The Rose (79)*, The Long Riders
    (80)*.
WEXLER, JEFF: Brinks (79), Being There (79), The Black Marble (80).

WHITMAN, DALE: Love in a Taxi (80).

WILBORN, CHARLES: The Jerk (79), Brubaker (80), Ordinary People (80).

YERSIN, LUKE: Union City (80).

YOSHIDA, RON: The Wizard Of Waukesha (80)*.

YOUDELMAN, BILLY: Divine Madness (80)*.

Choreographers

ALLEN, DEBRA: The Fish That Saved Pittsburgh (79).
BANAS, BOB: Skatetown Usa (79).
BASIL, TONI: The Rose (79), Divine Madness (80), First Family (80).
BIRCH, PATRICIA: Gilda Live (80).
BURGESS, HOVEY: Popeye (80)*.
DE ROLF, PAUL: 1941 (79).
DITCHBURN, ANNE: Slow Dancing In The Big City (78).
FALCO, LOUIS: Fame (80).
FAZAN, ELEANOR: Heaven's Gate (80).
FOLEY, BRIAN: Ice Castles (78).
FOSSE, BOB: Sweet Charity (69), Cabaret (72), All That Jazz (79).
GREGORY, GILLIAN: There Goes the Bride (80).
KIDD, MICHAEL: Movie Movie Baxter's Beauties (78).
KINNEY, SHARON: Popeye (80)*.
PHILLIPS, ARLENE: Can't Stop The Music (80).
ROMERO, ALEX: Love At First Bite (79).
SWAYZE, PATSY: Urban Cowboy (80).
TERRIO, DENEY: The Idolmaker (80).
THARP, TWYLA: Hair (79).
WILLS, LOU: Popeye (80)*.
WINTERS, DAVID: Roller Boogie (79).

Stunts

ARNETT, JAMES: Steel (80).
BAXLEY, CRAIG: The Warriors (79).
COMBS, GARY: The Villain (79).
CREACH, EVERETT: Time After Time (79).
HOOKER, HANK: Skatetown Usa (79).
HOWELL, CHRIS: Night Of The Juggler (80).
JANES, LOREN: Butch And Sundance (79).
JOHNSON, PAT: The Big Brawl (80).
LEONARD, TERRY: 1941 (79).
MATTSON, DENVER: The Main Event (79).
NICKERSON, JIM: Raging Bull (80).
NORRIS, AARON: The Octagon (80).
PALMISANO, CONRAD: Piranha (78).
SAVINI, TOM: Friday the 13th (80).
SAWAVA, GEORGE: The Concorde-Airport '79 (79).
SCOTT, WALTER: Comes A Horseman (78).
STACEY, EDDIE: ffolkes (80), Hawk the Slayer (80).
SULLIVAN, JOHN: Caravans (78).
VAN HORD, WAYNE: Every Which Way But Loose (78).
WARD, JOHN PARKER: Scavenger Hunt (79).
ZIKER, RICHARD: Smokey And The Bandit II (80).

Music

ADDISON, JOHN: Start the Revolution Without Me (69), Sleuth (72), Luther (74), Swashbuckler (76), The Seven Percent Solution (76), A Bridge Too Far (77).

ASHFORD, TED: Hickey And Boggs (72).

BACHARACH, BURT: Casino Royale (65), What's New Pussycat? (65), After The Fox (66), Butch Cassidy and the Sundance Kid (69), Lost Horizon (73).

BAND, RICHARD: The Day Time Ended (80).

BARRY, JEFF: The Idolmaker (80).

BARRY, JOHN: You Only Live Twice (67), Boom (68), Petulia (68), The Lion In Winter (68), Midnight Cowboy (69), Monte Walsh (70), Diamonds Are Forever (71), Murphy's War (71), The Last Valley (71), They Might Be Giants (71), The Day Of The Locust (75), King Kong (76), Robin And Marian (76), The Betsy (77), The Deep (77), Hanover Street (79), Moonraker (79), The Black Hole (79), Raise The Titanic (80), Somewhere In Time (80), Touched By Love (80).

BARTON, DEE: Play Misty For Me (71), High Plains Drifters (72), Thunderbolt And Lightfoot (74).

BASKIN, RICHARD: Nashville (75), Buffalo Bill and the Indians (76), Welcome To L A (77), Honeysuckle Rose (80)*.

BELL, THOM: The Fish That Saved Pittsburgh (79).

BENNETT, RICHARD RODNEY: Brinks (79), Yanks (79).

BENSON, ROBBY: Walk Proud (79), Die Laughing (80)*.

BERNSTEIN, CHARLES: Coast To Coast (80), Foolin' Around (80).

BERNSTEIN, ELMER: I Love You Alice B. Toklas (68), The Scalp Hunters (68), A Walk In The Spring Rain (69), The Gypsy Moths (69), The Midas Run (69), True Grit (69), The Liberation Of L B Jones (70), The Magnificent Seven Ride (72), McQ (74), Report To Commissioner (74), The Shootist (76), National Lampoon's Animal House (78), Meatballs (79), Airplane (80), Saturn 3 (80), The Great Santini (80).

BLAKE, HOWARD: Flash Gordon (80).

BOLCOM, WILLIAM: Hester Street (74).

BOLLING, CLAUDE: California Suite (78), The Awakening (80), Willie & Phil (80).

BOX, EVEL: The Double Mcguffin (79), Oh Heavenly Dog (80).

BRADLEY, OWEN: Coal Miner's Daughter (80).

BUDD, ROY: The Sea Wolves (80).

BUGATTI, DOMINIC: Fame (80)*.

BURGEON, GEOFFREY: Life Of Brian (79).

BURNS, RALPH: Movie Movie Baxter's Beauties (78), Movie Movie Dynamite Hands (78), All That Jazz (79), First Family (80), Urban Cowboy (80).

BUSBY, GERALD: Three Women (77).

CAMERON, JOHN: Lost And Found (79), Sunburn (79), The Mirror Crack'd (80).

CARMICHAEL, RALPH: Joni (80).

CARPENTER, JOHN: Halloween (78), The Fog (80).

CELMENTE, PAUL: Caligula (79).

CHAMBERLAIN, CATHY: Happy Birthday, Gemini (80)*.

COCKELL, JOHN MILLS: Terror Train (80).

COLOMBIER, MICHEL: Steel (80).

CONTI, BILL: The Garden Of Finzis Continis (72), Harry And Tonto (74), Rocky (76), Citizen's Band (Handle With Care) (77), An Unmarried Woman (78), Paradise Alley (78), The Big Fix (78), Uncle Joe Shannon (78), Dreamer (79), Goldengirl (79), Hurricane (79), Rocky II (79), The Seduction Of Joe Tynan (79), Gloria (80), Private Benjamin (80), The Formula (80).

COODER, RY: The Long Riders (80).

COPPOLA, CARMINE: The Black Stallion (79).

CORIGLIANO, JOHN: Altered States (80).

COSTA, DON: Madigan (68).

DAVIS, DAVID: H.O.T.S. (79).

DAVIS, MARK: Cheech And Chong's Next Movie (80).

DE VOL, FRANK: Krakatoa, East of Java (68), The Legend of Lylah Clare (68), Ulzana's Raid (72), The Longest Yard (74), Hustle (75), The Frisco Kid (79), Herbie Goes Bananas (80).

DE VORZON, BARRY: The Warriors (79), The Ninth Configuration (80), Xanadu (80).

DELERUE, GEORGES: Women In Love (69), The Horsemen (70), The Day Of The Dolphin (73), An Almost Perfect Affair (79).

DEODATO, EUMIR: The Onion Field (79).

DOERGE, CRAIG: Rich Kids (79).

DONAGGIO, PINO: Piranha (78), Home Movies (79), Dressed To Kill (80).

DRASNIN, ROBERT: The Kremlin Letter (70).

Richard Baskin.

DUNING, GEORGE: The Man With Bogart's Face (80).

EINHORN, RICHARD: Shock Waves (75).

ELLIOTT, JACK: Just You And Me, Kid (79), The Jerk (79).

ELLIS, DON: Kansas City Bomber (72), Natural Enemies (79).

ESTY, BOB: Roller Boogie (79).

FERGUSON, ALLYN: Avalanche Express (79).

FIELDING, JERRY: Suppose They Gave a War and Nobody Came (69), The Wild Bunch (69), Lawman (70), Chato's Land (71), Johnny Got His Gun (71), Straw Dogs (71), The Nightcomers (71), Junior Bonner (72), Scorpio (72), The Mechanic (72), The Outfit (73), The Super Cops (74), The Black Bird (75), The Killer Elite (75), The Outlaw Josey Wales (76), The Big Sleep (78), Beyond The Poseidon Adventure (79), Below The Belt (80).

FLICK, VIC: Hullabaloo Over Georgie and Bonnie's Pictures (79).

FOX, CHARLES: The Star Spangled Girl (71), The Last American Hero (73), The Laughing Policeman (73), The Other Side of the Mountain (75), Foul Play (78), Little Darlings (80), Nine To Five (80), Oh, God! Book II (80), Why Would I Lie? (80).

FRIED, GERALD: One Potato, Two Potato (64), The Killing of Sister George (68), Too Late the Hero (69), Whatever Happened to Aunt Alice (69), The Grissom Gang (71), Soylent Green (73), The Bell Jar (79).

FRONTIERE, DOMINIC: The Stunt Man (80).

GAGNON, ANDRE: Running (79), Phobia (80).

GALLO, PHIL: Mother's Day (80)*.

GARRETT, SNUFF: Any Which Way You Can (80), Bronco Billy (80).

GAYE, FRANKIE: Penitentiary (79).

GOLD, ERNEST: The Runner Stumbles (79), Tom Horn (80).

GOLDENBERG, BILLY: Scavenger Hunt (79).

GOLDSMITH, JERRY: In Like Flint (67), Planet of the Apes (68), 100 Rifles (69), Justine (69), Patton (69), The Chairman (69), The Illustrated Man (69), Rio Lobo (70), Tora! Tora! Tora! (70), The Last Run (71), The Mephisto Waltz (71), Wild Rovers (71), The Other (72), Papillon (73), Bring Me the Head of Alfredo Garcia (74), Chinatown (74), The Reincarnation of Peter Proud (74), Breakheart Pass (75), The Wind and the Lion (75), Logan's Run (76), The Last Hard Men (76), The Omen (76), Islands in the Stream (77), MacArthur (77), Capricorn One (78), Coma (78), Magic (78), The Boys from Brazil (78), Alien (79), Players (79), StarTrek-The Motion Picture (79), The Great Train Robbery (79).

GOODMAN, MILES: Skatetown Usa (79).

GORE, MICHAEL: Fame (80).

GROSS, CHARLES: On The Yard (79), Heartland (80).

GRUSIN, DAVE: Candy (68), The Heart is a Lonely Hunter (68), Tell Them Willie Boy Is Here (69), The Mad Room (69), Winning (69), Shootout (71), The Gang That Couldn't Shoot Straight (71), The Great Northfield Minnesota Raid (71), The Pursuit of Happiness (71), The Friends of Eddie Coyle (73), The Yakuza (75), Three Days of the Condor (75), W.W. And the Dixie Dancekings (75), Murder by Death (76), Bobby Deerfield (77), Heaven Can Wait (78), The Cheap Detective (78), ...And Justice For All (79), The Electric Horseman (79), My Bodyguard (80).

HALLIGAN, DICK: Cheaper to Keep Her (80), The Octagon (80).

HAMLISCH, MARVIN: The Swimmer (68), Take the Money and Run (69), The April Fools (69), Flap (70), Bananas (71), Kotch (71), Save the Tiger (71), Something Big (71), The War Between Men and Women (71), Fat City (72), The Sting (73), The Way We Were (73), The Prisoner of Second Avenue (75), Same Time Next Year (77), The Spy Who Loved Me (77), Ice Castles (78), Chapter Two (79), Starting Over (79), Ordinary People (80), Seems Like Old Times (80).

HARTLEY, RICHARD: The Lady Vanishes (79).

HARWOOD, BO: Minnie and Moskowitz (71), A Woman Under the Influence (74), The Killing of a Chinese Bookie (76), Opening Night (77).

HERRMANN, BERNARD: North by Northwest (59), Psycho (60), Obsessions (69), The Battle of Nererva (70), The Night Digger (71), Sisters (73), It's Alive (74), Obsession (76), Taxi Driver (76).

HOFFERT, PAUL: Circle Of Two (80), Double Negative (80).

HOLDRIDGE, LEE: Oliver's Story (78)*, French Postcards (79).

HORNER, JAMES: Battle Beyond The Stars (80), Humanoids From The Deep (80).

HUNDLEY, CRAIG: Schizoid (80).

JARRE, MAURICE: Isadora (68), Villa Rides (68), Topaz (69), Plaza Suite (71), Ryan's Daughter (71), The Life and Times of Judge Roy Bean (72), Ash Wednesday (73), The Mackintosh Man (73), Mandingo (75), Posse (75), The Man Who Would Be King (75), The American Success Company (79), Winter Kills (79), Resurrection (80), The Black Marble (80).

JENKINS, GORDON: First Deadly Sin (80).

JENSEN, MERRILL: Windwalker (80).

JONES, QUINCY: In Cold Blood (67), In the Heat of the Night (67), The Hell with Heroes (68), The Split (68), Bob & Carol & Ted & Alice (69), Cactus Flower (69), John and Mary (69), MacKenna's Gold (69), Brother John (70), The Out of Towners (70), $ (71), The Anderson Tapes (71), The Getaway (72), The Hot Rock (72), The New Centurions (72), The Wiz (78).

JUSTIS, BILL: The Villain (79).

KANE, ARTIE: Night Of The Juggler (80).

KAPLAN, SOL: Over The Edge (79).

KAPROFF, DANA: When A Stranger Calls (79), The Big Red One (80).

KARLIN, FRED: Up the Down Staircase (67), The Stalking Moon (68), Lovers and Other Strangers (69), The Sterile Cuckoo (69), The Little Ark (71), The Marriage of a Young Stockbroker (71), Westworld (73), Mixed Company (74), The Gravy Train (74), The Spikes Gang (74), Zandy's Bride (74), Leadbelly (76), Cloud Dancer (80), Loving Couples (80).

KELLAWAY, ROGER: Silent Scream (80).

KING, JEFF: Sunnyside (79).

LAI, FRANCIS: House of Cards (68), Hello Goodbye (70), Love Story (70), Visit to a Chief's Son (74), Oliver's Story (78)*.

LANCHBERY, JOHN: Nijinsky (80).

LANGHORNE, BRUCE: Melvin and Howard (80).

LAUBER, KEN: Hearts of the West (75), Head Over Heels (79), Wanda Nevada (79), The Little Dragons (80).

LAVIN, TOM: Out Of The Blue (80).

LEES, CAROL: The Last Word (79).

LEGRAND, MICHEL: How to Save a Marriage (68), Ice Station Zebra (68), Sweet November (68), The Thomas Crown Affair (68), The Happy Ending (69), The Lady in the Car with Glasses... (69), Le Mans (71), Summer of '42 (71), Lady Sings the Blues (72), One in a Million (72), Portnoy's Complaint (72), Breezy (73), Forty Carats (73), Atlantic City U S A (80), Falling In Love Again (80), The Hunter (80), The Mountain Men (80).

LEMMON, JACK: Tribute (80)*.

LEWIS, MICHAEL J.: The Legacy (79), ffolkes (80).

LEWIS, WEBSTER: The Hearse (80).

LOGAN, GARY: The Human Factor (79)*.

LOGAN, RICHARD: The Human Factor (79)*.

LOOK, RICH: Happy Birthday, Gemini (80)*.

MANCINI, HENRY: Me, Natalie (68), The Molly Maguires (68), Darling Lili (69), The Hawaiians (70), Sometimes a Great Notion (71), Oklahoma Crude (73), The Thief Who Came to Dinner (73), The White Dawn (73), 99 44/100 Percent Dead (74), Once is Not Enough (75), The Great Waldo Pepper (75), The Return of the Pink Panther (76), House Calls (78), The Revenge of Pink Panther (78), Who Is Killing the Great Chef's of Europe (78), 10 (79), Nightwing (79), The Prisoner Of Zenda (79), A Change of Seasons (80), Little Miss Marker (80).

MANDEL, JOHNNY: Pretty Poison (69), That Cold Day in the Park (69), MASH (70), The Last Detail (73), Summer Wishes, Winter Dreams (73), The Sailor Who Fell from Grace.... (76), Agatha (79), Being There (79), The Baltimore Bullet (80).

MANFREDINI, HARRY: Friday the 13th (80).

MANILOW, BARRY: Tribute (80)*.

MANN, PETER: Head On (80).

MANSFIELD, DAVID: Heaven's Gate (80).

MATZ, PETER: The Prize Fighter (79), The Private Eyes (80).

McCAULEY, MATTHEW: Middle Age Crazy (80).

McCRANE, PAUL: Fame (80)*.

MELLE, GIL: Borderline (80).

MINSKY, SUSAN: Love in a Taxi (80).

MONTENEGRO, HUGO: Lady in Cement (68), The Wrecking Crew (68), The Undefeated (69), Viva Max (69).

MORALI, JACQUES: Can't Stop The Music (80).

MORODER, GIORGIO: Midnight Express (78), American Gigolo (80), Foxes (80).

MORRICONE, ENNIO: Bloodline (79), Travels With Anita (79), The Island (80), Windows (80).

MORRIS, JOHN: The In-Laws (79), In God We Trust (80), The Elephant Man (80).

MUSKER, FRANK: Fame (80)*.

MYERS, STANLEY: The Deer Hunter (78), The Watcher In The Woods (80).

MYROW, FREDRIC: On The Nickel (80).

NELSON, WILLIE: Honeysuckle Rose (80)*.

NILSSON, HARRY: Popeye (80).

NITZSCHE, JACK: Hardcore (79), Heart Beat (79), Cruising (80).

NORTH, ALEX: Wise Blood (79), Carny (80).

PARKS, VAN DYKE: Goin' South (78).

PHILIPPS, ART: The Lucky Star (80).

PHILLIPS, STU: Buck Rogers (79).

POLEDOURIS, BASIL: Blue Lagoon (80), Defiance (80).

PRICE, GEORGE S.: Guyana:Cult Of The Damned (80)*.

RAMSEY, WILLIS ALAN: Second-Hand Hearts (80).

RENZETTI, JOE: Fatso (80).

RIDDLE, NELSON: The Great Gatsby (74), Guyana:Cult Of The Damned (80)*, Rough Cut (80).

ROBBINS, RICHARD: Jane Austen In Manhattan (80).

ROBERTSON, HARRY: Hawk the Slayer (80).

ROBINSON, HARRY: There Goes the Bride (80).

ROMANUS, RICHARD: Sitting Ducks (79).

ROSENMAN, LEONARD: Countdown (68), A Man Called Horse (70), The Todd Killings (70), Barry Lyndon (75), Race with the Devil (75), An Enemy of the People (76), The Lord of the Rings (78), Promises In The Dark (79), Hide In Plain Sight (80).

ROSENTHAL, LAURENCE: Brass Target (78), Meteor (79).

ROTA, NINO: Hurricane (79).

ROZSA, MIKLOS: Last Embrace (79), Time After Time (79).

RUBIN, LANCE: Motel Hell (80).

RUBINSTEIN, JOHN: Jeremiah Johnson (72), The Candidate (72), Kid Blue (73).

SCHIFRIN, LALO: Cool Hand Luke (67), Bullitt (68), Coogan's Bluff (68), Hell in the Pacific (68), The Brotherhood (68), Che! (69), I Love My Wife (70), Kelly's Heroes (70), Mrs. Pollifax-Spy (70), THX 1138 (70), W.U.S.A (70), Dirty Harry (71), Pretty Maids All in a Row (71), The Beguiled (71), Charley Varrick (72), Joe Kidd (72), Prime Cut (72), Rage (72), The Wrath of God (72), Harry in Your Pocket (73), Hit!. St. Ives (73), Magnum Force (73), Man on a Swing (73), Special Delivery (76), The Eagle Has Landed (77), Nunzio (78), Boulevard Nights (79), Escape to Athena (79), The Amityville Horror (79), The Concorde-Airport '79 (79), Brubaker (80), Serial (80), The Big Brawl (80), The Competition (80), The Nude Bomb (80), When Time Ran Out (80).

SCOTT, JOHN: North Dallas Forty (79), The Final Countdown (80).

SCOTT, TOM: Stir Crazy (80).

SEGAL, JERRY: Die Laughing (80)*.

SHIRE, DAVID: Drive, He Said (70), One More Train to Rob (71), Summertree (71), The Skin Game (71), Showdown (72), Two People (73), The Conversation (74), The Taking of Pelham 1-2-3 (74), Farewell My Lovely (75), The Hindenburg (75), All the President's Men (76), Harry and Walter Go to New York (76), The Big Bus (76), Saturday Night Fever (77), Norma Rae (79), The Promise (79).

SHKOLNIK, SHELDON: Tell Me a Riddle (80).

SILVERMAN, STANLEY: Simon (80).

SIMON, PAUL: One Trick Pony (80).

SMALL, MICHAEL: Puzzle of a Downfall Child (70), The Revolutionary (70), Klute (71), Child's Play (72), Dealing (72), Love, Pain and the Whole Damn Thing (72), The Parallax View (74), The Stepford Wives (74), Night Moves (75), Comes a Horseman (78), Girl Friends (78), The Driver (78), Going In Style (79), Those Lips Those Eyes (80).

SMITH, ARTHUR: Lady Grey (80)*.

SMITH, CLAY: Lady Grey (80)*.

SNOW, MARK: Something Short Of Paradise (79).

STEIN, CHRIS: Union City (80).

STEINMAN, JIM: A Small Circle Of Friends (80).

STROUSE, CHARLES: Just Tell Me What You Want (80).

SUMMERS, BOB: Guyana:Cult Of The Damned (80)*, In Search Of Historic Jesus (80).

THOMAS, PETER: Breakthrough (79).

THORNE, KEN: The Magic Christian (70), Royal Flash (75), The Ritz (76), The Outsider (79), Superman II (80)*.

VICARI, CLEM: Mother's Day (80)*.

WANNBERG, KEN: Tribute (80)*.

WECHTER, JULIUS: Midnight Madness (80).

WILKINS, RICK: The Changeling (80).

WILKINSON, MARC: Eagle's Wing (79), The Fiendish Plot Of Dr. Fu Manchu (80).

WILLIAMS, JOHN: The Reivers (69), Images (72), Pete 'n Tillie (72), The Poseidon Adventure (72), The Long Goodbye (73), The Man Who Loved Cat Dancing (73), The Paper Chase (73), The Sugarland Express (73), Cinderella Liberty (74), Conrack (74), The Towering Inferno (74), Jaws (75), The Eiger Sanction (75), Midway (76), The Missouri Breaks (76), Black Sunday (77), Close Encounters of the Third Kind (77), Star Wars (77), Superman (78), The Fury (78), 1941 (79), Dracula (79), Superman II (80)*, The Empire Strikes Back (80).

WILLIAMS, PATRICK: Breaking Away (79), Butch And Sundance (79), Cuba (79), Hot Stuff (79), Hero At Large (80), It's My Turn (80), Used Cars (80), Wholly Moses! (80).

WILLIAMS, PAUL: Phantom of The Paradise (74), A Star is Born (76), Bugsy Malone (76), The End (78), The Muppet Movie (79).

WILSON, PHILIP: Clarence And Angel (80).

WORTH, JODY TAYLOR: Up The Academy (80).

WYMAN, DAN: Without Warning (80).

YOUNG, NEIL: Where The Buffalo Roam (80).

ZAZA, PAUL: Prom Night (80)*, The Kidnapping Of The President (80).

ZEITLIN, DENNY: Invasion Of The Bodysnatchers (78).

ZITTRER, CARL: Prom Night (80)*.

Special Effects
and visual effects

ALBAIN, RICHARD, Jr.: The Fog (80), The Kidnapping Of The President (80)*.
ALLDER, NICK: Alien (79)*.
ALLEN, DAVID: The Day Time Ended (80)*.
AUER, GREG: The Promise (79).
BAUMGARTNER, KARL: Brass Target (78), Caravans (78).
BEDIG, SASS: Breakthrough (79).
BERG, JON: Piranha (78).
BINDER, MAURICE: The Final Countdown (80).
BLOUNT, JIM: Time After Time (79)*.
CALVERT, ADAMS R.: Motel Hell (80).
CARTER, JOHN: In Search Of Historic Jesus (80).
CHILVERS, COLIN: Saturn 3 (80), Superman II (80)*.
COLWELL, CHUCK: Galaxina (80).
COMISKY, C.: Battle Beyond The Stars (80).
COOK, RANDY: The Day Time Ended (80)*.
CORY, PHIL: Scavenger Hunt (79)*.
CRUICKSHANK, ART: The Black Hole (79)*, Herbie Goes Bananas (80)*.
DAWSON, ROBERT: Prophecy (79).
DAY, JOE: Hurricane (79)*.
DOCKREY, SAM: Chapter Two (79).
DYKSTRA, JOHN: Star Trek (79)*.
EDLUND, RICHARD: The Empire Strikes Back (80)*.
ELLENSHAW, HARRISON: The Empire Strikes Back (80)*.
ELLENSHAW, PETER: The Black Hole (79)*.
EVANS, JOHN: Moonraker (79)*.
EWING, BUD: Buck Rogers (79)*.
FAGGARD, JACK: Buck Rogers (79)*.
FERREN, BRAN: Altered States (80)*.

Douglas Trumbull.

FIELD, ROY: Superman II (80)*.
FLOWERS, A. D.: 1941 (79).
FUENTES, LARRY: Time After Time (79)*.
GASPAR, CHUCK: Every Which Way But Loose (78), Altered States (80)*, Nine To Five (80)*.
GENTRY, PAUL W.: The Day Time Ended (80)*.
GEORGE, ROGER: Steel (80).
GIBBS, GEORGE: Flash Gordon (80).
GREENBERG, RICHARD: Resurrection (80)*.
GREENBERG, ROBERT: Resurrection (80)*.
GRIGG, GENE: The Changeling (80).
GRISWOLD, AL: Hair (79).
GUTTERIDGE, MARTIN: Hanover Street (79).
HESSEY, RUSS: Invasion Of The Bodysnatchers (78)*.
HUTCHINSON, PETER: The Kidnapping Of The President (80)*.
JOHNSON, BRIAN: Alien (79)*, The Empire Strikes Back (80)*.
JOHNSON, RICHARD: Over The Edge (79).
KARKUS, STEVE: Silent Scream (80).
LEE, DANNY: Herbie Goes Bananas (80)*, Midnight Madness (80).
LOHMAN, AUGIE: The Electric Horseman (79).
LOMBARDI, JOE: Seven (79).
MATTEY, ROBERT A.: Jaws (75).
MEDDINGS, DEREK: Moonraker (79)*, Superman II (80)*.
MILLAR, HENRY: The Last Word (79).
MILRAD, ABE: The Concorde-Airport '79 (79).
PETERSON, ROBERT: Private Benjamin (80).
PUCCINI, ALDO: Hurricane (79)*.
RABIN, JACK: The Bees (78).

RAMBALDI, CARLO: Nightwing (79).

RHEAUME, DELL: Invasion Of The Bodysnatchers (78)*, The Amityville Horror (79).

RICHARDSON, JOHN: Moonraker (79)*, ffolkes (80).

ROBINSON, GLEN: Hurricane (79)*, Meteor (79)*.

ROBINSON, LARRY: 1941 (79).

SAVINI, TOM: Martin (78), Friday the 13th (80).

SILVER, TONY: Resurrection (80)*.

STEAPLES, ROBERT: Meteor (79)*.

SULLIVAN, MICHAEL: Can't Stop The Music (80).

SVEDIN, RAY: Scavenger Hunt (79)*.

SWEENEY, MATT: Nine To Five (80)*.

TRUMBULL, DOUGLAS: 2001: A Space Odyssey (68), Silent Running (71), Close Encounters of the Third Kind (77), Star Trek (79)*.

WAYNE, JAMES: Fade to Black (80).

WELDON, ALEX: Raise The Titanic (80).

WELLMAN, HAROLD: Beyond The Poseidon Adventure (79).

WHITLOCK, ALBERT: Earthquake (74), The Hindenburg (75), King Kong (76), High Anxiety (78), The Wiz (78), Dracula (79), The Prisoner Of Zenda (79), Cheech And Chong's Next Movie (80), The Island (80).

WILSON, PAUL: Superman II (80)*.

WINGROVE, IAN: The Legacy (79).

WOOLMAN, HARRY: Hangar 18 (80).

Editors

ALBERTSON, ERIC: Sunnyside (79)*, First Deadly Sin (80), Union City (80)*.

ALDRIDGE, RICHARD: Living Legend (80).

ALLEN, DEDE: Bonnie and Clyde (67), Rachel Rachel (68), Alice's Restaurant (69), Little Big Man (70), Slaughterhouse Five (72), Serpico (73), The Highest (73), Dog Day Afternoon (75), Night Moves (75), The Missouri Breaks (76), Slapshot (77), The Wiz (78).

ALLEN, STANFORD: The Fifth Floor (80), The Hollywood Knights (80)*.

APPLEBY, GEORGE: Double Negative (80), Nothing Personal (80).

ASHBY, HAL: The Russians Are Coming, The Russians Are Coming (66), In the Heat of the Night (67), The Thomas Crown Affair (68).

AVAKIAN, ARAM: Honeysuckle Rose (80)*.

AVILDSEN, JOHN: W.W. And the Dixie Dancekings (75), Slow Dancing in the Big City (78), The Formula (80)*.

BAIRD, STUART: Superman (78).

BARON, SUZANNE: Atlantic City U S A (80).

BARRERE, ROBERT: Over The Edge (79).

BEAUMAN, NICK: The Earthling (80).

BECK, REGINALD: Don Giovanni (79).

BERGER, PETER E.: The Promise (79), Oh, God! Book II (80), The Last Married Couple In America (80).

BERNDT, GEORGE: The Hearse (80).

BEYER, EDWARD: Rich Kids (79), One Trick Pony (80)*.

BIERY, EDWARD: When Time Ran Out (80)*.

BLANGSTED, FOLMAR: Camelot (67), Up The Down Staircase (67), Bandolero (68), Hell Fighters (68), The Forbin Project (69), The Pursuit Of Happiness (71), The Summer Of '42 (71), Man Of La Mancha (72), The Other (72), Oklahoma Crude (73).

BLANKETT, BETSY: Penitentiary (79).

BLEWITT, DAVID: In God We Trust (80), Steel (80), The Competition (80).

BLOOM, JOHN: Magic (78), Dracula (79).

BOCK, LARRY: Galaxina (80).

BOISVERT, DOMINIQUE: Hog Wild (80).

BOOTH, MARGARET: The Owl & The Pussycat (70), To Find A Man (71), Fat City (72), The Way We Were (73), Funny Lady (75), The Sunshine Boys (75), Murder By Death (76), California Suite (78)*, The Goodbye Girl (78).

BORDEN, MARSHALL: Cloud Dancer (80).

BORNSTEIN, CHARLES: The Fog (80)*.

BOUCHE, CLAUDINE: The Fiendish Plot Of Dr. Fu Manchu (80)*.

BRACHT, FRANK: Something Short Of Paradise (79).

BRADY, JERRY: The Baltimore Bullet (80).

BRAME, BILL: Beyond The Poseidon Adventure (79).

BRANDT, BYRON: Roller Boogie (79)*, It's My Turn (80)*.

BRENNER, GORDON D.: Herbie Goes Bananas (80).

BRETHERTON, DAVID: Villa Rides (68), Lovers and Other Strangers (69), On a Clear Day You Can See Forever (70), Fool's Parade (71), Cabaret (72), Slither (72), Save The Tiger (73), Westworld (73), The Man In The Glass Booth (75), Harry and Walter Go to New York (76), That's Entertainment, Part 2 (76), Winter Kills (77), Coma (78), The Great Train Robbery (79), The Big Red One (80)*, The Formula (80)*.

BRICMONT, WENDY GREEN: On The Nickel (80).

BROCKMAN, SUSAN: The Wizard Of Waukesha (80).

BROWN, ROBERT: The Amityville Horror (79), Brubaker (80).

BRUMMER, DICK: Schizoid (80)*.

BURCH, CURTIS: Without Warning (80).

BURNETT, JOHN F.: Moment By Moment (78), ...And Justice For All (79), Can't Stop The Music (80).

BUTLER, BILL: Lost And Found (79), How To Beat The High Cost of Living (80).

CAHN, DANN: The Octagon (80).

CAMBAS, JACQUELINE: Falling In Love Again (80)*.

CAMBERN, DONN: Easy Rider (69), Drive, He Said (70)*, The Last Picture Show (71), Steelyard Blues (72), Blume in Love (73), Cinderella Liberty (74), The Hindenburg (75), Alex And The Gypsy (76), The Other Side Of Midnight (77), Time After Time (79), Smokey And The Bandit II (80)*, Willie & Phil (80).

CARRUTH, WILLIAM: Saint Jack (79).

CARTER, JOHN: Mikey And Nicky (76), Between the Lines (77), The Formula (80)*.

CHULACK, FRED: Touched By Love (80).

CLARK, JIM: Agatha (79), Yanks (79).

CLARK, ROBIN: Rockshow (80).

CLIFFORD, GRAEME: Images (73), F.I.S.T. (78).

COATES, ANNE V.: The Legacy (79), The Elephant Man (80).

COBLENZ, JAMES: Foxes (80), It's My Turn (80)*.

COLE, STAN: Murder By Decree (79), Phobia (80).

CONRAD, SCOTT: Wanda Nevada (79), Cheech And Chong's Next Movie (80), The Hollywood Knights (80)*.

COOKE, MALCOLM: Flash Gordon (80).

CORNWELL, TOM: A Woman Under The Influence (74), The Killing of a Chinese Bookie (76), Opening Night (77).

COX, JOEL: Bronco Billy (80)*.

CRAVEN, GARTH: Avalanche Express (79).

CRUZ, EDIBERTO: Roller Boogie (79)*.

DALVA, ROBERT: The Black Stallion (79).

DANTE, JOE: Piranha (78)*.

DAVIES, FREEMAN A.: The Long Riders (80)*, When Time Ran Out (80)*.

DAVIS, T. BATTLE: The Ninth Configuration (80)*.

DE PALMA, BRIAN: The Wedding Party (63), Greetings (68), Murder a la Mod (68), Dionysus in 69 (70)*.

DIXON, HUMPHREY: Hullabaloo Over Georgie and Bonnie's Pictures (79).

DOW, HERBERT H.: Sunnyside (79)*.

DOYLE, JULIAN: Life Of Brian (79).

DUMAS, JOHN J.: Buck Rogers (79).

DYCK, DORIS: Out Of The Blue (80).

EGLESON, JAN: Billy In The Lowlands (79)*.

ERBER, ALICE: On Company Business (80)*.

FANFARA, STEPHEN: Happy Birthday, Gemini (80).

FARR, GLENN: Divine Madness (80), Fatso (80).

FEINBERG, NINA: Simon (80).

FENN, SUZANNE: Pretty Baby (78).

FERRIOL, CAROLINE: The Stunt Man (80)*.

FETTERMAN, RICHARD: Take Down (79).

FIELD, CONNIE: The Life and Times of Rosie the Riveter (80)*.

FIELDS, VERNA: Targets (68), Medium Cool (69), What's Up Doc? (72), American Graffiti (73), The Sugarland Express (73), Daisy Miller (74), Jaws (75).

FINFER, DAVID: Defiance (80).

FITZGERALD, ROBERT: Schizoid (80)*.

FITZSTEPHENS, JOHN J.: Just Tell Me What You Want (80).

FOLSEY, GEORGE, Jr.: The Blues Brothers (80).

FOOT, GEOFFREY: Sunburn (79), The Watcher In The Woods (80).

FOWLER, GENE, Jr.: Skatetown Usa (79).

FOWLER, MARJORIE: It's My Turn (80)*.

FOX, GREY: Loving Couples (80)*.

FRANCE, CHUCK: The War At Home (79).

FREDA, BILL: Friday the 13th (80), Love in a Taxi (80).

FRUCHTMAN, LISA: Heaven's Gate (80)*.

GARFIELD, DAVID: Hero At Large (80).

GAY, NORMAN: Shock Waves (75), Honeysuckle Rose (80)*.

GIBBS, ANTHONY: Butch And Sundance (79)*.

GLEN, JOHN: Moonraker (79), The Sea Wolves (80).

GOLDBLATT, MARK: Piranha (78)*, Humanoids From The Deep (80).

GORDEAN, WILLIAM: Smokey And The Bandit II (80)*.

GORDON, ROBERT: Blue Lagoon (80).

GOURSON, JEFF: Somewhere In Time (80).

GREENBERG, GERALD: Bye Bye Braverman (68), The Subject Was Roses (68), Alice's Restaurant (69), The French Connection (71), Electra Glide In Blue (73), The Seven Ups (73), The Taking of Pelham 1-2-3 (74), The Missouri Breaks (76), Apocalypse Now (79), Kramer vs. Kramer (79), Dressed To Kill (80), Heaven's Gate (80)*.

GREENBURY, CHRISTOPHER: The Muppet Movie (79), Sunday Lovers (80), Where The Buffalo Roam (80).

GREENE, DANFORD B.: That Cold Day In The Park (69), MASH (70), Myra Breckinridge (70), Blazing Saddles (74), Aloha Bobby and Rose (75), Fun With Dick And Jane (77), Outlaw Blues (77), Rocky II (79), Voices (79), The Hollywood Knights (80)*.

GRENVILLE, GEORGE: The Last Word (79), The Big Brawl (80), Tom Horn (80).

GRIBBLE, BERNARD: Motel Hell (80).

HALSEY, RICHARD: Harry And Tonto (74), Next Stop Greenwich Village (76), Boulevard Nights (79), American Gigolo (80), Tribute (80).

HAMBLING, GERRY: Fame (80).

HAMPTON, JANICE: Windwalker (80)*.

HANNEMANN, WALTER: The Villain (79), The Nude Bomb (80)*.

HANSON, JOHN: Northern Lights (79).

HARRIS, RICHARD A.: Smile (75), The Bad News Bears (76), Semi-Tough (77), An Almost Perfect Affair (79), The Island (80).

HARTZELL, DUANE: Joni (80).

HEIM, ALAN: All That Jazz (79).

HENDERSON, ANNE: Terror Train (80).

HERRING, PEMBROKE J.: Little Darlings (80), Nine To Five (80).

HILL, DENNIS: Nashville (75), Three Women (75), Health (80).

HIRSCH, PAUL: The Empire Strikes Back (80).

HIRSCH, TINA: More American Graffiti (79).

HIRSCHLER, KURT: Running (79).

HIRSH, PAUL: Sisters (73), Carrie (76), Obsession (76), Star Wars (77), King Of The Gypsies (78), The Fury (78).

HIVELY, GEORGE: Movie Movie Baxter's Beauties (78), Movie Movie Dynamite Hands (78).

HOFSTRA, JACK: The Stunt Man (80)*.

HOLDEN, DAVID: The Warriors (79), The Long Riders (80)*.

HOLMES, CHRISTOPHER: Five Easy Pieces (70), Sergeant Pepper's Lonely Hearts Club Band (78), Scavenger Hunt (79).

HOLMES, JOHN W.: Just You And Me, Kid (79), Popeye (80)*.

HORGER, JACK: The Frisco Kid (79)*.

HOWARD, JOHN C.: Americathon (79), Nightwing (79), Why Would I Lie? (80).

HURWITZ, LEO: Dialogue With a Woman Departed (80).

JACKSON, DOUG: Falling In Love Again (80)*.

JENKINS, ERIC: Heart Beat (79), Altered States (80).

JOHNSON, STEPHEN J.: Windwalker (80)*.

JONES, ALAN: There Goes the Bride (80).

JONES, AMY HOLDEN: Second-Hand Hearts (80).

JONES, ROBERT C.: I Love You Alice B Toklas (68), Man Of La Mancha (72), The Last Detail (73), Shampoo (75), Bound for Glory (76), Heaven Can Wait (78).

KAHN, MICHAEL: Close Encounters of the Third Kind (77), Ice Castles (78)*, 1941 (79), Used Cars (80).

KAHN, SHELLY: An Enemy Of The People (76), Bloodbrothers (78), Same Time Next Year (78), The Electric Horseman (79), Private Benjamin (80).

KAMEN, JAY: North Dallas Forty (79).

KANEW, JEFF: Natural Enemies (79), Ordinary People (80).

KAREN, DEBRA: Meatballs (79).

KARIN, DEBBIE: Final Assignment (80).

KELBER, CATHERINE: The Outsider (79).

KELLER, HARRY: Stir Crazy (80).

KELLY, JOHN: Middle Age Crazy (80).

KENNEDY, PATRICK: Airplane (80).

KLINGMAN, LYNZEE: Hair (79).

KRESS, CARL: Meteor (79), Hopscotch (80).

KRESS, HAROLD F.: I Walk The Line (70), The Horsemen (71), The Poseidon Adventure (72), The Iceman Cometh (73), 99 44/100 Percent Dead (74), The Towering Inferno (74), Gator (76), The Other Side Of Midnight (77), Viva Knievel (77).

KUNIN, HOWARD: Roller Boogie (79)*, Fade to Black (80).

LAMBERT, ROBERT K.: Brinks (79)*, The Final Countdown (80).

LANE, DAVID: Brass Target (78).

LANGLOIS, YVES: The Lucky Star (80).

LAUB, MARC: Honeysuckle Rose (80)*.

LAUDENSLAGER, JIM: Lady Grey (80).

LAWSON, TONY: Bad Timing (80).

LEDERSEN, LILLA: The Changeling (80).

LEE-THOMPSON, PETER: The Ninth Configuration (80)*.

LEEDS, LINDA: You Better Watch Out (80)*.

LEVIN, SIDNEY: Mean Streets (73), Nashville (75), The Cheap Detective (78), Norma Rae (79), Wholly Moses! (80).

LEWIS, TERRY: Pilgrim, Farewell (80).

LINDER, STU: First Family (80)*, My Bodyguard (80).

LINK, JOHN F., II: The King Of Marvin Gardens (72), Stay Hungry (76), Borderline (80).

LITTLETON, CAROL: French Postcards (79), Roadie (80)*.

LLOYD, RUSSELL: The Lady Vanishes (79), The Fiendish Plot Of Dr. Fu Manchu (80)*.

LOMBARDO, LOU: Brewster McCloud (70), McCabe And Mrs. Miller (71), The Long Goodbye (73), California Split (74), Thieves Like Us (74), The Black Bird (75), The Late Show (77).

LOMBARDO, TONY: A Wedding (78), A Perfect Couple (79), Popeye (80).

LOTTMAN, EVAN: The Seduction Of Joe Tynan (79), Honeysuckle Rose (80)*.

LOVEJOY, RAY: The Shining (80).

LOVETT, ROBERT Q.: Once In Paris (78).

LUCAS, GEORGE: THX 1138 (70).

LUCAS, MARCIA: American Graffiti (73), Alice Doesn't Live Here Anymore (74), Taxi Driver (76), New York New York (77), Star Wars (77).

MALKIN, BARRY: Apocalypse Now (79), Last Embrace (79), One Trick Pony (80)*, Windows (80).

MARDEN, RICHARD: Saturn 3 (80), The Mirror Crack'd (80).

MARSH, D'ARCY: Billy In The Lowlands (79)*.

MARTIN, SUSAN: First Family (80)*.

McCREA, PETER L.: Windwalker (80)*.

McKAY, CRAIG: Melvin and Howard (80).

McLAUGHLIN, GREGG: The Black Hole (79).

McLAVERTY, MICHAEL: The Kidnapping Of The President (80).

MICHAELS, J.: Union City (80)*.

MILLER, ALAN: Mr. Mikes Mondo Video (79)*.

MITCHELL, JAMES: Capricorn One (78), Hanover Street (79).

MOLIN, BUD: Bloodline (79), The Jerk (79), Up The Academy (80).

MOORE, MILLIE: Those Lips Those Eyes (80).

MORRIS, FRANK: Hometown USA (79).

MORSE, SUSAN E.: Manhattan (79), Stardust Memories (80).

MURCH, WALTER: The Conversation (74), Julia (77).

NELSON, ARGYLE: Night Of The Juggler (80).

NERVIS, SANDY: The Bees (78).

NEWMAN, EVE: Little Miss Marker (80).

NICHOLSON, GEORGE: Goldengirl (79), Coast To Coast (80).

NICOLAOU, TED: The Day Time Ended (80).

NILSSON, ROB: Northern Lights (79).

NOCHOLS, DAVID: Circle Of Two (80).

NORRIS, GEORGE T.: He Knows You're Alone (80).

NUNEZ, VICTOR: Gal Young Un (79).

O'HARA, CORKY: Home Movies (79), You Better Watch Out (80)*.

O'MEARA, C. TIMOTHY: Going In Style (79)*.

O'STEEN, SAM: The Graduate (67), Rosemary's Baby (68), The Sterile Cuckoo (69), Catch-22 (70), Carnal Knowledge (71), Portnoy's Complaint (72), The Day Of The Dolphin (73), Chinatown (74), Hurricane (79).

OPPENHEIMER, GARY: Head On (80).

PALMER, NORMAN R.: Midnight Madness (80)*.

PAPPE, STUART H.: Bob & Carol & Ted & Alice (69), Alex In Wonderland (70), An Unmarried Woman (78), Oliver's Story (78), The Wanderers (79)*, Carny (80).

PERKINS, ERIC BOYD: Hawk the Slayer (80).

PETTIT, SUZANNE: Tell Me a Riddle (80).

PHENIX, LUCY MASSIE: The Life and Times of Rosie the Riveter (80)*.

POKRAS, BARBARA: H.O.T.S. (79).

POULTON, RAYMOND: Breakthrough (79).

PRIESTLEY, TOM: Deliverance (72), The Great Gatsby (74), The Return Of The Pink Panther (75), Voyage Of The Damned (76), Times Square (80).

RAMSAY, TODD: Star Trek (79).

RASE, KENDALL S.: In Search Of Historic Jesus (80).

RAVOK, BRIAN: Prom Night (80).

RAWLINGS, TERRY: Alien (79), The Awakening (80).

RAWLINS, DAVID: The Bingo Long Traveling All-Stars (76), Saturday Night Fever (77), The Last Remake Of Beau Geste (77), The China Syndrome (79), Urban Cowboy (80).

RAY, DAVID: One Trick Pony (80)*.

REYNOLDS, BILL: Old Boyfriends (79).

REYNOLDS, WILLIAM: Star! (68), Hello Dolly (69), The Great White Hope (70), What's the Matter with Helen? (71), The Godfather (72), The Sting (73), Two People (73), The Great Waldo Pepper (75), The Seven Percent Solution (76), The Turning Point (77), A Little Romance (79), Heaven's Gate (80)*, Nijinsky (80).

ROBERTS, RANDY: Players (79), A Small Circle Of Friends (80).

ROBLEE, JAN: The Last Waltz (78).

ROLAND, RITA: Resurrection (80).

ROLF, TOM: Taxi Driver (76), New York New York (77), Blue Collar (78), Hardcore (79), Prophecy (79), Heaven's Gate (80)*.

ROOSE, RONALD: The Wanderers (79)*.

ROSENBLUM, IRVING: The Frisco Kid (79)*.

ROSENBLUM, RALPH: Bananas (71), Born to Win (71), Bad Company (72), Sleeper (73), Love And Death (75), Annie Hall (77), Interiors (78).

ROTHMAN, MARION: Comes A Horseman (78), Starting Over (79).

RUBAN, AL: Faces (68).

RUGGIERO, EVA: The Mountain Men (80).

SAETA, EDDIE: The Man With Bogart's Face (80).

SALIER, EDWARD: Roller Boogie (79)*, Silent Scream (80).

SALMINI, AMBROSE: American Odyssey (80).

SAYLES, JOHN: Return Of The Secaucus Seven (80).

SCHEIDER, CYNTHIA: Breaking Away (79), Head Over Heels (79).

SCHENKEIN, MICHAEL: Joe Albany...a Jazz Life (80).

SCHMIDT, ARTHUR: Coal Miner's Daughter (80).

SCHOONMAKER, THELMA: Raging Bull (80).

SEITH, LEON: The Double Mcguffin (79), Oh Heavenly Dog (80).

SEKELY, JACK: Midnight Madness (80)*.

SELVER, VERONICA: On Company Business (80)*.

SHAPIRO, MELVIN: Ice Castles (78)*.

SHERIDAN, MICHAEL J.: The Champ (79).

SHUGRUE, ROBERT F.: Raise The Titanic (80)*.

SILVI, ROBERTO: Wise Blood (79), The Ninth Configuration (80)*.

SIMMONS, DAVID: Popeye (80)*.

SMITH, BUD: Brinks (79)*, Cruising (80), Falling In Love Again (80)*.

SMITH, JOHN VICTOR: Cuba (79), Superman II (80).

SPANG, RON: Any Which Way You Can (80)*.

SPENCE, MICHAEL: Hangar 18 (80).

SPENCER, DOROTHY: Happy Birthday Wanda June (71), Limbo (72),
Earthquake (74), The Concorde-Airport '79 (79).

STEINKAMP, FREDERIC: They Shoot Horses, Don't They? (69), The
Strawberry Statement (70), A New Leaf (71), The Marriage of a
Young Stockbroker (71), Freebie And The Bean (74), The Yakuza
(75), Three Days Of The Condor (75), Bobby Deerfield (77), Hide
In Plain Sight (80)*.

STEINKAMP, WILLIAM: Hide In Plain Sight (80)*.

STEVENSON, HOUSELEY: The Great Santini (80).

STEVENSON, MICHAEL: California Suite (78)*, Chapter Two (79),
Seems Like Old Times (80).

STEWART, DOUGLAS: The Shootist (76), Telefon (77), Invasion of the
Bodysnatchers (78), Walk Proud (79), Rough Cut (80).

STRACHAN, ALAN: ffolkes (80).

SWINK, ROBERT: Going In Style (79)*, The In-Laws (79).

TISCHLER, BOB: Mr. Mikes Mondo Video (79)*.

TOKEL, LANA: Union City (80)*.

TORDJMANN, FABIEN: The Prize Fighter (79), The Private Eyes (80).

TRAVIS, NEIL: Die Laughing (80), The Idolmaker (80).

TREVOR, RICHARD: The Human Factor (79).

TRIROGOFF, GEORGE: Butch And Sundance (79)*.

TUBOR, MORTON: The Big Red One (80)*.

TUCKER, PHIL: The Nude Bomb (80)*.
URIOSTE, FRANK: Loving Couples (80)*.
VILLASENOR, GEORGE C.: Gloria (80).
VIRKLER, DENNIS: Xanadu (80).
VITALE, SAM: When A Stranger Calls (79).
WALKER, LESLEY: Eagle's Wing (79).
WALLACE, TOMMY: The Fog (80)*.
WALLOWITZ, MARVIN: The Bell Jar (79).
WALLS, TOM: Roadie (80)*.
WALTER, ERNIE: Circle Of Iron (79).
WARSCHILKA, EDWARD: The Main Event (79), Cheaper to Keep Her (80).
WATSON, EARL: Guyana:Cult Of The Damned (80).
WATTS, RAY: It's Not The Size That Counts (79).
WEBSTER, FERRIS: Ice Station Zebra (68), Start the Revolution Without Me (69), A Walk in the Spring Rain (70), ZigZag (70), Glory Boy (71), The Organization (71), High Plains Drifter (72), Joe Kidd (72), Breezy (73), Magnum Force (73), The Eiger Sanction (75), The Enforcer (76), The Outlaw Josey Wales (76), The Gauntlet (77), Every Which Way But Loose (78), Escape From Alcatraz (79), Any Which Way You Can (80)*, Bronco Billy (80)*.
WELD, JONATHAN: Clarence And Angel (80).
WHEELER, JOHN W.: The Onion Field (79), Serial (80).
WILLIAMS, J. TERRY: Raise The Titanic (80)*.
WINETROBE, MAURY: Ice Castles (78)*, The Frisco Kid (79)*, The Black Marble (80).
WINTERS, RALPH E.: 10 (79), The American Success Company (79).
WISEMAN, FREDERICK: Manoeuvre (79).
WOHL, IRA: Best Boy (79).
WOLFE, ROBERT L.: The Wild Bunch (69), Drive, He Said (70)*, Straw Dogs (71), Junior Bonner (72), The Getaway (72), Pat Garrett & Billy The Kid (73), The Terminal Man (74), The Wind And The Lion (75), All the President's Men (76), The Deep (77), The Rose (79), The Hunter (80).
WYMAN, BOB: Promises In The Dark (79).
YAHRUS, BILL: Heartland (80).
YEE, YEU-BUN: The Last Waltz (78).
ZAILLION, STEPHEN: Below The Belt (80).
ZIEGLER, WILLIAM: Pretty Poison (69), The Big Bounce (69), Topaz (69), El Condor (70), The Omega Man (71), 1776 (72), McQ (74).
ZIMMERMAN, DON: Heaven Can Wait (78), Uncle Joe Shannon (78), Being There (79), A Change of Seasons (80).
ZINNER, PETER: The Godfather (72), The Deerhunter (78), The Fish That Saved Pittsburgh (79), Foolin' Around (80).